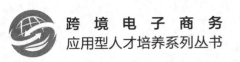

跨境电子商务
应用型人才培养系列丛书

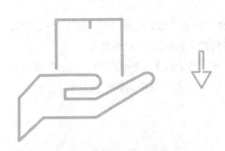

跨境电子商务
实用英语

■ 主编◎崔新红　徐赢光　邹益民

清华大学出版社
北京

内 容 简 介

本书共八章，包括跨境电子商务概述，跨境电子商务平台，建立商务关系，跨境电子商务支付与结算，跨境电子商务物流，跨境电子商务市场理论，跨境电子商务订单管理，跨境电子商务服务。

本书内容全面、实例丰富，既适合普通高等院校跨境电子商务、电子商务、物流管理、国际经济与贸易、市场营销等专业作为教材使用，也适合跨境电子商务创业者、从业者和培训机构参考使用。

图书在版编目（CIP）数据

跨境电子商务实用英语 / 崔新红，徐赢光，邹益民主编. —北京：清华大学出版社，2024.1
（跨境电子商务应用型人才培养系列丛书）
ISBN 978-7-302-65311-0

Ⅰ. ①跨⋯　Ⅱ. ①崔⋯　②徐⋯　③邹⋯　Ⅲ. ①电子商务—英语　Ⅳ. ①F713.36

中国国家版本馆 CIP 数据核字（2024）第 019879 号

责任编辑：邓　婷
封面设计：刘　超
版式设计：文森时代
责任校对：马军令
责任印制：杨　艳

出版发行：清华大学出版社
　　　　网　　　址：https://www.tup.com.cn，https://www.wqxuetang.com
　　　　地　　　址：北京清华大学学研大厦 A 座　　　　邮　　编：100084
　　　　社 总 机：010-83470000　　　　　　　　　　　邮　　购：010-62786544
　　　　投稿与读者服务：010-62776969，c-service@tup.tsinghua.edu.cn
　　　　质量反馈：010-62772015，zhiliang@tup.tsinghua.edu.cn
印 装 者：大厂回族自治县彩虹印刷有限公司
经　　销：全国新华书店
开　　本：185mm×260mm　　　印　　张：17.75　　　字　　数：427 千字
版　　次：2024 年 1 月第 1 版　　　　　　　　　　印　　次：2024 年 1 月第 1 次印刷
定　　价：59.80 元

产品编号：088419-01

前　言

近年来，跨境电商的快速发展不仅带来了传统国际贸易企业的快速转型，也催生了对跨境电商专业人才的巨大需求。为适应经济社会发展需要，许多高校纷纷开设跨境电商专业或课程，培养专业人才，这对推动我国跨境电商发展、深化外贸经济改革具有十分重要的作用。

本书共八章，包括跨境电子商务概述，跨境电子商务平台，建立商务关系，跨境电子商务支付与结算，跨境电子商务物流，跨境电子商务市场理论，跨境电子商务订单管理，跨境电子商务服务。

英语是跨境电商最重要的技能之一，关系到整个交易过程的顺利进行。跨境电商交易中的定价、营销、订单处理、物流和售后都需要专业的英语知识和技能做支撑。

本教材旨在培养了解跨境电商基础知识，精通专业英语运用，熟悉跨境电商运营管理，能够独立从事跨境电商相关工作的具有过硬职业素质、专业能力和专业知识的专业人才。

本书设置了以下版块。

新词：本书汇集了专业、实用、基础、全面的专业词汇。只有有针对性地学习，才能轻松地掌握跨境电商的实用英语。

短语：本书汇集了常用的专业短语，有助于更好地理解全文。

句子：本书汇集了各种表达方式，简单实用，帮助使用者灵活表达和运用跨境电商实用英语。

对话：本书设置了真实场景对话，真正实用的语言交流。

本书实用直观，通俗易懂，适合相关专业的大中专学生以及涉足跨境电商、希望进一步拓展销售渠道的创业者和准备从事跨境电商的人员阅读。

本书由崔新红、徐赢光、邹益民主编，他们负责本书的整体起草工作。由于编者水平有限，书中的不足和疏漏在所难免，请各位读者多多指教。

编者

Preface

In recent years, the rapid development of cross-border E-commerce has not only brought about the rapid transformation of traditional international trade enterprises, but also given rise to a huge demand for cross-border E-commerce professionals. In order to meet the needs of economic and social development, many colleges and universities have set up cross-border E-commerce majors or courses to train professional talents, which plays a very important role in promoting the development of cross-border E-commerce and deepening the economic reform of foreign trade in China.

This book is divided into eight chapters, including the overview of cross-border E-commerce; platform of cross-border E-commerce; establishment of business relations; payment and settlement of cross-border E-commerce; cross-border E-commerce logistics; cross-border E-commerce market theory; the cross-border E-commerce order management; the services of cross-border E-commerce.

English is one of the most important skills in cross-border E-commerce, which is related to the smooth progress of the whole transaction process. Pricing, marketing, order processing, logistics and after-sales in cross-border E-commerce transactions all require professional English knowledge and skills.

The purpose of this course is to train professionals with excellent professional quality, professional ability and professional knowledge who understand the basic knowledge of cross-border E-commerce, be proficient in the use of professional English, be familiar with the operation and management of cross-border E-commerce, and be able to independently engage in a series of cross-border E-commerce work.

The features of this book are as follows:

New words: This book collects the most professional, practical, basic and comprehensive professional vocabulary. Only by studying pertinently can we change quantitatively to qualitatively and easily master practical English in cross-border E-commerce.

Phrases: This book is a collection of commonly used professional phrases, which is helpful to better understand the full text.

Sentences: This book brings together a variety of expressions, simple and practical, to help you flexibly express and use practical English for cross-border E-commerce.

Conversations: Actual combat scene dialogue, real practical dialogue and communication.

This book is practical, intuitive and easy to understand. It is suitable for individuals, entrepreneurs, small and medium-sized enterprises, large enterprises and those engaged in cross-border E-commerce who want to set foot in cross-border E-commerce, and who want to further expand their sales channels.

Cui xinhong, Xu yingguang, Zou yimin are the editor-in-chief of this book and they are responsible for the overall draft of the book. Due to the limited level of the editor, the mistakes and omissions in the book are inevitable, please do not hesitate to give us advice from readers.

Authors

目　　录

Contents

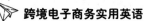

Chapter 1 Overview of Cross-border E-commerce

跨境电子商务概述

【Ability Objectives】

- ❑ Be able to introduce the E-commerce in English 能够用英语介绍电子商务；
- ❑ Be able to communicate with customers in English 能够用英语与顾客交流；
- ❑ Be able to read and comprehend some articles related to cross-border E-commerce 能够阅读和理解与跨境电子商务有关的文章。

【Knowledge Objectives】

- ❑ Master typical expressions about cross-border E-commerce 掌握跨境电子商务的经典表达；
- ❑ Memorize new words and phrases in the texts 能够记忆文章中的单词与短语。

【Key Words】

E-commerce（电子商务）；cross-border E-commerce（跨境电子商务）

Section 1.1 Overview of E-commerce 电子商务概述

New Words

E-commerce	*n.*	电子商务
infrastructure	*n.*	（国家或机构的）基础设施
commercial	*adj.*	贸易的；商业的；盈利的；以获利为目的的
	n.	（电台或电视播放的）广告
sphere	*n.*	球；领域；球体；球形
	v.	使成球形；包围；把……放在球内；使处于天体之间
external	*n.*	外部；外观；形式；外部情况
	adj.	外部的；外面的；外界的；外来的
separate	*v.*	分离；区分；隔开；区别
	adj.	单独的；独立的；分开的；不同的
corporate	*adj.*	公司的；组成公司（或团体）的；法人的；社团的

browser	n.	浏览器；浏览程序；浏览图书报刊者；逛商店的人
extranet	n.	【计】外联网
intranet	n.	【计】内联网
concept	n.	概念；观念；设想；观点
perspective	n.	观点；远景；景观；透视法
	adj.	（按照）透视画法的；透视的
implement	v.	实施；执行；落实（政策）；使生效
	n.	工具；器具；〈英〉【法】履行（契约等）
facilitate	v.	促进；促使；使便利
accelerate	v.	加快；加速
transactions	n.	事务；交易；学报；处理
extended	adj.	延长了的；扩展了的
geographic	adj.	地理学的
irrelevant	adj.	无关紧要的；不相关的
competitors	n.	竞争者；敌手
cyberspace	n.	网络空间
multimedia	n.	【计】多媒体；混合舞台效果；【画】混合画法
	adj.	多媒体的；使用多媒体的
icons	n.	偶像；人像；肖像；画像
trademark	n.	商标；标记；招牌动作；特征
accurate	adj.	正确无误的；精确的；准确的；准确的（掷、射、击等）
inventory	n.	库存；财产清单；（建筑物里的物品、家具等的）清单
	v.	开列清单
consumption	n.	消费；消耗量
perishable	adj.	易腐烂的；易变质的
	n.	易腐败的东西
antiques	n.	古董；古风
	adj.	过时的；古时制造的；古风的；古董的
	v.	使显得古色古香
inspect	v.	检查；视察；检阅；审查
ultimately	adv.	最终；最后；归根结底；终究
frequent	adj.	频繁的；经常发生的
	v.	常到（某处）
turnover	n.	成交量；人事变更率；人员调整率；销售比率
impediments	n.	阻碍；障碍物；口吃；同 impedimenta
integrate	v.	使一体化；使（黑人等）不受歧视；表示（面积、温度等的）总和
	adj.	完整的

resistant	*adj.*	抵抗的；有抵抗力的；抵制的；阻止的
	n.	抵抗者；有抵抗力的东西
conflicting	*adj.*	互相斗争的；相冲突的
merchant	*n.*	商人；批发商；（尤指）进出口批发商；（某活动的）爱好者
	adj.	海上货运的
vendors	*n.*	〈正式〉供应商；小贩

Phrases

at the request of	应……的要求
in addition	另外；除此之外；并且
to concentrate on	专心于；把思想集中于
Internet protocol(IP)	互联网协议
business transactions	商务交易；经济业务；业务事务
electronic data interchange(EDI)	电子数据交换
generalized E-commerce	广义电子商务
workflow automation	工作流自动化
medium-sized enterprises	中型企业；中小企业的客户；中等规模企业
outdated information	信息过时；过时信息；过时的内容

Sentences

1. Hello, welcome to my Internet shop.
   你好，欢迎光临我的网店。

2. Welcome to my store on the Internet.
   欢迎光临我的网店。

3. Starting an online store has advantages over having a physical storefront.
   开通网上商铺比实体店铺有优势。

4. After all, starting an online store today has become simpler than ever.
   毕竟现在开通网上商铺已经变得比以前简单多了。

5. Can I be of some help?
   有什么可以帮助您的吗？

6. Thank you for shopping at my Internet store.
   感谢您来我们网店购物。

7. Are you being helped?/ Are you being served?
   你需要帮忙吗？

8. Hello, this is seller No. 1. Are there any questions?
   你好，我是 1 号销售员，你有什么要咨询的吗？

9. Have a nice shopping.
   祝您购物愉快。

10. We can start thinking about who can help to handle some of the product management.
我们开始考虑谁能帮助处理一些产品管理的事宜。

11. He has worked in the cross-border electricity business for more than ten years, with roles in management, technical marketing, product marketing, and product management.
他已经在跨境电商行业工作了十多年，曾做过管理、技术市场、产品市场以及产品管理工作。

12. As with other aspects of product management, spending extra time and effort defining the problem in advance can save more time and effort after carrying out task.
与产品管理中的其他许多方面类似，多花些时间和精力提前明确问题，可以在开展工作时节省更多时间和精力。

13. There are big differences between product management and project management.
产品管理和项目管理之间有着巨大的差别。

14. To fulfill both the strategic and the new tactical product management functions, we must pick personalities compatible with the task at hand.
为了实现战略和新战术上的产品管理功能，我们选才时必须对号入座。

15. Product management is concerned with the life of the product, from conception, development and eventually to discontinuation.
产品管理关心的是产品的整个生命周期：从概念、发展到废弃。

Conversations

1. Welcome

salesman: Good morning, madam. Is there anything can I do for you?

customer: Yes. I'd like to buy the dress.

salesman: You mean this one? It's the latest fashion.

customer: What is this dress made of ?

salesman: It's made of silk. It's perfect, isn't it?

customer: I want to buy the purple one.

salesman: What size do you wear?

customer: Size L. I will pay for it. How much is it?

salesman: 698 yuan.

 (A few days later)

salesman: Hello, how does the dress fit?

customer: It's perfectly. I will give a positive review for you.

salesman: Thanks. Welcome back again.

1. 欢迎

售货员：早上好，太太。我能为您做点什么吗？

顾客：是的。我想看看这件礼服。

售货员：您是说这一件吗？这是最新款。

顾客：这件礼服是什么材料做的？

售货员：这是丝绸做的。很漂亮，不是吗？

顾客：我想买件紫色的。

售货员：您穿多大号的？

顾客：L 号。我准备付费。这件礼服多少钱？

售货员：698 元。

（几天后）

售货员：你好，礼服合身吗？

顾客：很合身。我会给好评的。

售货员：谢谢。欢迎下次再来。

2. Inferior/Unqualified Products Faulty Materials

A: Have you seen our surveyor's report of your products?

B: Yes. I'm feeling very sorry.

A: There are too many faulty materials in the goods which you have shipped to us.

B: I'm sorry. That's quite unusual for our company. What can we do to make things better?

A: We would like to ship back all the goods to you.

B: No better way?

A: I think this is the best solution.

B: That is all right. We will send you a replacement right now.

A: Thanks for your cooperation.

2. 劣质品

A：您看过我方的产品检查报告了吗？

B：是的，我感到十分抱歉。

A：你们寄过来的那批货中劣质品太多了。

B：不好意思。我们公司向来很少发生这种事情。那现在我们应该怎么办？

A：我们想把整批货送回去。

B：没有更好的办法了吗？

A：我想这就是最佳的解决方案。

B：那好吧。我们会马上补寄一批货过去。

A：谢谢你的合作。

Text

1.1.1   The Concept and Characteristics of E-commerce 电子商务的概念和特征

At present, it's certain that E-commerce will become an important part of the global economy. The infrastructure of E-commerce is a computer network. Today, whether it is in the commercial sphere, family or government agencies, computer network has become standard computer application environment. Through communicate network, many computers and its external devices can be connected. In this way, the computer user can communicate with different computer users in the network but in different locations to obtain or exchange information on the computer. More and more people have connected to the Internet global network environment, or joined to corporate Internet.

如今，电子商务成为国际经济中的重要部分已成定局。电子商务的基础是计算机网络。现如今，不论是商业领域、家庭还是政府机构，计算机网络已经成为计算机应用环境的标准。通过数据通信网络，许多计算机及其延伸设备得到连接。通过这种方式，计算机使用者可以与不同地区的不同的计算机使用者交流以获得或者交换信息。

1. Definition of E-commerce 电子商务的定义

E-commerce is a new concept, which describes the process of trading, the exchange of goods, services and information via computer networks (including the Internet).

电子商务是一个新的概念，它描述了货物、服务以及信息通过计算机网络（包括互联网）交易的过程。

E-commerce is defined from the following angles: From the communication point of view, E-commerce transmits information, product/service or pay through the telephone line, computer network or other electronic means. From the business perspective, E-commerce is the technology application implemented to facilitate business transactions and workflow automation. From the service perspective, E-commerce is the tool used to help companies, consumers, or managers reduce service costs, improve product quality, and accelerate the speed of service. From the online perspective, E-commerce supplies the information of purchase and sale of goods through the Internet and other online services.

电子商务可以从以下角度被定义：从交流的角度来说，电子商务通过电话付费、计算机网络或者其他电子方式传送信息、产品或服务；从商业角度来说，电子商务是用于促进商务交易和工作流程自动化的科技应用；从服务角度来说，电子商务是用来帮助公司、客户或者经营者减少服务费用，提高产品质量和提升服务效率的工具；从线上的角度来说，电子商务通过互联网或者其他线上服务提供买卖信息。

People regard the commercial affairs as the behavior of transactions between business partners. Therefore, for some people, the concept of E-commerce is narrow. So many people use the term E-business, that is, generalized E-commerce. Generalized E-commerce is not just about buying and selling, also includes service for customer, cooperation between business partners and the electronic transaction within corporate organizations. As Lou Gerstner, the IBM CEO, remarks: "the generalized E-commerce is a complete cycle, which means high-speed, globalization, increase of production, acquiring new customers, and sharing competitive advantage. "

人们认为商务是商业伙伴之间的交易行为。因此对某些人来说，电子商务的概念是狭义的。许多人用的 E-business 就是广义的电子商务。广义的电子商务不仅是关于买卖的，还包括对顾客的服务、商务伙伴之间的合作、企业之间的电子交易。正如美国国际商用机器公司的总裁路易·郭士纳所言："广义的电子商务是一个完整的闭环，这意味着高速、全球化、产量的增长、新顾客的获得还有竞争优势的分享。"

2. Characteristics of E-commerce 电子商务的特征

1) The Benefits of E-commerce 电子商务的优势

As the computer network can promote the exchange of information in a quick and inexpensive way, Internet has now extended to every corner of the world. Small and medium-sized enterprises can establish contacts with trading partners around the world. The high-speed network makes the geographic distance become irrelevant.

由于计算机网络可以促使信息以快速廉价的方式得到交换，互联网在这个世界上已经无处不在。中小型企业可以与世界各地的交易伙伴建立联系。高速的网络使物理距离不再重要。

Companies can more easily sell goods, explore new markets and identify business opportunities outside the traditional markets. Small and medium-sized enterprises that are unable to establish overseas offices before can now show themselves to every corner of the world. Enterprises may gather information about products, buyers and competitors through the Internet to enhance their competitiveness.

公司可以更容易地售卖商品，探索新的市场，发现传统市场外的商业机会。那些之前不能建立海外办事处的中小型企业现在可以在世界的任何角落展示自己。企业可以通过互联网收集产品、买家以及竞争对手的信息，以增强自身的竞争力。

Companies will maintain their competitive advantage by establishing close contact with customers via the Internet, and providing the latest information about product and service 24 hours a day. In addition, the data can be updated at any time, so the problem of outdated information does not exist. Internet companies can supply many markets and endless marketing opportunities in cyberspace, and also it can enhance contact with the buyer.

企业可以通过互联网与顾客保持密切的联系，提供最新的产品信息以及全天候服务来保持其竞争优势。另外，互联网可以在任何时间更新数据，所以信息老旧的问题不复存在。互联网公司可以在网络空间提供许多市场以及无尽的市场机会，而且它可以增强买家之间的联系。

Use of multimedia features can effectively make people accept a group of icons, as well as the trademark of products and services via the Internet. Detailed and accurate sales data can help to reduce inventory levels, thus reducing operating costs. Detailed customer information, such as consumption patterns, personal preferences and purchasing power etc., can help companies develop marketing strategies more effectively.

运用互联网中多媒体的特性可以有效地使人们接受图标，以及产品的商标和服务。详细和精确的销售数据可以降低最低库存量，从而降低运用成本。详细的客户信息，如消费方式、个人喜好以及购买力等可以有效地帮助公司开发营销策略。

2) Disadvantages of E-commerce 电子商务的劣势

(1) Technologies are changing rapidly, and keeping pace with change will ultimately become too costly.

归根结底，科技飞速变化，要跟上科技的变化财务消耗巨大。

(2) There is frequent employee turnover. Many skilled employees leave and start their own businesses or for higher salaries.

人事变更频繁，许多有技能的员工为了自己创业或者高工资离开。

(3) Many companies face cultural and legal impediments when they start E-commerce business.

许多企业在开展电子商务的时候面临着文化与法律障碍。

(4) There is difficulty in integrating existing database into the E-commerce software.

把已有的数据库整合到电子商务软件中是有困难的。

(5) Some consumers are still fearful of sending their credit card information on the Internet.

有些顾客仍然对把他们的信用卡信息输入互联网有顾虑。

(6) Other consumers are simply resistant to purchase online and are uncomfortable viewing merchandise on a computer screen.

其他顾客只是单纯地排斥在网上购物，他们觉得在电脑屏幕上浏览商品不舒服。

(7) Internet laws are confusing and conflicting.

互联网法律混乱冲突。

3) E-commerce Safety Problems

Tips for safe shopping on-line:

安全购物的要点如下：

(1) Know the merchant. Find the company physical location.

了解商家，找到商家公司的实际位置。

(2) Know the refund and return policy.

了解退款以及退货政策。

(3) Protect our Internet passwords.

保护自己的支付密码。

(4) Protect your privacy. Input your credit card and social security information only in secure environment.

保护自己的隐私，在安全环境中输入自己的信用卡和社交安全信息。

(5) Keep accurate shopping records.

精准保存购物记录。

(6) Know your consumer rights.

了解自己的消费权益。

As the traditional markets, there are lots of fakes in shopping online. Consumers and vendors should beware.

和传统市场一样，网上购物有许多虚假信息，消费者与供应商应该警惕。

1.1.2   The Development History of E-commerce 电子商务的发展

The development of China's E-commerce presents typical block economic characteristic.

中国电子商务的发展展现出中国块状经济的典型特色。

With gradual establishment and improvement of domestic logistics, payment system, and further development of information infrastructure, E-commerce market in China obviously got resuscitated, and market vigor of E-commerce market significantly strengthens.

随着国内物流、支付系统以及信息基础设施的逐渐建立与完善，中国的电子商务市场明显活跃起来，电子商务市场的活力明显增强。

Indeed, E-commerce in China worth many hundreds of billions of dollars. Online retail sales in China have soared in recent years.

实际上，中国的电子商务价值数以亿计，近几年网上零售业突飞猛进。

Generally speaking, the China E-commerce market contains huge commercial opportunities, and the development prospect is extremely broad.

总体来说，中国的电子商务市场有着巨大的商业机会，发展前景极其广阔。

Section 1.2   Overview of Cross-border E-commerce
跨境电子商务概述

New Words

blog	*n.*	博客
platform	*n.*	平台
memorandum	*n.*	备忘录
custom	*n.*	海关，关税
transaction	*n.*	交易，业务，事务；办理，处理
logistics	*n.*	物流；后勤
definition	*n.*	定义；解释
argument	*n.*	争论，争吵；论据
distribution	*n.*	分配，分布
consumer	*n.*	消费者，顾客
individual	*adj.*	个人的；个别的
	n.	个人；个体
process	*n.*	过程
import	*v.*	进口；引进；输入
	n.	进口；重要；意义；进口货

export	*n.*	出口；【无线电】呼叫；出口货；输出额
	v.	出口；排出
	adj.	输出的
cumbersome	*adj.*	大而笨重的；难以携带的；缓慢复杂的；冗长的
exhibition	*n.*	展览；展出；表演；（一批）展览品
disseminate	*v.*	传播；散播；扩散
express	*v.*	表达；表示；表露；代表
	adj.	特快的；快速的；快递的；用快递寄送的
	n.	特快列车；快件服务；快递服务；快运服务
qualification	*n.*	合格；学历；资历；限定条件
retail	*v.*	零售；以……价格销售
	n.	零售
	adv.	零卖
self-operated	*un.*	自营的
warehousing	*n.*	仓储；仓储业
facilitate	*v.*	促进；促使；使便利
wholesaler	*n.*	批发商
retailer	*n.*	零售商；零售店
operational	*adj.*	可使用；操作的；运转的；运营的
community	*n.*	社区；社团；公众；社会团体
ecosystem	*n.*	生态系统
small-scale	*adj.*	小型的；小范围的；小规模的；按小比例绘制的
dilemma	*n.*	（进退两难的）窘境
integration	*n.*	一体化；结合；融入群体或社会；
procurement	*n.*	（尤指为政府或机构）采购
utmost	*n.*	极限；最大限度；最大量；最大可能
	adj.	最大的；极度的
constraint	*n.*	约束；限制；限定；严管
bottleneck	*n.*	障碍；瓶颈路段（常引起交通阻塞）
	v.	限制；交通堵塞
	adj.	（街道等）狭隘的
restriction	*n.*	限制；约束；制约因素；限制规定
undeniably	*adv.*	不可否认地
convert	*v.*	转换；可转变为；可变换成
vigorous	*adj.*	充满活力的；充满激情的；激烈的；精力旺盛的
boldly	*adv.*	大胆地；大模大样地；理直气壮地
reshuffle	*v.*	改组；进行岗位调整；更改职责配置
	n.	〈比喻〉（政府等的）改组；重新配置；（牌的）重洗

vertical	*n.*	垂直线；垂直位置
	adj.	竖的；垂直的；直立的；纵向的
subdivide	*v.*	再分；超级细分；把……再分
practitioner	*n.*	（尤指医学或法律界的）从业人员；习艺者；专门人才
rationalization	*n.*	（尤指事业等的）合理化；【数】有理化；【心】文饰（作用）；理论解释

Phrases

cross-border E-commerce	跨境电子商务
capital market	资本市场
free trade zone	自由贸易区
international business	国际商业
foreign trade	对外贸易
to confuse …with…	把……与……混淆
to be concentrated on	集中在
overseas logistics company	海外物流公司
as much as possible	尽可能
ways of spread	传播方式
information flow	信息流，数据流
investment platform	投资平台
return service	退货服务
direct purchasing	直接采购
television set	电视机
business model	业务模式，商务模式
private individual	个人
direct mail	直接邮寄
supply chain	供应链
content sharing	内容共享，内容分享
third-party platform	第三方平台
systematic docking	系统对接
self-operated platform	自营平台
after-sales service	售后服务
supply channel	供应渠道
operating cost	营业费用，营业成本
third-party payment	第三方支付
customs clearance	结关，验关
tax refund	退税
quality inspection rate	质量检验率

technical level	技术层面
series of	一系列
annual growth rate	年增长速度
tuyere industry	风口行业
subdivided market	细分市场
to keep up with	继续做；熟悉；保持联系
B2B（business to business）	企业对企业电子商务
B2C（business to customer）	企业对个人电子商务
M2C（manufacturer to consumer）	生产厂家对消费者电子商务
C2C（consumer to consumer）	个人对个人电子商务
SKU（stock keeping unit）	库存量单位，最小存货单位

Sentences

1. These are new products from our warehouse.
   这都是我们仓库的新产品。

2. There are as many as 100 new products on show.
   展出的新产品不少于 100 种。

3. Do you want to see the samples?
   您想看样品吗?

4. I'd like to give you a detail introduction of the new products.
   我现在向您详细介绍一下我们的新产品。

5. Our new products are among the most popular ones on the Internet.
   我们的新产品在网上是最受欢迎的产品之一。

6. The new products are suitable for 1-18 age groups.
   这种产品适合 1～18 岁年龄段使用。

7. The new products are very much to the taste of our market.
   这种产品在我国市场上大受欢迎。

8. It is a busy season for our new products now.
   我们的新产品正值旺季。

9. They are in large demand.
   这种产品销路非常大。

10. Our new products will be launched into market at the end of this month.
    我们的新产品将在本月末投放市场。

11. Let me explain the specifications of this new product.
    让我来解释一下这款新产品的规格。

12. Are you interested in our new products?
    您对我们的新产品感兴趣吗?

13. I have searched that the foods of that quality will never sell.

我搜索了一下，那样质量的商品绝对卖不出去。

14. Have you searched? What about quality control?

你搜索了没有？质量控制怎么办？

15. We found the quality of the goods is much inferior to the samples.

我们发现这批货物的品质大大低于样品。

Conversations

1. Introduction of New Products

David: What can I do for you?

Tom: I've been attracted by your products. Could you give me more information on them?

David: I'm pleased to be of any help to you. Our company specializes in making better quality office furniture and equipment. Please have a look at the pictures of our newest products.

Tom: How do you ensure quality?

David: All of our new products have a 1-3 year testing period.

Tom: What happens if I'm not satisfied with my purchases?

David: Your satisfaction is guaranteed, or you can return products without reasons in seven days and we refund your money.

Tom: I see. But I have to talk it over with my boss before I make a decision.

David: OK. I hope we will get in touch soon.

1. 新产品发布

大卫：需要什么帮助吗？

汤姆：我对你们的产品很感兴趣。能告诉我有关你们产品的更多信息吗？

大卫：很乐意为您效劳。我们公司专门生产优质的办公设备。请看一下我们最新产品的图片。

汤姆：你们怎么保证产品质量呢？

大卫：我们所有的新产品都有 1～3 年的保质期。

汤姆：买了之后不满意怎么办？

大卫：我们保证用户满意，你可以七天无理由退货，退货后我们就退款。

汤姆：我知道了，但我必须在做决定之前跟我的老板商量一下。

大卫：好的，希望我们不久就可以联系。

2. Searching

A: Have you ever tried searching some products online?

B: No, never. I prefer to actually seeing and touching what I'm buying before paying for it, especially for clothes and shoes. So I always try it on in the store first and then go searching online and purchase it online.

A: That's right. Seeing is believing.

B: I've heard some friends say when they get the goods, it's quite different from what they see on the website advertisement.

A: That happens. Without close quality examination, we may encounter fraud, and the E-shop may suddenly disappear.

B: What's more, it's not always so safe for us to pay online as hackers might steal the user's name and password.

A: It's said that some measures have been taken to deal with this problem. Paying online is much safer than before, but I still have the feeling that it's not safe enough.

B: I can't agree more. That's why I only do street shopping.

A: Me too. Sometimes I surf online shops to check some related information, and then go to the physical store to do the actual shopping.

B: That's a good idea.

2. 网上搜索

A：你在网上买过东西吗？

B：没买过，我还是喜欢在买之前亲自感受一下，特别是衣服和鞋。现在我总是会先在实体店试好了，再从网上买。

A：没错，眼见为实。

B：我听朋友说过他们在网上买到的东西和网站广告上看到的很不一样。

A：确实有这种事。不好好检查质量，可能会买到假货，网店也没准儿突然消失。

B：而且网上付费有时也不安全，黑客可能会偷走用户名和密码。

A：听说已经出台措施解决这个问题了。现在网上付费比以前安全多了，但我还是觉得不够安全。

B：你说得太对了。所以我只在实体店买东西。

A：我也是。有时候我会逛逛网店，查一下产品信息，然后到实体店去买。

B：那真是一个好主意。

Text

1.2.1　The Definition of Cross-border E-commerce 跨境电子商务的概念和特征

Cross-border E-commerce is a kind of E-commerce. As the largest E-commerce platform in the world, Amazon entered Shanghai Free Trade Zone on August 20, 2014. The memorandum signed on cooperation shows that "Amazon will open its new cross-border E-commerce platform in the free trade zone". From here we know that cross-border E-commerce must have been translated from the English. So, what exactly is the definition of cross-border E-commerce?

　　跨境电子商务是一种电子商务。作为全球最大的电子商务平台，亚马逊于 2014 年 8 月 20 日进入上海自由贸易区。签署的合作备忘录显示，"亚马逊将在自由贸易区开设新的跨境电子商务平台"。从这里我们知道跨境电子商务一词应该是由英语翻译而来的。那么，跨境电子商务到底该如何定义？

In Wikipedia, cross-border E-commerce refers to an international business activity where the trading entities that belong to different customs achieve transactions, payments, and cross-border logistics delivery through the E-commerce platform.

在维基百科中，跨境电子商务是指一种国际商业活动，其中属于不同海关的交易实体通过电子商务平台实现交易、支付和跨境物流交付。

1.2.2　The Classification of Cross-border E-commerce 跨境电子商务的分类

1. Import Cross-border E-commerce 进口跨境电子商务

1) M2C Model　M2C 模式

It is an investment platform, and it is manufacturer-to-customer. In this model, merchants need to obtain qualifications and authorization for overseas retail sales. The products are directly mailed overseas and can provide local return service, but usually the price is relatively high.

这是一个投资平台，是厂家对客户的。在这种模式下，厂家需要获得海外零售的资格和授权。直接邮寄到海外的产品可以提供本地退货服务，但价格通常比较高。

2) B2C Model　B2C 模式

It means self-operated and direct purchasing, and it is business-to-customer. In this model, the platform will generally directly participate in the flow of goods purchasing and logistics warehousing. For example, buying a television set from an electronics retailer would be a B2C transaction.

这指的是自营和直接采购，即企业对客户。在这种模式下，平台一般会直接参与物流采购和物流仓储。例如，从电子产品零售商处购买电视机是 B2C 交易。

3) C2C Model　C2C 模式

Consumer-to-consumer, or C2C, is the business model that facilitates commerce between private individuals. Whether it's for goods or services, this category of E-commerce connects people to do business with one another. The goal of a C2C is to enable these relationships, helping buyers and sellers locate each other. Customers can benefit from the competition for products and easily find products that may otherwise be difficult to locate.

客户对客户，即 C2C，是促进个体与个体之间交易的商业模型。无论商品还是服务，这种电子商务把人们联系在一起，让他们互相做生意。C2C 的目标是实现这些关系，帮助匹配买方和卖方。客户可以从产品竞争中获益，并且很容易找到在其他模式下可能很难找到的商品。

4) B2B Model　B2B 模式

That is business-to-business which refers to commerce between two or more businesses such as those involving a manufacturer and wholesaler or retailer. In general, it is used to improve efficiency for companies.

这是企业对企业，指的是两个或更多企业之间的商业行为，如涉及制造商和批发商或零售商的企业。一般来说，它用于提高公司的效率。

5) Overseas E-commerce Direct Mail 海外电子商务直邮

The representative company is Amazon. The model is characterized by having a global high-quality supply chain system and a wealth of SKUs.

代表公司是亚马逊。该模式的特点是拥有全球高品质的供应链系统和大量库存。

6) Third Partner 第三方

In fact, there are two types of this model: One is technical, and the other is operational. Generally, there are advantages in the early stage of cross-border E-commerce. It is easy to start with low cost, rich SKUs, but lacks competitiveness, and needs real-time updates and other strong technical support.

事实上，这种模式有两种类型：一种是技术型，另一种是运营型。一般来说，跨境电子商务初期具有优势。它易启动，低成本，有丰富的库存，但缺乏竞争力，需要实时更新和其他强有力的技术支持。

7) Content Sharing/Community Information 内容共享/社区信息

This model is the promotion base for brands, because it mainly achieves natural conversion through content.

这种模式是品牌的推广基础，因为它主要通过内容实现自然转换。

2. Export Cross-border E-commerce 出口跨境电子商务

1) B2B Model B2B 模式

It is divided into two types: information service platform and transaction service platform. For the information service platform, it is mainly to conduct information distribution or information search to complete transaction through a third-party platform. The representative companies are Alibaba International Station and Global Sources. The transaction service platform is to build a platform business model that enables online transactions and payments between supply and demand parties. Representative companies include Dunhuang. com and etc.

它分为两种类型：信息服务平台和交易服务平台。对于信息服务平台而言，主要是通过第三方平台进行信息发布或信息搜索来完成交易。其代表公司是阿里巴巴国际站和环球资源。交易服务平台是建立一个平台业务模型，支持供需双方之间的在线交易和支付，其代表公司包括敦煌网等。

2) B2C/C2C Model B2C/C2C 模式

It is divided into an open platform and a self-operated platform. The open platform realizes the systematic docking of applications and platforms, and builds an ecosystem around the platform itself. The representative platform includes Amazon, Wish, AliExpress, eBay, Lazada, and other small-scale platforms. The self-operated platform manages the products in a unified way. It trades online and delivers products to consumers through logistics.

它分为开放平台和自营平台。开放平台实现了应用程序和平台的系统对接，并围绕平台自身构建了一个生态系统。代表性平台包括亚马逊、Wish、AliExpress、eBay、Lazada

和其他小型平台。自营平台以统一的方式管理产品。它实现在线交易，通过物流向消费者提供产品。

1.2.3　The Development of Cross-border E-commerce in China 中国跨境电子商务的发展形式

1. Dilemmas of Cross-border E-commerce 跨境电子商务的困境

When the cross-border E-commerce has been developing at a high speed in recent years, it has also received great support with policies. However, the entire process of cross-border E-commerce needs the integration and cooperation of procurement supply, logistics, distribution, payment, and after-sales service to achieve stable development. At present, it still faces the following dilemmas.

近年来跨境电子商务发展迅速，同时也有很多政策支持。但是，跨境电子商务需要整合采购、供应、物流、配送、支付和售后服务才能实现稳定发展。目前，它仍然面临以下困境。

1) Logistics Constraints 物流限制

Logistics is a core factor in both cross-border E-commerce and traditional trade. At present, logistics is also a major bottleneck among cross-border E-commerce. Restrictions are mainly reflected in two aspects. First, there are still large gaps between the logistics companies in different countries. If trans-shipping the goods, the supply chain will easily break and eventually affect the logistics speed of goods. The usual solution is to establish overseas warehouses. Another dilemma is how to increase the turnover of overseas warehouses and reduce operating costs.

物流是跨境电子商务和传统贸易的核心因素。目前，物流也是跨境电子商务的主要瓶颈。限制主要体现在两个方面。首先，不同国家的物流公司存在较大差距，导致运送货物的供应链很容易断裂，最终影响物流速度。通常的解决方案是建立海外仓库。其次，物流的困境是如何增加海外仓库的营业额并降低运营成本。

2) Online Payment Dilemma 在线支付困境

The development of the third-party payment industry is undeniably rapid. For example, Alipay and PayPal have been eligible for cross-border E-commerce. Even so, payment still face many difficulties like customs clearance and tax refunds. In cross-border business, convert, credit, security and risk are also factors of restricting.

第三方支付行业的发展无疑是迅速的。例如，支付宝和 PayPal 已经能进行跨境电子商务了。即便如此，付款仍然面临着诸如清关和退税等许多困难。在跨境业务中，换汇、信贷、安全和风险也是限制因素。

3) After-sales Service Problems 售后服务问题

After-sales services are very important links. The after-sales problem of cross-border E-commerce is also an important factor that discourages consumers because of the numerous links in the entire process, such as customs clearance, logistics, and so on. The after-sale cost is high. With the continuous development of cross-border E-commerce, the above problems are in fact still

inevitable. However, when you understand China brands, these problems can be solved.

售后服务是非常重要的环节。跨境电子商务的售后问题也是消费者关注的焦点，因为整个过程中有许多环节，如通关、物流等。售后服务的成本很高。

随着跨境电子商务的不断发展，实际上上述问题仍然是不可避免的。但是，当你了解了中国品牌后，这些问题都可以解决。

(1) China brands have more than one million products covering more than 100 categories. The entire suppliers are more than 10,000 with more than 1,000 brand suppliers.

The quality inspection rate is 100%, guaranteeing the quality of all products on the platform.

中国拥有超过100万种的品牌产品，涵盖100多品类。供应商超过10 000家，其中1000多家是品牌供应商。质量检验率为100%，能够保证平台上所有产品的质量。

(2) China brands cooperate with 1000+ leading logistics companies in the world, with more than 10,000 logistics lines, covering more than 200 countries and regions in the world and China brands storage covers more than 20 countries around the world.

中国品牌与全球1000多家领先的物流公司合作，拥有10 000多条物流专线，覆盖全球200多个国家和地区，中国品牌仓储覆盖全球20多个国家。

(3) For the after-sales services, after cooperating with China brands, we will provide 6×24 hours of customer service, 100% real-time online reply, and the customer service language covers Chinese, English, German, French, and other 10 languages.

对于售后服务，与中国品牌合作后，我们将提供6×24小时的客户服务，100%的实时在线回复，客户服务语言涵盖汉语、英语、德语、法语等10种语言。

2. Trends of Cross-border E-commerce 跨境电子商务的趋势

Most of the above-mentioned cross-border E-commerce dilemma exist at the technical level. The difficulties will be solved one by one with the vigorous development of the cross-border E-commerce industry and the support of the governments' series of policies. Let's forecast the future trend of cross-border E-commerce.

上述跨境电子商务困境大多数存在于技术层面。随着跨境电子商务产业的蓬勃发展和政府的一系列政策的支持，这些困难将逐一解决。我们来预测一下跨境电子商务的未来趋势。

1) Rapid Growth 快速增长

Throughout the past few years, the average annual growth rate of the cross-border E-commerce industry has been above 30%. In fact, few industries can maintain such a high growth rate, because the premise is that the environment will not change within a few years. Therefore, we can boldly predict that the cross-border E-commerce industry will continue to maintain rapid growth in the next 3-5 years.

在过去几年中，跨境电子商务行业的年均增长率已超过30%。事实上，很少有行业能够保持如此高的增长率，因为前提是环境不会在几年内发生变化。因此，我们可以大胆预测，跨境电子商务行业在未来3~5年将继续保持快速增长。

2) Big Seller 大卖家

Any tuyere industry will experience a process of reshuffle. In the future, the overall resources of the cross-border E-commerce industry will be further concentrated on the large platforms and big sellers. This trend is unavoidable, but it does not mean that small and medium sellers have no chance at all. They will generally enter the vertical and subdivided markets.

任何风口行业都将经历重新洗牌的过程。未来，跨境电子商务行业的整体资源将进一步集中于大型平台和大卖家。这种趋势是不可避免的，但这并不意味着中小卖家根本没有机会，它们通常会进入垂直市场和细分市场。

3) Professional Competition 专业竞争

For the high-speed-development of the cross-border E-commerce industry, it can be said that the package does not keep up with the pace of development, but it does not mean this will always be the case. For cross-border E-commerce players, the requirements must be higher. In the future, the competition will be more professional.

由于跨境电子商务行业的高速发展，可以说一揽子计划跟不上发展的步伐，但并不意味着总是如此。对于跨境电子商务参与者来说，要求必须更高。未来，竞争将更加专业化。

4) Standardization 标准化

For an industry to have a benign development, there must be standardized policies. For the cross-border E-commerce industry, whether import or export, there are now more and more related policies. The industry will be more standardized in the future, and for the practitioners, there will be more rationalization requirements.

一个行业想要良性发展，就必须有标准化的政策。对于跨境电子商务行业，无论是进口还是出口，现在都有越来越多的相关政策。未来行业将更加标准化，对于从业者来说，将会有更多的合理化要求。

【 Exercise 】

1. Translate the following phrases into Chinese.

　　at the request of＿＿＿＿＿＿＿＿＿＿＿＿＿＿＿＿＿＿＿＿＿＿＿＿＿

　　concentrate on ＿＿＿＿＿＿＿＿＿＿＿＿＿＿＿＿＿＿＿＿＿＿＿＿＿

　　Internet protocol(IP) ＿＿＿＿＿＿＿＿＿＿＿＿＿＿＿＿＿＿＿＿＿＿

　　generalized E-commerce＿＿＿＿＿＿＿＿＿＿＿＿＿＿＿＿＿＿＿＿＿

　　electronic data interchange(EDI)＿＿＿＿＿＿＿＿＿＿＿＿＿＿＿＿＿

2. Translate the following phrases into English.

　　资本市场＿＿＿＿＿＿＿＿＿＿＿＿＿＿＿＿＿＿＿＿＿＿＿＿＿＿＿

　　自由贸易区＿＿＿＿＿＿＿＿＿＿＿＿＿＿＿＿＿＿＿＿＿＿＿＿＿＿

　　国际商业＿＿＿＿＿＿＿＿＿＿＿＿＿＿＿＿＿＿＿＿＿＿＿＿＿＿＿

　　直接采购＿＿＿＿＿＿＿＿＿＿＿＿＿＿＿＿＿＿＿＿＿＿＿＿＿＿＿

　　细分市场＿＿＿＿＿＿＿＿＿＿＿＿＿＿＿＿＿＿＿＿＿＿＿＿＿＿＿

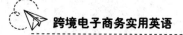

3. Please give the definition of the following words or items in English.

B2B model

B2C model

C2C model

4. Please answer the following questions.

(1) What is E-commerce?

(2) What is cross-border E-commerce?

(3) What are the trends of cross-border E-commerce?

Chapter 2   Platform of Cross-border E-commerce
跨境电子商务平台

【Ability Objectives】

- ❑ Be able to introduce the E-commerce in English 能够用英语介绍电子商务；
- ❑ Be able to communicate with customers in English 能够用英语与顾客交流；
- ❑ Be able to read and comprehend some articles related to cross-border E-commerce 能够阅读和理解与跨境电子商务有关的文章。

【Knowledge Objective】

- ❑ Master typical expressions about cross-border E-commerce 掌握跨境电子商务的经典表达；
- ❑ Memorize new words and phrases in the texts 能够记忆文章中的单词与短语。

【Key Words】

Amazon（亚马逊）；Wish；AliExpress（阿里巴巴速卖通）；Tmall Global（天猫国际）

Section 2.1   The Main Platform of Cross-border E-commerce 跨境电子商务主要平台

New Words

visionary	*n.*	空想家；有远见的人；有智慧的人；幻想者
	adj.	有远见的；空想的；不切实际的；有想象力的
entitiy	*n.*	实体；统一体；存在（物）；（有别于属性等的）本质
headquartered	*adj.*	总部在某地
retailers	*n.*	零售商
commodity	*n.*	商品；产品；货物；商品经济
subsidiary	*n.*	子公司；附属公司
	adj.	辅助的；附带的；次要的；附属的
refurbish	*v.*	翻新；整修；再刷新；重新擦亮
classify	*v.*	分类；归类；划分；界定

rebate	n.	折扣；退还款
	v.	削弱；给……回扣；使钝（刀刃）
stimulate	v.	刺激；激发；促进；激励
staff	n.	五线谱；拐杖；权杖；全体职工（或雇员）
	v.	在……工作；任职于；为……配备职员
exquisite	adj.	精美的；精致的；剧烈的；强烈的
immersive	adj.	（计算机系统或图像）沉浸式虚拟现实的
commitments	n.	诺言；（受）约束；（承担）义务；债务
quota	n.	配额；定额；指标；限额
specifically	adv.	具体来说；明确地；具体地；特意
vouchers	n.	证件；证书；收据；（付款）凭单
diverse	adj.	不同的；相异的；多种多样的；形形色色的
thrift	n.	节俭；节约
undoubtedly	adv.	无疑；毋庸置疑地
extraordinary	adj.	意想不到的；令人惊奇的；奇怪的；不平常的
giant	n.	巨人；伟人；巨兽
	adj.	巨大的；特大的；伟大的
cornerstone	n.	基石；基础；奠基石；最重要的部分
violently	adv.	激烈地；猛烈地；强烈地；厉害地
fuel	n.	燃料；燃油；【新闻传媒】推动力；燃料；刺激物
	v.	（给船等）上煤；（给……）加油；【新闻传媒】加速
pillar	n.	支柱；（尤指兼作装饰的）柱子；纪念柱；柱状物
	v.	用柱子装饰（支持）；成为……的栋梁
entity	n.	独立存在物；实体
browse	v.	浏览；（在商店里）随便看看；翻阅
	n.	嫩枝；放牧
bubble	n.	泡沫；气泡；肥皂泡；（欲表达的）一点感情
	v.	冒泡；起泡；（移动时）发出冒泡的声音；洋溢着（某种感情）
audacious	adj.	敢于冒险的；大胆的
downturn	n.	（商业经济的）衰退
adequate	adj.	足够的；合格的；合乎需要的
enclosure	n.	圈地；围场；圈占地；圈用地
effective	n.	精兵
	adj.	产生预期结果的；有效的；实际的；事实上的
erode	v.	侵蚀；腐蚀；损害；削弱
inventory	n.	库存；财产清单；（建筑物里的物品、家具等的）清单
	v.	开列清单

forecast	*n.*	预测；预报
	v.	预测；预报
display	*v.*	显示；展示；陈列；展出
	n.	展示；陈列；表现；展览
vendor	*n.*	〈正式〉供应商；小贩
subsequent	*adj.*	随后的；后来的；之后的；接后的
entrust	*v.*	委托；托付；交托
delivery	*n.*	分娩；交付；传送；递送
postage	*n.*	邮资；邮费
return	*n.*	返回；回报；回来；收益；退款
	v.	返回；回报；回来；恢复
replication	*n.*	（绘画等的）复制；拷贝；【统】重复（实验）；
		（尤指对答辩的）回答
recommend	*v.*	建议；推荐；介绍；劝告
marketplace	*n.*	市场；集市
innovations	*n.*	创新；改革；新发明
plain	*adj.*	清楚的；明显的；浅白的；坦诚的
	v.	发牢骚；叹惜；哀悼；痛哭
	adv.	绝对地
	n.	平原
commonplace	*n.*	老生常谈；常见的事；平常的事；平淡无奇的言语等
	adj.	平凡的；普通的；普遍的
	v.	把……记入备忘录；由备忘录中摘出
thrive	*v.*	繁荣；茁壮成长；蓬勃发展；兴旺发达
empower	*v.*	授权；使能
tangible	*adj.*	有形的；实际的；真实的；可触摸的
launch	*v.*	发射；发起；开展；开始
	n.	发射；汽艇
primarily	*adv.*	主要地；根本地
automatically	*adv.*	自动地；自然地；无意识地；不自觉地

Phrases

according to		根据；按照；据（……所说）；按（……所报道）
to aspire to		渴望；立志
to be located in		位于；坐落于
to be committed to		承担；致力于；完全旨在
online bookstore		网上书店
Amazon River		亚马孙河

Fortune 500 company	世界五百强公司
home and garden	家居园艺；家居与园艺
health and personal care products	健康和个人护理用品
sports and outdoor goods	运动与户外用品
automotive and industrial products	汽车与工业产品
product strategy	产品战略；商品策略
customer-centric	以客户为中心；以顾客为中心；以客户为中心的
marketing strategies	销售策略；行销策略；营销策略
electronic goods	电子产品
discount pricing strategy	折扣价格策略
public relations	公共关系；公关工作（或活动）
sales promotion	推销；促销活动；销售推广
multimedia pictures	多媒体图片
authoritative book	权威著作
multimedia advertising	多媒体广告；影视广告；多媒体广告艺术
dynamic real-time	动态实时性
authoritative comments	权威点评
regardless of	不管；不顾；不理会
referral fee	介绍费；介绍人费；转介费
cooperative partnership	合作性伙伴关系；合作伙伴关系
wide variety of	各种各样
distribution centers	分配中心；配销中心
free delivery service	免费送货服务
scientific and technological	科学与科技
headquartered in	总部设在
investment bank	投资银行；商业银行
commodity price	商品价格
in any way	无论如何；以任何方式；在任何方面
to rush into	一拥而上；冲进；投到；推行
capital investment	基建投资；资本投资；基本投资；基本建设投资
third-party platform	第三方平台
at that time	在当时；那时候；在那个时候
pointed out	指出
preferential prices	优惠价格
warehousing logistics	仓储物流
back-end	后端
point of view	观点；态度；意见；看法
to be conducive to	有助于；有益于

beneficial cycle	良性循环
Amazon global merchant services	亚马逊全球商家服务
senior vice president	高级副总裁
is voted by	由……来投票的
worldwide category expansion	全球范围的品类扩张
accumulated a lot of experiences	积累了很多经验
back tracking parcel bill	返程包裹单
be very fond of	非常喜欢
independent retail category	自主零售的品类
third-party merchant	第三方商家
entity retail	实体零售
one key shopping	一键购物
high-definition images	高清晰度图像
front and back covers	封面和封底
sample chapters	样章
one-of-a-kind	独一无二的
connected commerce	互联商务
affiliate marketing	联盟营销
cloud computing	云计算
country boundaries	国界
mainland China	中国大陆
millions of	数百万
used items	二手物品；二手商品；二手宝贝
to set up	建立；创立；发起；开办
so-called	（表示不认同）所谓的；（引出约定俗成的称谓）人称……的
corporate DNA	商业利益的本质；组织基因；公司基因；企业 DNA
to focus on	集中于；专注在
to be obsessed in	沉迷于

Sentences

1. Best choice and best discounts.
   最佳选择，最大优惠。

2. I think it seems very well.
   我觉得这个很好。

3. As many repairs as you need, it is free of charge in our store of the website.
   在我们网店，随时免费维修。

4. There is a promotion going on for 10% off. Have you chosen some?

九折促销。您要选购一些吗？

5. There are two new styles in the website, I think they must be suitable for you.

这个网站有两款新款，我想会适合你。

6. I recommend you the ××× website.

我给你推荐×××网。

7. It's the latest fashion.

这是最新的款式。

8. It's a lovely dress, and it's very smart. Short skirts are in fashion now. I have searched in the website, and it is cheaper than in the store.

这件裙子很好看，非常时髦。短裙现在很流行。我在网上搜了一下这件裙子，比店里边的便宜。

9. I take a fancy to this shirt on the×××.com. This shirt matches my skirt well.

我在×××网上相中了一件衬衫，它和我的裙子很配。

10. This is the latest design. You can buy it in the ×××.com.

这是最新款。你们可以在×××网上买到。

11. The website just launched a new project. Would you like to take a look?

这个网站又推出了一个新的项目。您要看看吗？

12. This is the website I will not hesitate to recommend. It is so attractive and also reliable.

这个网站是我毫不犹豫要推荐的。它很吸引人而且也很可靠。

13. Hello, this is the Skin II website. Do you know your skin type?

你好，这是 Skin II 旗舰店。你知道你肌肤的类型吗？

14. This kind of electric product is our bestseller. You can buy some to have a try.

这款电器是我们卖得最好的。你可以拍下试用一下。

15. Please forgive me just being frankly, madam. We don't have this kind of products because we have sold out.

请原谅我的坦诚，夫人。这款产品已经卖完了。

Conversations

1. What Express to Choose?

A: I am very interested in this sunglasses. When can I get it if I place the order?

B: Our default mode of free shipping is China Post Air Mail, it takes about 15-20 days to arrive.

A: I'd like to receive the goods as soon as possible, preferably within 10 days.

B: How about EMS? You can choose priority, express or standard mail. Well, standard mail can take up to 10 working days. Priority is a bit faster and will arrive in about 5 to 7 working days. Express is the fastest, but it's also the most expensive. It only takes 3 days.

A: Oh, I see. I choose Priority.

1. 选择什么快递？

A：我对这副墨镜很感兴趣。如果下单，大概什么时候能到呢？

B：我们默认的包邮方式是中邮小包，15～20 天到达。

A：我想尽快收到货，最好在 10 天以内。

B：EMS 如何？您可以选择优先快递、特快快递或普通快递。普通快递需要至少 10 个工作日。优先快递快一些，5～7 个工作日能送到。特快快递是最快的，但也是最贵的，只需要 3 天就能送到。

A：哦，我明白了。我选择优先快递。

2. Detention of Goods

A: Hello.

B: Hello, may I help you?

A: I just entered the DHL tracking site to view the logistics information of the goods, and found that my package has been stuck in Hong Kong for 10 days. I think you should give me a reasonable explanation.

B: Dear customer, I'm sorry. Due to the typhoon, all goods transshipped in Hong Kong have been stuck. Please understand.

A: Well then, do you have any idea of what's going on?

B: We have been in contact with the Hong Kong side during this period. They stopped working now and will resume their work in the next two or three days. Please be patient.

A: I hope it can be delivered as soon as possible.

B: Please be assured that once the red alarm is lifted, I will call the relevant staff immediately to ask them to deliver the goods. To show our apologize, we have a small gift for you.

A: Okay, I'll wait for a few more days.

2. 货物滞留

A：你好。

B：您好，能为您效劳吗？

A：我刚刚登录 DHL 站点查询商品的物流信息，结果发现我的东西在香港滞留了 10 天。请你给我一个合理的解释。

B：对不起，亲，由于台风的关系，所有在香港转运的货物都受到了影响，还请您理解。

A：那么，你有没有了解现在是什么情况？

B：在此期间，我们一直与香港方面保持联系。他们现在处于停工的状态，会在未来两三天内恢复工作，还请您耐心等待。

A：希望能尽快送到。

B：请您放心，一旦解除警报，我会立即致电相关工作人员，请他们运送货物。为了表示我们的歉意，我们再额外送您一份小礼物。

A：好吧，我就再等几天吧。

Text

2.1.1　Amazon Platform 亚马逊平台

1. Profile of Amazon Company 亚马逊公司简介

Amazon(Amazon.com) is the American largest E-commerce net company, located in Seattle, Washington and is one of the earliest E-commerce company operating on the network.

亚马逊公司（Amazon.com，简称亚马逊）是美国最大的一家网络电子商务公司，位于华盛顿州的西雅图，是网络上最早开始经营电子商务的公司之一。

Amazon company was founded by Jeff Bezos on July 16, 1995. At the beginning, it was called Cadabra, whose nature is the basic online bookstore. However, visionary Bezos saw the potential and characteristics of the network. When entities large bookstores provided 200,000 books, online bookstore can provide more than 200,000 books for the reader to choose. Bezos renamed the net with Amazon River which gave birth to the most variety of biological on earth and reopened in July 1995. The company had registered in the state of Washington in 1994, changed to register in Delaware in 1996, and went public on May 15, 1997, with Code AMZN, one share for $18.

亚马逊公司是在 1995 年 7 月 16 日由杰夫·贝索斯（Jeff Bezos）成立的，一开始叫 Cadabra，性质是基本的网络书店。然而具有远见的贝索斯看到了网络的潜力和特色，当实体的大型书店提供 20 万本书时，网络书店能够提供比 20 万本书更多的选择给读者。因此，贝索斯将 Cadabra 以地球上孕育最多种生物的亚马孙河重新命名，于 1995 年 7 月重新开张。该公司原于 1994 年在华盛顿州登记，1996 年时改到特拉华州登记，并在 1997 年 5 月 15 日上市，代码是 AMZN，一股为 18 美元。

Amazon, Fortune 500 company, is headquartered in Seattle, Washington, United States. It has become an online retailers with the global most commodity and the world's second largest Internet company, including Alexa Internet, a9, lab126, and the Internet Movie DataBase(IMDB) and other subsidiaries under its name. Amazon. com and other sellers offer consumers millions of unique, new, refurbished and used items, such as books, film, television, music, games, digital downloads, electronics and computers, home and garden, toys, baby products, food, clothing, shoes and jewelry, health and personal care products, sports and outdoor goods, toys, automotive and industrial products.

亚马逊公司是一家世界财富 500 强公司，总部位于美国华盛顿州的西雅图。亚马逊目前已成为全球商品品种最多的网上零售商和全球第二大互联网公司，在公司名下，也包括了 Alexa Internet、a9、lab126 和互联网电影数据库（Internet Movie DataBase, IMDB）等子公司。亚马逊及其他销售商为客户提供数百万种独特的全新、翻新及二手商品，如图书、影视音乐和游戏、数码下载、电子和计算机、家居园艺用品、玩具、婴幼儿用品、食品服饰、鞋类和珠宝、健康和个人护理用品、体育及户外用品、玩具、汽车及工业产品等。

2. Amazon Sales Strategy 亚马逊销售策略

1) Product Strategy 产品策略

Amazon is committed to be the world's "most customer-centric" company, and has become an online retailer with the widest range of global commodity.

亚马逊致力于成为全球最"以客户为中心"的公司。目前已成为全球商品种类最多的网上零售商。

2) Discount Pricing Strategy 折扣价格策略

Amazon uses discount pricing strategy. The so-called discount strategy is that the business gave a rebate on the original price of the commodity to stimulate consumers and increase the purchase. Amazon makes up for the discount and increasing profits by expanding the sales and it gave a considerable amount of rebates for most commodities. For example, for music commodities, it promises: "You'll enjoy everyday savings of up to 40% on CDs, including up to 30% off Amazon's 100 the best-selling CDs(CD class, to a 40% discount, which including 30% rebate on the best-selling CD)."

亚马逊采用了折扣价格策略。所谓折扣价格策略，是指企业为了刺激消费者增加购买，在商品原价格上给予一定的折扣。它通过扩大销量弥补折扣费用和增加利润。亚马逊对大多数商品都给予了相当数量的折扣。例如，在音乐类商品中承诺："对 CD 类给予 40%的折扣，其中包括对亚马逊 100 种最畅销 CD 给予 30%的折扣。"

3) Promotion Strategy 促销策略

There are four tools for businesses to communicate with consumers. They are advertising, personal selling, public relations and sales promotion. Except for the marketing staff, the rest of what are reflected in Amazon pages.

在商业活动中与顾客交流的工具有四种，它们分别是广告、人员推销、公共关系和营业推广。在亚马逊的网页中，除了行销人员，其余部分都有体现。

Joy of shopping is not just buying books with enough money, but the book selection process. Holding the book in hands, looking at the beautiful cover, and reading the introduction is often one of the great pleasures during book shopping. At home page of Amazon, the joy will not be reduced apart from not being able to hold the book directly, exquisite multimedia pictures, clear profile, and authoritative book comment can make people feel immersive. The advertising position at home page is also very reasonable. The first is the best book on the day, then a recent best-selling book, recommended books from the book club, and the latest books from famous authors. Multimedia advertising, not only in the pages of Amazon, but also other networking sites can be seen, such as Yahoo! Visiting the websites and searching books, you can see Amazon advertising.

购物的乐趣并不一定在于是否有足够的钱来买想要的书，而在于挑选书的过程。手里捧着书，看着精美的封面，读着简介往往是购书的一大乐趣。在亚马逊的主页上，除了不能直接捧到书，这种乐趣并不会减少。精美的多媒体图片、明了的内容简介和权威人士的书评都可以使人有身临其境的感觉。主页上广告的位置也很合理，首先是当天的最佳书，而后是最近的畅销书介绍，还有读书俱乐部的推荐书，以及著名作者的近期书籍，等等。不仅在亚马逊的网页上有大量的多媒体广告，在其他相关网络站点上也经常可以看到亚马逊的广告，例如，在雅虎上搜索书籍网站时就可以看到亚马逊的广告。

A major feature of advertising is its dynamic real-time. The ads replaced daily makes customer learn the latest publications and most authoritative comments. The ads changed every day, in addition, you can read the news updated hourly from "Check out the Amazon Hot 100".

广告的另一大特点就在于其动态实时性，每天都更换的广告使得顾客能够了解到最新的出版物和最权威的评论。不但广告每天更换，还可以从"Check out the Amazon Hot 100"中读到每小时都在更换的消息。

Amazon did everything possible to promote their own sites, and continue to seek associate. Associates and brokers enable customers to get more opportunities to enter its sites and shop, even generously made the following commitments: As long as you become a partner in Amazon, and then the book sold by sites, regardless of reaching the certain quota or not, Amazon will pay you 15% referral fee. It's rare in other cooperative partnership. Amazon has got many associates, from the following words on the pages — "In fact, five of the six most visited web sites are already Amazon associates. Yahoo and Excite are marketing products from their web sites. So are AOL.com, Geocities, Netscape, and tens of thousands of other sites both large and small". We can see that five most frequently visited sites including Yahoo and Excite have become a partner of Amazon.

亚马逊千方百计地推销自己的网点，不断寻求合作伙伴。由于有许多合作伙伴和中间商，从而使得顾客进入其网点的方便程度和购物机会都大大增加。它甚至慷慨地做出了如下的承诺：只要你成为亚马逊的合作伙伴，那么由贵网点售出的书不管是否达到一定的配额，亚马逊都将支付你 15%的介绍费。这是其他合作型伙伴关系中很少见的。目前，亚马逊的合作伙伴已经有很多，从其网页上的这段话我们可以得知，事实上，包括雅虎和 Excite 在内的 5 个最经常被访问的站点已经成为亚马逊的合作伙伴。此外，亚马逊的合作伙伴还有 AOL.com、地球村、Netscape 以及其他大大小小数以万计的网站。

Amazon has specifically set up a gift page that prepares wide variety of gifts for adults and children. This is actually sales promotion activities of a promotional strategy. It aims to attract customers to have long-term purchase in the store by providing vouchers or small gifts to customers of all ages. In addition, Amazon also gives preferential treatment for long-term customers to buy their goods, which is a business promotion measures.

亚马逊专门设置了一个礼品页面，为大人和小孩都准备了各式各样的礼物。这实际上是促销策略的营业推广活动。它以向各个年龄层的顾客提供购物券或者精美小礼品的方法吸引顾客长期购买本商店的商品。另外，亚马逊还为长期购买其商品的顾客给予优惠，这也是一种营销推广的措施。

Amazon's special gift page provides small gifts for online customers (including adults and children), which both belong to a sales promotion activities, also a kind of public relations activities.

亚马逊在专门的礼品页面为网上购物的顾客（包括大人和小孩）提供小礼品。这既属于一种营业推广活动，也属于一种公共关系活动。

Amazon often eliminates some of the freight when customers are at university campus, or fit for a certain amount of order.

当客户在大学校园或是订单已满一定金额，亚马逊经常会免去一些运费。

Amazon has its own distribution centers, with diverse ways of payment, and in return for consumer, it will offer free delivery service "at least 29 yuan".

亚马逊配有自己的配送中心，支持的付款方式多样，并且为了回报消费者，商品"满29 元"即可享受免费配送服务。

3. Quest Amazon's Secret of Success 探索亚马逊成功的秘密

1) Thrift Gene 节俭基因

If there is so-called "corporate DNA", the most successful scientific and technological enterprises have undoubtedly vividly reflected this in the past decade. Apple obsessed in simplicities, and Facebook set up the world's largest social network. Amazon's success qualities seem extraordinary—thrift.

倘若果真存在所谓的"企业 DNA"，那么过去十年最成功的一批科技企业无疑已经淋漓尽致地体现了这一点。苹果痴迷于简约，脸书则构建了全球最大的社交网络。亚马逊赖以成功的特质似乎要平凡得多——节俭。

The online bookstore headquartered in Seattle has grown into an E-commerce giant by carrying forward the thrift concept, applying it to operation, brands, and a variety of new products such as Kindle Fire. "Cost reduction is the cornerstone of success for Amazon". R. J. Hottovy, the equity research director of the U.S. investment research firm Morningstar said. Not having to bear the cost pressures of the store helps Amazon depress price.

通过发扬节俭的理念，并将其贯彻到运营、品牌和 Kindle Fire 等各种新品中，这家总部位于西雅图的网上书店已经成长为一家电子商务巨头。"成本压缩是亚马逊成功的基石。"美国投资研究公司晨星股权研究总监 R. J. 霍托维说。不必承受实体店的成本压力，帮助亚马逊压低了售价。

According to the Chicago Investment Bank William Blair& Company data, Amazon's highest commodity price is cheaper by 13% than other online stores or the real store.

根据芝加哥投资银行 William Blair & Company 的数据，亚马逊的商品售价最高可比其他网上商店或实体店便宜 13%。

This makes Amazon's brand win popular support. Amazon challenges competitors more violently, and it even played a role in fueling the bankruptcy of Circuit City, Borders and other retailers.

这使得亚马逊的品牌形象深入人心。亚马逊对竞争对手发起的挑战越来越猛烈，它甚至对电路城和 Borders 等零售商的破产起到了推波助澜的作用。

2) A Wealth of Choice 丰富的选择

Continue increase the varieties of commodities is an important pillar of the Amazon to improve the customer experience. From the first day of creation, Bezos believes that "We want to provide customers with a certain thing that they are difficult to get in any way".

不断地增加商品的丰富性是亚马逊提高客户体验的一个重要措施。从创立亚马逊的第一天起，贝索斯就认为，"我们要为客户提供某种他们以任何方式都难以得到的东西"。

Amazon's books selling online in 1997 is far more than any one entity bookstore, and these books are presented to the user with useful, easy way to search and browse in 365×24 not closing store.

早在 1997 年，亚马逊在线销售的图书数量就远远多于任何一个实体书店销售的图书数量，而且这些书籍是在 365×24 小时的不打烊的店里，以一种有用的、容易搜索和浏览的方式呈现给用户的。

The second year of being on the market, Amazon began the category expansion. In 1998, Amazon added online music, video, gifts, and other categories, Amazon rushed into the leading online video only in six weeks' on-line time.

上市的第二年，亚马逊就开始了品类扩张。1998 年，亚马逊新增加了在线音乐、视频、礼物等品类，仅仅上线 6 周，亚马逊就冲到了在线视频的领先地位。

The Internet bubble experience in 2000 made Bezos realize the importance of the size and the category. Although he thought it should make audacious investments in new areas, but living.com and Pets.com, the two small-scale E-commerce businesses invested by Amazon closed down with the downturn of the economic situation, which make Bezos reflect its exceptional difficulty for small and medium-scale and single category of B2C Internet to be successful. Bezos thought, compared with physical retail formats, the characteristics of the online retail is high fixed costs and low variable costs, so the expansion of category and scale of operations are an effective way to decrease the fixed cost of online retail business. Also because of the high fixed costs, medium-sized companies are difficult to succeed without adequate capital investment. "Enclosure" on the Internet is an effective strategy.

2000 年互联网泡沫的破灭令贝索斯更加深刻地意识到规模和增加品类的重要性。尽管他认为要对新领域做出大胆的投资，但是亚马逊投资的两家小规模的电子商务企业 living.com 和 Pets.com 却随着经济形势的不景气而倒闭了。这让贝索斯反思了在互联网上中小规模和单一品类的 B2C 要获得成功异常艰难。贝索斯认为，和实体零售业态相比，在线零售的特点是固定成本高、可变成本低，因此扩充品类和规模化运营是摊薄在线零售企业固定成本的有效途径。也正是因为固定成本高的特点，在没有充足资本投入的情况下，中等规模的公司很难成功。在互联网上，"圈地"是有效的策略。

Amazon invited businesses to shop at the third-party platform (Market Place). At that time, the industry thought that there was risk for goods from third-party merchants and Amazon's own retail goods, and the goods from third-party may erode Amazon's retail business. It was pointed out that the third-party merchants shopping would make Amazon's inventory forecasting difficult, and there may not be enough product information display in the third-party page.

亚马逊邀请商家来第三方平台（Market Place）开店。当时业界都认为第三方商家的商品和亚马逊自己的零售商品放在一起销售会有风险，或许会蚕食它们自己的零售业务。有人指出第三方商家开店，会让亚马逊的库存预测变得困难，而且有可能没有足够的商品信息展示在第三方卖家的商品页面。

But Bezos thought if third-party vendors provide preferential prices or satisfying commodity, customers will accept, which will benefit Amazon's own goods category expansion. In the subsequent development, the third-party merchants without B2C warehousing logistics experience entrust the back-end logistics to Amazon, namely FBA (Fulfillment By Amazon), which also effectively decrease Amazon's warehousing and logistics cost. Now, third-party platform has become an important business in Amazon.

不过贝索斯认为，第三方商家如果提供优惠的价格或者符合市场需求的商品，顾客就会接受，这对亚马逊自己的商品品类扩充非常有益。在随后的发展中，那些没有 B2C 仓储物流经验的第三方商家也将后端的物流外包给亚马逊管理，即 FBA（Fullfillment By Amazon），这也有效地摊薄了亚马逊的仓储物流中心的成本。现在，第三方平台已经成为亚马逊一个重要的业务。

"From the customer's point of view, the competition between third-party merchants and Amazon, and the competition between the businesses and merchants, is conducive to create a fair and beneficial cycle shopping environment", said Sebastian Gunningham, the Amazon Global Merchant Services, senior vice president. Amazon is more concerned to provide the best shopping experience for consumers. In this competition, sometimes Amazon win, and sometimes the businesses win, which is voted by consumers.

"从顾客的角度看，第三方商家和亚马逊之间的竞争、商家和商家之间的竞争有利于创造一个公平和良性循环的购物环境。亚马逊全球商家服务高级副总裁塞巴斯蒂安·吉宁汉姆（Sebastian Gunningham）说，亚马逊更关注为消费者提供最好的购物体验，因此在这种竞争中，有时候亚马逊赢，有时候商家胜出，这都是由消费者投票的。

At present, Amazon extends its category expansion to global scale, including automotive supplies in Japan, baby products in France, footwear and apparel in China.

如今，亚马逊将品类扩张的步伐延伸到全球范围，包括在日本推出汽车用品，在法国推出婴儿用品，在中国推出鞋类和服饰。

For the worldwide category expansion, Amazon usually first take the rule to promote mature category. Diego Piacentini, the senior vice president of Amazon Worldwide Sales said, the expansion in various countries, Amazon launched the shoe business first, and then clothing. In the United States, Amazon purchased Zappos and Endless shoe enterprises, and has accumulated a lot of experiences on selling shoes.

对于全球范围的品类扩张，亚马逊通常会采用先推广运营成熟的品类的法则。亚马逊全球销售高级副总裁迭戈·皮亚琴蒂尼（Diego Piacentini）介绍，在各个国家的扩张中，亚马逊会先推出鞋的业务，再推出服装，因为在美国，亚马逊收购了 Zappos 和 Endless 等卖鞋的企业，积累了很多卖鞋的经验。

Piacentini said: "in the United States, Amazon allows customers to buy two pairs of the same shoes, after try on, consumers keep the suitable one, and return the other for free." Selling clothes is the same, and with delivery goods, UPS will offer Amazon's back tracking parcel bill with postage paid to customer.

皮亚琴蒂尼说：“在美国，亚马逊允许顾客买两双同样的鞋，送到后试一下，留下最合适的一双，另一双免费退货。"卖衣服也一样，送货的时候，UPS 会同时将付完邮资的亚马逊的返程包裹单交给顾客。

"We found that Chinese consumers are also very fond of the free return shoes service." Piacentini said, Amazon global category expansion is mainly the replication of mature experience.

"我们发现中国的消费者也非常喜欢免费退鞋的服务。"皮亚琴蒂尼说，亚马逊全球的品类扩张都以复制成熟经验为主。

Independent retail category expansion and third-party merchant sales have greatly enriched Amazon's products selection, which attract more customers for Amazon.

自主零售的品类扩张和第三方商家的销售都极大地丰富了亚马逊的商品选择，这为亚马逊吸引了更多的顾客。

3) Convenience 便利

Bezos once said: "We are not making money by selling things, but by helping consumers make better buying decisions." After providing a wealth of goods, how to help customers find the needed goods quickly, how to recommend goods according to consumers' behavior, as well as how to deliver goods to customers, is what Amazon concerned, and it's the second pillar for Amazon to enhance customer experience: convenience.

"我们不是通过卖东西赚钱，而是通过帮助消费者做出更好的购买决策而赚钱。"贝索斯曾经说。在提供了丰富的商品后，亚马逊会关注如何帮助顾客快速找到需要的商品，甚至根据其消费行为推送其可能喜欢的商品，并快速地交付顾客。这是亚马逊提升顾客体验的第二个支柱——便利。

Different from entity retail, Amazon can display large commodity-related information for consumers on the Internet, including not only the introduction of goods, a large number of reviews, browse options, recommended merchandise, but also the functionality of one key shopping.

和实体零售不同的是，亚马逊可以在互联网上为消费者呈现丰富的商品相关信息，不仅包括商品的介绍，还有大量的评论、浏览选项和推荐商品，以及一键购物的功能。

In Amazon, it creates more convenience for consumers through strong technical ability. For example, Amazon books category launched a new service, that is, "look inside the book". Customers can first check the high-definition images of the book, see the front and back covers, as well as a contents and some sample chapters, and then decide whether to buy this book.

亚马逊更多地通过强大的技术能力为消费者创造更多的便利。比如亚马逊在图书品类推出的一项新的服务是"看看书的内容"，顾客可以先查看书的高清晰度图像，再看封面和封底，以及目录和一些样章，再决定是否购买这本书。

"Our aim is to deliver the goods chosen by customers to them quickly." An Amazon engineer said. In front, Amazon provided customers with the convenience, such as, rich merchandise selection, more accurate search and information delivery, smoother orders process; while on the back end, Amazon are committed to its rapid delivery whether it is physical or virtual goods.

"我们的宗旨是将顾客选择的东西快速地交付到他手上。"一位亚马逊的工程师说。在前端，亚马逊为顾客提供的便利表现为丰富的商品选择、更精准的搜索和信息推送、下单的流程更为顺畅；而在后端，无论是实体还是虚拟的商品，亚马逊都在致力于将其快速交付。

2.1.2　EBay Platform EBay 平台

Founded in 1995, eBay connects a diverse and passionate community of individual buyers and sellers, as well as small businesses. EBay marketplace is a leader in mobile commerce. No other commerce provider has delivered as many innovations across as many devices in as many countries as they have. EBay are available in eight languages and 190 countries on iPhone, iPad, Android and BlackBerry devices.

eBay 成立于 1995 年，是一个连接了个人买家和卖家以及小企业的多样化的和充满激情的社区。eBay 市场是移动商务领域的领先者。没有任何其他商务提供商能在如此多的国家和地区通过如此多的设备提供如此多的创新。eBay 在 iPhone、iPad、Android 和黑莓设备上有 8 种语言的版本，覆盖 190 个国家。

eBay: 20 years development:

eBay：20 年的发展：

What we do:

我们所做的：

eBay is where the world goes to shop, sell, and give. Whether you are buying new or used, plain or luxurious, commonplace or rare, trendy or one-of-a-kind—if it exists in the world, it probably is for sale on eBay. Our mission is to be the world's favorite destination for discovering great value and unique selection. We give sellers the platform, solutions, and support anything they need to grow their businesses and thrive. We measure our success by our customers' success.

易趣是全世界购物、销售和捐赠的地方。无论您购买的物品是新的还是旧的，普通的还是奢华的，平凡的还是罕见的，流行的还是独一无二的，只要它在世界上存在，它就可能在 eBay 上售卖。我们的任务是成为消费者发现巨大价值与独特选择的目的地。我们为供应商提供平台、解决方案，并且支持任何它们在商业成长与繁荣的过程中需要的东西，我们以我们顾客的成功来衡量我们的成功。

What sets us apart:

是什么让我们与众不同：

Our vision for commerce is one that is enabled by people, powered by technology, and open to everyone. We empower people and create opportunity through connected commerce. We focus on empowering our sellers, not competing with them. We are building stronger connections between buyers and sellers with product experiences that are fast, mobile, and secure. And we are transforming the individual selling experience to help you turn the things you no longer need into cash you can use.

我们认为电子商务是一种由人实现的、由技术驱动的、向每个人开放的商务。我们通过互联商务赋予人们权利以及创作机会。我们专注于增强我们的卖家的能力，而不是与它们竞争。我们正在通过快速、移动和安全的产品体验在买家和卖家之间建立更紧密的联系。我们正在转变个人销售体验，帮助您将不再需要的东西转化为您可以使用的现金。

How we work:

我们怎样工作：

At eBay, our connected commerce purpose links us to something bigger than ourselves. We share a common drive to create uncommon economical opportunities, professional, and personal. And because our business is about people, we have a passion for what we do. We fight for it, every day. We employ extraordinary people who do meaningful work that has a tangible impact on the lives of individuals all over the world. And we aspire to make extraordinary things possible for each other, for our customers, and for you. We've been doing this for years. And we're just as passionate about it today as when we founded the company in 1995.

在 eBay，我们的互联商务目标将我们与比我们自己更重要的东西联系在一起。我们有着共同的动力来创造不同寻常的经济上的机会，无论是专业的还是个人的。因为我们的业务是关于人的，所以我们对我们所做的事情充满热情。我们每天都在为之奋斗。我们雇用了非凡的人才，他们所做的有意义的工作对世界各地的人们的生活都有切实的影响。我们立志使非凡的事情成为可能，包括彼此、我们的客户以及您。我们已经做了多年了。我们今天对它的热情就像我们在 1995 年创立该公司时一样。

2.1.3　Wish Wish 平台

1. Profile of Wish Wish 简介

Wish was founded in 2011 and is currently a mobile B2C cross-border E-commerce platform in the United States. The early version of Wish is a mobile App for users to create wish lists. Wish App can extract data from users' existing wish lists, predict other items they might like, and recommend them. From March 2013, Wish began to transform into E-commerce, where users can buy these products while sharing pictures.

Wish 创立于 2011 年，目前是美国一家移动 B2C 跨境电商平台。Wish 的早期版本是一个用户创建心愿清单的移动应用，Wish App 可以从用户现有的心愿清单中提取数据，预测出他们可能会喜欢的其他物品并给予推荐。从 2013 年 3 月起，Wish 开始转型做电子商务，用户在分享图片的同时，也可以购买图片所示的商品。

Unlike AliExpress, Amazon and other E-commerce platforms, Wish takes the mobile end as a starting point, and develops rapidly. With the development of mobile Internet, users are moving from PC to mobile, which is the advantage of Wish development. Although Amazon, AliExpress, eBay and other third-party cross-border E-commerce platforms have also seen this trend, they have launched their own mobile App, but more of them only achieve the mobility of the interactive interface. In terms of operational thinking, we also need to take into account both the PC side and the mobile mode.

与速卖通、亚马逊等电商平台不同的是，Wish 以移动端作为切入点迅速发展壮大起来。

随着移动互联网的发展，用户正在从 PC 端向移动端转移，这是 Wish 发展的优势所在，亚马逊、速卖通、eBay 这些第三方跨境电商平台虽然也看到了这样的变化趋势，推出了自己的移动 App，但更多的只是实现了交互界面的移动化，在运营思维上，还需要兼顾好 PC 端与移动端模式。

On the mobile side, Wish has obvious advantages and unique features. It really enables users to see and buy anytime and anywhere, not only providing users with a different interface experience, but also recommending technology through intelligent algorithms to recommend products that they may like, rather than products that the platform thinks is good. This not only strengthens the interaction between the platform and users, reflects the user care and humanized operation thinking, but also greatly enhances the user stickiness.

在移动端方面，Wish 就具有明显的优势和独特之处，真正地实现了让用户随时随地想看就看，想买就买，不仅给用户提供了不一样的界面体验，还通过智能化算法推荐技术，给用户推荐的是他们可能喜欢的，而不是平台自己认为好的产品。这就加强了平台与用户之间的互动性，体现了用户关怀与人性化运营思维，也大大增强了用户黏性。

2. Wish is a Marketplace Wish 是一个市场

You understand and agree that Wish is a marketplace and as such is not responsible or liable for any content, data, text, information, usernames, graphics, images, photographs, profiles, audio, video, items, products, listings, links or information posted by you, other merchants or outside parties on Wish. You use the services at your own risk.

您理解并同意，Wish 是一个市场，故概不对您、其他商家或外部各方在 Wish 中发布的任何内容、数据、文本、信息、用户名、图形、图像、照片、个人档案、音频、视频、项目、产品、列表、链接或信息承担责任或法律责任。您使用服务需要您自担风险。

To the fullest extent permitted by law, you and your affiliates (defined below) waive claims related to, and agree that Wish and Wish's affiliates, including any of their officers, directors, employees, consultants or agents, are not responsible for (1) any statements, guarantees, services in this agreement, and expected transactions, including merchantability, applying to particular purposes or any implied warranties; (2) implied warranties based on the transaction process, the performance of the contract or trading practices course of dealing; or (3) any duties, responsibilities, rights, claims or tort reliefs, whether or not they are due to Wish's negligence.

在法律允许的最大范围内，您和您的关联公司（定义见下文）放弃与以下各项相关的索赔，并同意 Wish 和 Wish 的关联公司，包括其任何高级职员、董事、员工、顾问或代理概不对以下各项负责：① 本协议中的任何声明、保证、服务，以及预期交易，包括适销性、适用于特定用途或任何默示保证；② 基于交易过程、合约履行、交易惯例或交易习惯的默示保证；③ 任何职责、责任、权利、索赔或侵权救济，不论是否因 Wish 的疏忽产生。

If you have disputes with any third-party over any product, offering or interaction over the services, you agree not to make any claim of any kind or nature against Wish or its affiliates, no matter whether such claims, requirements or compensation of damages are known, ensured or released.

如果您就服务上的任何产品、服务或互动与任何第三方产生争议，您同意不对 Wish 或其关联公司提出任何类型或性质的索赔，不论该等索赔、要求或损害赔偿是否已知、得到保证或已被解除。

3. Content of Wish Wish 的内容

1) License 许可

You hereby grant Wish a royalty-free, non-exclusive, worldwide, perpetual, sub-licensable (through multiple tiers), irrevocable right and license to use, reproduce, perform, display, distribute, adapt, modify, excerpt, analyze, re-format, create derivative works of, and otherwise commercially or non-commercially exploit in any manner your content in any medium or in any format and for any purpose, including, without limitation, for the advertising, marketing, or promotion of Wish or the services. For the sake of clarity, nothing in the terms will prevent or impair our right to use your content without your consent to the extent that such use is allowable without a license from you or your Affiliates under applicable law (e.g., fair use under United States copyright law, referential use under trademark law, or valid license from a third-party).

您特此向 Wish 授予免版税、非独家、全球、永久、可再许可（通过多个层级）、不可撤销的权利和许可，以任何方式使用、复制、执行、显示、分发、改编、修改、摘录、分析、重新格式化您载于任何媒体中或采用任何格式及用于任何目的（包括但不限于 Wish 或服务的广告、营销或推广）的内容，创建其衍生作品，以及以其他方式商业化或非商业化开发该等内容。为清楚起见，本文条款中的任何内容均不会阻止或损害我们不经您的同意使用您的内容的权利，前提是，根据适用法律可不经您或您的关联公司许可即可使用该等内容（例如，美国版权法下的公平使用、商标法下的参考使用或第三方的有效许可）。

2) Reposting Content 重新发布内容

By posting content on Wish, it is possible for an outside website or a third-party to repost that content. You agree to indemnify, defend and hold Wish harmless for any dispute relating to this use.

在 Wish 上发布内容可能会有外部网站或第三方重新发布该内容。您同意就对与该使用相关的任何争议向 Wish 做出赔偿，为其抗辩，并使其免受伤害。

3) Privacy, Legal Requirements, Protection of Wish and Others Wish 和其他人的隐私、法律要求和保护

When you use the services, such as when you fulfill a purchase, you may obtain personal information from or about a Wish user ("User Data"). Your use of User Data shall comply with applicable data protection law, including without limitation Europe's General Data Protection Regulation. Unless you obtain a valid consent from the individuals described by User Data, you shall only use User Data in connection with the corresponding transaction with such user (e.g. shipping and fulfillment) or as necessary to meet your statutory legal requirements, such as tax and reporting requirements. You shall employ reasonable and appropriate measures to safeguard User Data from misuse, loss, destruction or unauthorized access or use. You acknowledge and agree that if Wish determines in good faith that additional agreements are necessary for compliance with applicable data protection law, you will promptly review and accept such agreements or cease using the services or applicable portions thereof, such as sales into the European Union.

当您使用服务时，例如您履行购买订单时，您可以从 Wish 用户处获取或获取有关 Wish 用户的个人信息（"用户数据"）。您对用户数据的使用应遵守适用的数据保护法，包括但不限于欧洲的通用数据保护法规。除非您获得用户数据所述个人的有效同意，否则您仅可就与该用户进行的相应交易（如运输和履约）使用相关用户数据或在必要时用于满足您的法定法律要求，例如，税务和报告要求。您应采取合理和适当的措施保护用户数据免遭滥用、丢失、破坏或未经授权访问或使用。您确认并同意，如果 Wish 真诚地确定，为遵守适用的数据保护法需要签订其他协议，您将从速审查并接受该等协议或停止使用服务或其适用部分，例如，向欧盟销售。

Without limiting the foregoing, without express opt-in consent from the user, you shall not add any Wish user to your E-mail or physical mail list, and shall not upload, access or use tracking technologies (such as browser cookies, web beacons or flash cookies) as part of any item listing. Wish does not assume any responsibilities for disputes between you and your customers for using customer information without authorization.

在不限制前述规定一般性的前提下，未经用户明确做出选择加入同意，您不得将任何 Wish 用户添加到您的电子邮件或实体邮件列表中，亦不得上传、访问或使用跟踪技术（如浏览器 cookie、网络信标或闪存 cookie）作为任何商品上架的一部分。对于您和您的客户之间因未经授权使用客户信息而产生的争议，Wish 概不承担任何责任。

Furthermore, you acknowledge and agree that your own personal information will be collected and used as described in Wish's Privacy Policy. Wish reserves the right to access, read, preserve, and disclose any content or other information that Wish in good faith believes is necessary to comply with law or court order; respond to legal, regulatory, or commercial claims; enforce or apply Wish's policies, guidelines or other agreements; or protect the rights, property, or safety of Wish, its employees, users, or others. In connection with your use of the services, and subject to the above, you understand and agree that Wish may disclose certain information about you to suppliers, consumers, regulators or other third-parties, including without limitation your: name; E-mail address; payment method or financial account information; shipping address; phone number; social network account credentials; sales information; Wish identifications or usernames.

此外，您确认并同意，您自身的个人信息将按 Wish 隐私政策中所述被收集和使用。Wish 保留访问、阅读、保存和披露 Wish 认为对遵守法律或法院命令，回应法律、监管或商业索赔，强制执行或应用 Wish 的政策、指引或其他协议，或保护 Wish、其员工、用户或其他人的权利、财产或安全属必要的任何内容或其他信息的权利。就您使用服务而言，在不触犯上述条款的情况下，您需理解并同意，Wish 可能会向供应商、消费者、监管者或其他第三方披露有关您的某些信息，包括但不限于您的：名称；邮箱地址；付款方式或财务账户信息；收货地址；电话号码；社交网络账户凭据；销售信息；Wish 身份证明或用户名。

Section 2.2 The China Main Platform of Cross-border E-commerce 中国跨境电子商务主要平台

New Words

comprehensive	*adj.*	全部的；综合的；所有的；（几乎）无所不包的；详尽的
cosmetics	*n.*	化妆品
legitimate	*adj.*	正当合理的；合情合理的；合法的；法律认可的
	v.	使合法；认为正当
valid	*adj.*	（法律上）有效的；（正式）认可的；符合逻辑的；合理的
instruction	*n.*	指示；教导；命令；传授
	adj.	说明用法的；操作指南的
bonded	*adj.*	（织物）多层黏合的；有债券作保证的；有担保的
reputable	*adj.*	声誉好的；值得信赖的
priority	*n.*	优先；优先权；重点；优先事项
unify	*v.*	统一；使成一体；使一元化
notch	*n.*	等级；档次；位阶；（表面或边缘的）V形刻痕
	v.	赢取；获得；（在表面或边缘）刻V形痕
estimate	*v.*	估计；估算；估价
	n.	估价；（对大小、数量、成本等的）估计；估计的成本
supplier	*n.*	供货商；供应者；供货方
primary	*adj.*	主要的；最重要的；基本的；最初的
recommendation	*n.*	推荐；介绍；提议；正式建议
strength	*n.*	强度；力量；实力；力气；优势
weakness	*n.*	弱点；柔弱；薄弱；怯懦

Phrases

to be owned by	归……所有
round-the-clock	（全天候的）
proprietary trading	自营交易
brand authorizations	品牌授权
brand reputation	品牌声誉
direct shipping services	直接送货服务
bonded warehouse services	保税仓库服务
transported by sea	海运
bonded warehouse	保税仓库
cleared by customs	海关清关

vertical platform	垂直平台
comprehensive platforms	综合平台
sub platform	子平台
independent platform	独立平台
marketplace platforms	市场平台
bonded warehouse	保税仓库
to be operated by	由……运营
Cainiao Express	菜鸟快递
brand flagship store	品牌旗舰店
franchised store	特许经营店
exclusive store	专卖店
in terms of	依……；从……方面；用……特有的字眼
third-party logistic corporations	第三方物流公司
counties and districts	县区
application process	申请流程
xLobo Global Express	贝海国际速递
to be verified by	由……正式认证
in demand	要求

Sentences

1. Some are in your line of business, while others may be in an entirely different industry.
   有些是在你的业务范围之内的，而另一些可能是在完全不同的行业。

2. It's time to change the business pattern of the industry.
   是时候改变这个行业的经营模式了。

3. What do you see as the future trends for the industry?
   你如何看待将来这个行业的发展趋势？

4. If you or any of your management team have experience in the industry, you should share your experience with the bank in your business plan.
   如果你或你管理团队中的任何人在此行业有经验，那么你们在呈交给银行的创业报告中应该写明这点。

5. Chinese commodities available for export are varied.
   中国可供出口的商品种类繁多。

6. This result seems hard to believe: surely we are more likely to find something we like from a range four times as large.
   这一结果看起来令人难以置信：可供挑选的商品种类多了四倍，按道理我们应该更有可能找到自己喜欢的东西。

7. Because of the type of merchandise, we can only ship by rail.
   由于商品种类的关系，我方只能用火车来运送。

8. He runs a Chinatown shop that sells everything from 50-cent ceramic coffee cups to $10 Hannah Montana backpacks.

他在唐人街的商铺经营的商品种类繁多，有 50 美分一个的陶瓷咖啡杯，也有 10 美元一个的汉娜蒙塔娜背包。

9. However, the website offers the shopper great convenience since they contain such a wide variety of products.

不过这个网站为顾客提供了很大的方便，因为它们的商品种类如此繁多。

10. But usually on sale in the website economic commodity types little to the market in such commodities were traded collectively, "tradeable commodities".

但通常在网站上买卖的经济商品种类很多，能够在此类市场上进行交易的商品统称为"可交易商品"。

11. The company are looking forward to your enthusiasm manufacturers in the declaration charges for the ports and customs of different types of goods both for consultations.

本公司热诚期待与贵厂合作，因各报关口岸及商品种类不同，报关费双方可作协商。

12. It is in fashion now. Would you like to try to buy it?

这款现在正流行。您可以先试着拍下？

13. This is your size of this type, it's a lovely dress and very smart.

这款有您要的尺寸，这件衣服很漂亮，非常时髦。

14. Sheer robbery!

太贵了！

15. Casual elegance is the principal spirit of this season.

精致休闲是这一季的主格调。

Conversations

1. Payment Failure

A: Hi.

B: Hello, welcome to my shop. Glad to be of service.

A: I want to buy 2 wallets from your shop, but I failed to pay for my order. All is well with my account as I have checked it.

B: Dear customer, would you like to send the screenshot of the wallet you want to buy?

A: Well. It's this one. I want two wallets in different colors.

B: Sorry, this wallet is under special discount, each customer is limited to purchase one. That is why you can't pav for the two wallets successfully.

A: Is it? That's too bad. I will buy one of them.

B: Okay. Thank for your order. We will send your wallet as soon as possible.

1. 支付失败

A：你好。

B：您好，欢迎光临本店。非常高兴为您服务。

A：我想在你们店买两只皮夹，但支付失败了。我检查了付款账号，一切正常。

B：亲，可以将您想买的皮夹的截图发过来吗？

A：好的。就是这款，我想要两种颜色的皮夹各一只。

B：不好意思，这款皮夹是特价款，所以每位顾客限购一只。这就是您不能成功支付两只皮夹的原因。

A：是吗？那太遗憾了，我买一只吧。

B：好的，感谢您的订单。我们会尽快发货的。

2. Placing an Order

Paul: I looked over the catalog you gave me this morning, and I'd like to discuss prices on your computer speakers.

Leslie: Very good. Here is our price list.

Paul: Let me see. I see that your listed price for the K-two-one model is ten US dollars. Do you offer quantity discounts?

Leslie: We sure do. We give a five percent discount for orders of a hundred or more.

Paul: What kind of discount could you give me if I were to place an order for six hundred units?

Leslie: On an order of six hundred, we can give you a discount of ten percent.

Paul: What about lead time?

Leslie: We could ship your order within ten days of receiving your payment.

Paul: So, you require payment in advance of shipment.

Leslie: Yes. You could wire transfer the payment into our bank account or open a letter of credit in our favor.

Pau 1: I'd like to go ahead and place an order for six hundred units.

Leslie: Great!

2. 下订单

保罗：今天早上我已经详细看过你给我的目录了。我想讨论一下你们计算机扬声器的价格。

莱斯利：好的。这是我们的价目表。

保罗：我看看。你们 K-2-1 型的标价是 10 美元。如果大量订购，有折扣吗？

莱斯利：当然有。100 或以上的订单我们有百分之五的折扣。

保罗：如果我下 600 的订单，你们可以给我什么样的折扣？

莱斯利：我们可以给你百分之十的折扣。

保罗：交货时间呢？

莱斯利：在收到货款的 10 天内，我们就可以把货送出去。

保罗：那么，你们需要提前付款？

莱斯利：是的。你可以汇款到我们的银行账户，或者开一个以我们公司为抬头的信用证。

保罗：那我就先下 600 的订单。

莱斯利：好极了！

Text

2.2.1 AliExpress 阿里巴巴速卖通

Launched in April 2010, AliExpress is a global retail marketplace targeted at consumers worldwide, many of them located in Russia, Brazil and the United States. The platform enables consumers from around the world to buy directly from wholesalers and manufacturers in China and have access to a wide variety of products at competitive prices.

阿里巴巴速卖通成立于 2010 年 4 月，是一个面向全球消费者的全球零售市场，其中许多消费者位于俄罗斯、巴西和美国。该平台使来自世界各地的消费者能够直接从中国的批发商和制造商那里购买，并能够以具有竞争力的价格获得种类繁多的产品。

Great value: We offer competitive prices on our 100 million plus product range.
企业价值：我们为我们的 1 亿多种产品系列提供有竞争力的价格。

Worldwide delivery: With sites in 5 languages, we ship to over 200 countries & regions.
全球发货：我们有 5 种语言的网站，发货到 200 多个国家和地区。

Safe payment: Pay with the world's most popular and secure payment methods.
安全支付：使用世界上最流行、最安全的支付方式进行支付。

Shop with confidence: Our buyer protection covers your purchase from click to delivery.
放心购物：我们的买家保护涵盖了您从点击到送货的整个过程。

24/7 Help center: Round-the-clock assistance for a smooth shopping experience.
全天候帮助中心：全天候帮助您享受购物体验。

Shop On-the-go: Download the App and get the world of AliExpress at your fingertips.
随时随地购物：下载应用程序，让全球速卖通触手可及。

AliExpress is owned by Alibaba Group. Alibaba Group was founded in 1999 by 18 people led by Jack Ma, a former English teacher from Hangzhou, China. The founders started the company to champion small businesses, in the belief that the Internet would level the playing field by enabling small enterprises to leverage innovation and technology to grow and compete more effectively in the domestic and global economies.

阿里巴巴速卖通属于阿里巴巴集团。阿里巴巴集团成立于 1999 年，由来自中国杭州的前英语教师马云领导的 18 人领导。创始人创办公司是为了支持小企业，他们相信互联网将使小企业能够利用创新和技术在国内和全球经济中更有效地增长和竞争，从而创造公平的竞争环境。

Alibaba Group's mission is to make it easy to do business anywhere.
阿里巴巴集团的使命是让业务在任何地方都能轻松开展。

We operate leading online and mobile marketplaces in retail and wholesale trade, as well as cloud computing and other services. We provide technology and services to enable consumers, merchants, and other participants to conduct commerce in our ecosystem.

我们在零售和批发贸易以及云计算和其他服务领域运营领先的在线和移动市场。我们提供技术和服务，使消费者、商家和其他参与者能够在我们的生态系统中进行商业活动。

2.2.2　Kaola 考拉

Kaola is actually owned by NetEase Inc. which is a Chinese Internet company that provides online services focused on content, community, and commerce.

Kaola 实际上归网易公司所有。网易公司是一家中国互联网公司，提供专注于内容、社区和商业的在线服务。

Operation pattern: Comprehensive, B2C, proprietary trading, independent platform.

运营模式：综合、B2C、自营交易、独立平台。

Product categories: Fashion & apparel, jewelry & accessories, sports & outdoors, children's wear & shoes, home & personal care, nutrition and health food, digital appliances, fresh food & produce maternity & baby products, cosmetics.

产品类别：时装及服饰、珠宝及配饰、运动及户外用品、童装及鞋类、家居及个人护理、营养保健食品、数码家电、生鲜食品、母婴用品、化妆品。

Application process: Since Kaola. com is a proprietary trading platform, their main method of cooperation will be to purchase directly from the brand. Because Kaola.com mostly handle their own operations in terms of selling and logistics, you must apply to become a merchant in order to sell on Kaola.

申请流程：由于网易考拉是一个自营交易平台，其主要合作方式是直接从品牌商家那里购买。因网易考拉在销售和物流方面主要自己处理业务，因此要在考拉实现销售，就必须申请成为商家。

To become a merchant, you must first possess legitimate corporate entities, valid brand authorizations, good brand reputation, and operation status. And if you're interested in applying to Kaola.com, simply follow these 3 steps to become a partner with Kaola.

要成为商家，必须首先拥有合法的公司实体、有效的品牌授权、良好的品牌声誉和运营状态。如果你有兴趣申请网易考拉，只需执行以下 3 个步骤就能成为考拉的合作伙伴：

(1) Submit an application on Kaola's website.

在网易考拉的网站上提交申请。

(2) Wait for your application to be approved by Kaola.

等待网易考拉批准你的申请。

(3) If you're approved by Kaola, you'll then receive an offer letter via E-mail. Follow the instruction to finish the registration process.

如果网易考拉批准了，你就会通过电子邮件收到审批通知书。按照说明完成注册过程。

Logistics: Kaola also offers both bonded warehouse services and direct shipping services. If you choose to use their bonded warehouse services, your product will go through the following procedure.

物流：考拉也提供保税仓库服务以及直接送货服务。如果选择使用其保税仓库服务，你的产品将执行以下程序。

(1) Kaola will purchase products from you.

网易考拉将向你购买产品。

(2) Your products will be transported either by sea or by air.

你的产品将通过海运或空运。

(3) Once your product arrives in China they will be inspected.

一旦你的产品到达中国，产品将接受检查。

(4) After inspection, they will be transferred and stored in a bonded warehouse.

检查后，产品将转移并存放在保税仓库中。

(5) Upon an order is placed by a customer on Kaola, your product will be taken to be cleared by customs.

当客户在网易考拉下订单时，你的产品将在海关清关。

(6) Finally, your product will be shipped by domestic logistics to ensure it is delivered to the customer's hand on time.

最后，你的产品将通过国内物流运送，以确保按时交付客户。

Alternatively, if you want to use Kaola's direct mailing or shipping services, you will be shipping the product directly from an overseas warehouse to the Chinese consumer. Below is the general procedure:

或者，如果你想使用考拉的直接邮寄或运送服务，则可以直接从海外仓库把产品运送给中国消费者，以下是一般程序：

(1) Kaola will purchase products from you.

考拉将向你购买产品。

(2) Instead of shipping your product to China, they will store it in an overseas warehouse.

不是将产品运往中国，而是将其存放在海外仓库中。

(3) Upon an order is placed by a customer on Kaola, your product will be shipped via international logistics.

当客户在考拉下订单时，你的产品将通过国际物流运送。

(4) Once your product arrives in China, it will be inspected and wait for customs clearances in a bonded area.

一旦你的产品到达中国，产品将接受检查并等待保税区内的清关。

(5) Finally, your product will be shipped by domestic logistics to ensure it is delivered to the customer's hand on time.

最后，你的产品将通过国内物流运输，以确保按时交付客户。

2.2.3　TMall Global 天猫国际

TMall Global is the child platform of TMall which is ultimately all owned and operated by

Alibaba Group, while in China TMall is the leading E-commerce website.

天猫国际是天猫的子平台，由阿里巴巴集团拥有并运营。而在中国，天猫是领先的电子商务网站。

Operation patterns: Comprehensive, B2C, marketplace, sub-platform.

运营模式：综合、B2C、市场、子平台。

Product categories: Cosmetics, maternity & baby, food & health care, apparels & luggages, digital appliances.

产品类别：化妆品、母婴用品、食品及保健品、服装及行李箱、数码家电。

Application process: TMall Global has the most significantly special application process. TMall Global does not accept any application for setting up stores on their platform. TMall Global will actively look for international brands that are in demand or urgent need by the consumer and the market.

申请流程：天猫国际拥有最重要的特殊申请流程。它不接受任何在其平台上设置商店的申请。它会积极寻找消费者和市场需要或迫切需要的国际品牌。

Logistics: For logistics, TMall Global has appointed Cainiao Express as the exclusive bonded warehouse service provider. This means that if you want to sell on TMall Global and want to use a bonded warehouse as your part of your logistics you must use Cainiao Express. But if you want to sell on TMall Global and want to use direct shipping as your logistics, then you're open to using Cainiao or any other international logistic company of your choice.

物流：对于物流，天猫国际已指定菜鸟快递为其独家保税仓库服务提供商。这意味着如果想在天猫国际销售并希望使用保税仓库作为物流的一部分，就必须使用菜鸟快递。但是，如果想在天猫国际销售，并希望使用直接运送的物流方式，那么既可以使用菜鸟快递，也可选择其他国际物流公司。

2.2.4　JD Worldwide 京东国际

JD Worldwide, which is also known as Joybuy.com, is the brainchild of JD. com, the second largest E-commerce website in China.

京东国际也被称为 Joybuy.com，是中国第二大电子商务网站京东的创意产品。

Operation pattern: Comprehensive, B2C, marketplace, sub-platform.

运营模式：综合、B2C、市场、子平台。

Product categories: Maternity & baby, cosmetics & personal care, nutrition & health food, digital appliances, watches jewelry, sports outdoors, car accessories, home luxury.

产品类别：母产品、化妆品及个人护理、营养及保健食品、数码家电、手表及珠宝、运动及户外用品、汽车配件、家居及奢侈品。

Application process: JD Worldwide offers 4 different store types for their merchants. You can create a Brand Flagship Store, Outlet Flagship Store, Franchised Store, and Exclusive Store. In order to be accepted and set up your store on JD Worldwide, you must have a legal registered corporate entity, a public bank account, a reputable brand and meet the specific requirements for the store type you want to open.

申请流程：京东国际为其商家提供 4 种不同类型的商店。你可以创建品牌旗舰店、Outlet 旗舰店、特许经营店和专卖店。为了能让京东国际接受和在其上建立商店，你必须拥有合法注册的公司实体、公共银行账户、信誉良好的品牌，并满足开立的商店类型的特定要求。

However, because you meet these basic requirements it does not mean JD Worldwide will accept your application and allow you to open a store. However, JD Worldwide has a priority list and if your brands fit within the list, then your application will be approved right away.

然而，仅仅因为符合此基本要求，并不意味着京东国际就会接受你的申请并允许你开设商店。京东国际有一个优先级列表，如果你的品牌符合列表，那么你的申请将立即获得批准。

Here is the current priority list:
这是当前的优先级列表：

(1) Famous retailers (for example, Costco).
著名零售商（如开市客）。

(2) Famous international brands (for example, Apple).
著名的国际品牌（如苹果）。

(3) Famous foreign brands that have never entered the Chinese market before.
以前从未进入中国市场的著名外国品牌。

(4) If your brand is selling products in one of the following industries — maternity baby, nutrition & health, food, wear & shoes, bags and suitcase, and cosmetics, you may also be qualified for priority recruiting.

如果销售的品牌属于以下行业——母婴产品、营养和健康产品、食品、服装和鞋子、行李箱和手提箱以及化妆品，也可能有资格优先被接受。

Logistics: In terms of logistics, JD Worldwide is far more superior than the other platforms. JD operates its own logistic company with one unified logistic system that ensures efficient shipping and delivery of any products sold on JD.

物流：在物流方面，京东国际远远优于其他平台。京东运营自己的物流公司，拥有统一的物流系统，可确保在京东上销售的任何产品都能高效运输和交付。

As for direct shipping from countries where JD's logistics do not cover, they are currently cooperating with international third-party logistic corporations such as Kuehne & Nagel, Schenker, etc. Overall JD Worldwide covers more than 50 countries and regions around the world.

对于那些京东物流没有覆盖的国家的直接运送，它们目前正在与国际第三方物流公司（如 Kuchne & Nagel，Schenker 等）合作。京东国际物流覆盖了全球五十多个国家和地区。

Apart from the third-party partnerships, JD Worldwide also owns multiple overseas warehouses in countries like USA, Europe, South Korea, Japan, Australia and so on. This allows JD to carry out external drop shipment in multiple warehouses and deliver products upon an order immediately.

除了与第三方伙伴合作，京东国际还在美国、欧洲、韩国、日本、澳大利亚等国家和地区拥有多个海外仓库。这使得 JD 可以在多个仓库中进行外部卸货，并立即交付订单产品。

JD's logistics is a truly touched notch with superior customer service and excellent user experience. As for JD national, it is currently the only E-commerce platform with its own logistic team covering 2661 counties and districts in China that guarantees fast delivery when the product from overseas warehouse reaches China.

JD 的物流真正触及了卓越的客户服务和卓越的用户体验这一点。至于国内的 JD，它是目前唯一拥有自己物流团队的电子商务平台，覆盖了中国 2661 个县区，保证海外仓库产品到达中国时能够快速交付。

2.2.5　YMatou 洋码头

It is one of the first cross-border E-commerce platform and marketplace that allows an overseas franchise to sell directly to Chinese consumers.

它是首个跨境电子商务平台和市场之一，允许海外特许经营店直接向中国消费者销售商品。

Operation pattern: Comprehensive, B2C, C2C, marketplace, independent platform.

运营模式：综合、B2C、C2C、市场、独立平台。

Product categories: Appliance, electric appliance car accessories, home products, pets products, cosmetics, sports & outdoors, bags & suitcases, watches & jewelry, health & nutrition, maternity & baby, apparels.

产品类别：家电、电器及汽车配件、家居产品、宠物用品、化妆品、运动及户外用品、箱包、手表及珠宝、健康与营养用品、母婴用品、服饰。

Application process: The application process for YMatou is pretty straight forward and simple. Just follow these 5 steps to submit your brand for approval on YMatou.

申请流程：洋码头的申请流程非常简单明了，只需按照以下这 5 个步骤提交你的品牌就可以，以获得洋码头的批准。

(1) Estimate and assess your sales.

估算和评估你的销售。

(2) Submit the estimated sales along with merchant information and E-mail them to YMatou.

提交估算的销售额和商家信息，并通过电子邮件发送给洋码头。

(3) Wait for YMatou to process your application which will usually take several working days.

等待洋码头处理申请，这通常需要几个工作日。

(4) If approved, YMatou will E-mail you back an agreement for you to sign and resubmit back to them.

如果获得批准，洋码头将通过电子邮件向你发送协议，你签署并重新提交。

(5) Finally, you're not a YMatou merchant, so create your store and start listing your products.

最后，你不是洋码头商家，因此请创建商店并开始列出你的商品。

Logistics: In terms of logistics, YMatou has 3 different types of direct mailing services and 2 different types of bonded warehouse services. It is worth noting that YMatou actually has one of the fastest direct mailing services. The average arrival time for a package from aboard supplier to a Chinese buyer is about 5 days. It's amazing because it is faster than the average time of the bonded warehouse logistic model.

物流：在物流方面，洋码头有三种不同类型的直接邮寄服务和两种不同类型的保税仓库服务。值得注意的是，洋码头实际上拥有最快的直接邮件服务之一。从供应商到中国买家的包裹平均到货时间约为五天。这太棒了，因为它比保税仓库物流模式的平均时间更短。

Direct mailing using xLobo Global Express: xLobo Global Express is YMatou's official international logistics company, and it offers direct mail from most countries around the world. The whole direct mailing process is highly controlled by YMatou, so it is more efficient compared to other logistics companies.

使用贝海国际速递直接邮寄：贝海国际速递是洋码头的官方国际物流公司，提供来自世界上大多数国家的直邮服务。整个直接邮寄过程由洋码头严格控制，因此与其他物流公司相比效率更高。

Direct mailing by verified third-party international logistic companies: Alternatively, you can also use one of the many third-party international logistic companies that are officially verified by YMatou to handle all your logistics.

通过认证的第三方国际物流公司直接邮寄：你也可以使用由洋码头正式认证的任何一家第三方国际物流公司处理你的所有物流。

Direct mailing by unverified third-party international logistic companies: You can also use any third-party international logistic companies that are not verified by YMatou for your shipping and delivery, but it will not be as efficient and fast as the other two options above.

通过未经认证的第三方国际物流公司直接邮寄：你也可以使用未经 YMatou 认证的任何第三方国际物流公司进行运送和交付，但与上述其他两个选项相比，它不会那么高效和快捷。

Using bonded warehouse from xLobo Global Express: xLobo Global Express also provides bonded warehouse service should you want to go that route.

使用来自贝海国际速递的保税仓库：如果你有这个意愿，贝海国际速递还提供保税仓库服务。

Using bonded warehouse from unverified third-party international logistic companies: If you don't want to use xLobo Global Express for your bonded warehouse services, you can also use any third-party international logistic company that offers bonded warehouse services.

使用未经认证的第三方国际物流公司的保税仓库：如果你不想将贝海国际速递用于保税仓库服务，还可以使用任何提供保税仓储服务的第三方国际物流公司的服务。

2.2.6　VIP International VIP 国际

VIP International is the cross-border E-commerce platform of vip.com or vipshop.com. VIP is currently the third largest E-commerce platform in China right after JD. com and TMall.com. Its primary focuses are on online discount sales and discount shopping.

VIP 国际是 vip.com 或者 Vipshop.com（唯品会）的跨境电子商务平台。VIP 目前是中国第三大电子商务平台，排在京东和天猫之后，它主要关注在线折扣销售和折扣购物。

Operation pattern: Vertical platform, B2C, proprietary trading, sub-platform.

运营模式：垂直平台、B2C、自营交易、子平台。

Product categories: Cosmetics & beauty, maternity & baby, food & nutrition, home & personal care, fashion apparels.

产品类别：化妆品及美容、母婴产品、食物及营养、家居及个人护理、时装及服饰。

Application process: In order to become supplier for VIP international, you need to have at least one of the qualifications below.

申请流程：要成为 VIP international 的供应商，你需要至少具备以下一种资格：

(1) The owner of famous brand.

著名品牌的所有者。

(2) The authorized sole agent of a famous brand.

著名品牌的授权独家代理商。

(3) The authorized sole distributor of a famous brand.

著名品牌的授权独家经销商。

(4) A branch of a famous brand.

著名品牌的一个分支。

(5) Chinese agency of a famous global brand.

著名全球品牌中国代理商。

Logistics: As for logistics, VIP currently owns overseas warehouses and 4 bonded warehouses in China. Hence VIP International provides support for both direct mail and bonded warehouse service.

物流：在物流方面，VIP 目前在中国拥有 11 个海外仓库和 4 个保税仓库。因此，VIP International 为直邮和保税仓库服务提供支持。

2.2.7　Little Red Book（RED）小红书

Little Red Book (RED) is an online sharing community which enables users to post their recommendations based on their previous experiences. It naturally adds cross-border sales features as well. Unlike other social media, the platform aims to offer more informative and detailed content in order to make it more authentic and build trust with the Chinese users. Previously RED was mainly focused on beauty and cosmetics, however it has been expanding to other segments such as fashion food, traveling, and lifestyle. RED is one of the largest and fastest growing social E-commerce Apps in China.

小红书是一个在线分享社区，允许用户根据自己以前的经验发布他们的推荐。它自然也增加了跨境销售功能。与其他社交媒体不同，该平台旨在提供更多信息和详细内容，以使其更真实，并与中国用户建立信任关系。以前小红书主要专注于美容和化妆品，但它已经扩展到其他领域，如时尚食品、旅游和生活方式。小红书是中国最大、增长最快的社交电商应用之一。

Each of these platforms has their own strengths and weaknesses, so it is really important to understand how they could benefit or hurt your business. Furthermore, depending on your business and strategy in China it might not be recommended to sell on too many different platforms since you will need to allocate resources to manage and promote each one of them. Besides that, each platform has different application process, rules for their logistics and users focus, which makes it harder to successfully manage different platforms at the same time. Finally, it is suggested that you enter the Chinese online market by selling a limited number of SKUs, adding volume as your business grows.

这些平台中的每一个都有自己的优势和劣势，因此了解它们对您的业务有利或有害很重要。此外，根据您在中国的业务和战略，可能不建议在太多不同的平台上销售，因为您需要分配资源来管理和推广每个平台。此外，每个平台都有不同的申请流程、物流规则和用户关注点，这使得同时成功管理不同的平台变得更加困难。最后，建议您通过销售有限数量的 SKU 进入中国在线市场，随着业务的增长而增加销量。

As you can see, in order to succeed in China, a lot of research and planning is required. It is also important to be persistent, flexible, and creative to adjust to different consumers' needs.

正如您所看到的，为了在中国取得成功，需要大量的研究和规划。为了适应不同消费者的需求，坚持不懈、灵活和富有创造力也很重要。

【 Exercise 】

1. Translate the following phrases into Chinese.

online bookstore _____

Amazon River_____

Fortune 500 company_____

product strategy_____

electronic goods_____

2. Translate the following phrases into English.

保税仓库_____

综合平台_____

市场平台_____

品牌旗舰店_____

第三方物流公司 _____

3. Please explain the following words or items.

vertical platform

comprehensive platforms

sub platform

4. Please answer the following questions.

(1) What are the sales strategies of Amazon?

(2) What are the Amazon's secrets of success?

(3) Name the main platforms of cross-border E-commerce in China.

Chapter 3　Establishment of Business Relations
建立商务关系

【Ability Objectives】

- ❑ Be able to introduce the E-commerce in English 能够用英语介绍电子商务；
- ❑ Be able to communicate with customers in English 能够用英语与顾客交流；
- ❑ Be able to read and comprehend some articles related to cross-border E-commerce 能够阅读和理解与跨境电子商务有关的文章。

【Knowledge Objectives】

- ❑ Master typical expressions about cross-border E-commerce 掌握跨境电子商务的经典表达；
- ❑ Memorize new words and phrases in the texts 能够记忆文章中的单词与短语。

【Key Words】

seeking business cooperation（寻求商务合作）；after-sale E-mail（售后邮件）；pre-sale E-mail（售前邮件）；on-sale E-mail（售中邮件）；online store（线上商店）；Amazon（亚马逊）

Section 3.1　Seeking Business Cooperation 寻求商务合作

New Words

recommend	vt.	推荐
manufacturer	n.	生产商，制造商
annual	adj.	每年的
approximately	adv.	大约，接近
capable	adj.	有能力的
tailored	adj.	（衣服）定做的，合身的，特制的
prevailing	adj.	普遍的，盛行的
explore	vt.	探讨，研究
available	adj.	可获得的；有空的；可购得的
preferably	adv.	更可取地，更好地

venue	*n.*	场地，地点
supplier	*n.*	供应商
leading	*adj.*	主要的
experience	*n.*	经验，经历
	vt.	经历
line	*n.*	行业，行当
version	*n.*	版本
latest	*adj.*	最新的
hesitate	*vi.*	犹豫
inquiry	*n.*	询盘
assure	*vt.*	向保证，使确信
coincide	*vi.*	与一致，与……相符
specialize	*vi.*	专门从事，专门经营
popularity	*n.*	普及，流行
request	*n.*	要求
	vt.	要求
quotation	*n.*	报价
exporter	*n.*	出口商
regret	*n.*	遗憾；懊悔；痛惜；失望
	v.	懊悔；感到遗憾；惋惜
represent	*vt.*	代表
advise	*vt.*	劝告，告知，通知
item	*n.*	商品，物品

Phrases

craftsmanship evaluation	工艺评价
licensed export intermediary	持牌出口中介
as well	也，一样
business line	业务范围
to be in line with...	与……相一致/相符
to be out of line with...	与不一致/不相符
to enter into business relations with sb.	与某人建立业务关系
to establish/set up/build up trade relationship with sb.	与某人建立业务关系
to open an account with sb.	与某人建立业务关系
on the basis of	在……基础上
a general idea	大致情况，概况
for your information	供你方参考
for your reference	供你方参考

for your consideration	供你方考虑
look forward to (sth./doing sth.)	期待（某物/做某事）
general inquiry	一般询盘
specific inquiry	具体询盘
to assure sb. that...	使某人确信
to assure sb. of sth.	使某人确信某事
rest assured	确信无疑，放心
with reference to	关于，有关
date of delivery	交货期
date from/date back to	追溯到……，从……开始
to be delighted to do sth.	乐于做某事
light industrial product	轻工业产品
to be specialized in	专门从事，专门经营
in compliance with	依从，遵照，依照
to meet one's interest	迎合某人的兴趣
quotation sheet	报价单
without delay	立即，立刻
in the meantime	同时
to provide sb. with sth.	为某人提供某物
to provide sth. for sb.	为某人提供某物
prior to	先于，在……之前
to be willing to do sth.	乐意做某事
to be in a position to do sth.	能够做某事
to supply sb. with sth.	为某人提供某物
at your end	你地，你处
get in touch with sb.	与某人取得联系
make sb. an offer	为某人报盘

Sentences

1. The director is expected to explore the opportunity of investing in that country.
   董事长预计将会探讨在那个国家的投资机会。

2. There is no stock available at present.
   当前没有库存可供。

3. The manager is not available right now. He is attending a meeting.
   经理在开会，现在没空。

4. Orders are expected to be placed next month, preferably at the end of this month.
   预计下个月下订单，最好是本月底。

5. We mainly export our products through a licensed export intermediary.
　我们的产品主要是通过持牌出口中介出口的。

6. Xiamen's International Convention Centre is the venue for "the Sept. 8th Trade and Investment Show".
　厦门国际会展中心是"9月8日投洽会"的主要场所。

7. A man who doesn't learn from others can't be hoped to achieve much.
　一个不向别人学习的人不能指望有多大成就。

8. Britain's future as a leading industrial nation depends on investments.
　作为主要工业国，英国的未来依赖投资。

9. The company has very rich experience in manufacturing such kind of machines.
　该公司在生产这种机器方面有丰富的经验。

10. Attending the 100th Canton Fair is undoubtedly a great experience to a beginner in foreign trade like me.
　参加第100届广交会对于像我这样的外贸新手来说无疑是重要的经历。

11. American business is now experiencing a severe recession.
　美国商业现在正经受着严重的衰退。

12. We have been in the line of textiles for many years.
　我们经营纺织品已经好多年了。

13. In my line of work, I often get home too late for dinner.
　干我们这一行，经常回家太迟赶不上吃饭。

14. We desire to enter into business relations with you in the near future.
　我方期待在不久的将来与贵方建立业务关系。

Conversations

1. Market Survey Report

A: Lance, here is our market survey report.

B: Good. Please brief your research result.

A: OK. 60% of the people are attracted by the style of our products. The customers always pay more attention to the package. In my view, these goods didn't sell well merely because of the poor package.

B: Yeah, I think so. How about our brand effect?

A: Well, most people like the idea of being able to buy a Chinese brand rather than a foreign one. In other words, being a Chinese brand is one of our major strengths.

B: That's great. So we have confidence now. And what about the price?

A: Almost 40% of the customers can't accept the price. Maybe we should lower our price.

B: Yes, I agree with you. We should express our opinions to the general manager.

A: Absolutely.

1. 市场调查报告

A：这是我们的市场调查报告。

B：好的，请简短地说一下你们的调查结果。

A：好的，有 60%的人被我们产品的款式所吸引。顾客通常更注意包装，在我看来，这些商品销售不好是由于包装不好引起的。

B：嗯，我也这么认为。我们的品牌效应怎么样？

A：哦，大多数人更愿意买中国的品牌而不是国外的品牌。换句话说，作为一个中国品牌，这是我们的一个主要优势。

B：太好了，那我们现在就有信心了。价格怎么样？

A：大约有 40%的顾客不能接受这个价格，也许我们应该降价。

B：是啊，我同意你的说法。我们应该把我们的想法告诉总经理。

A：那是一定的。

2. E-business

Spark: Why did you close your office?

Ailsa: Well, it's all E-business these days, so I can just work from home on my computer.

Spark: E-business? What's the meaning?

Ailsa: Well, E-business is electronic business. It means any business can be done using the Internet.

Spark: Do you think we should start an E-business service?

Ailsa: Why not? It could bring in sales in 24-7. I'm sure our customers would love it.

Spark: How wonderful! I've never thought we can make money via the Internet.

Ailsa: Well, you should learn about it or you'll be out of date.

Spark: You're right.

2. 电子商务

斯帕克：你为什么关闭你的办公室？

艾丽莎：哦，这些日子都是电子商务，所以我在家通过电脑就可以工作。

斯帕克：电子商务？什么意思呢？

艾丽莎：哦，电子商务就是电子的商务，是使用互联网的商务运作。

斯帕克：你觉得我们该开展电子商务服务吗？

艾丽莎：为什么不呢？每周 7 天，每天 24 小时都可以买卖。我相信顾客也会喜欢的。

斯帕克：太神奇了！我从来没有想过我们可以通过互联网挣钱。

艾丽莎：嗯，你应该学习，要不然你会被淘汰出局的。

斯帕克：你说得对。

Text

3.1.1　Introduction 简介

The development and expansion of a business depends largely on customers. It goes without saying that no customers means no business. To set up business relations is the first and fundamental step in the international trade, because no transactions can be concluded before the establishment of business connections.

企业的发展和壮大在很大程度上取决于客户。不用说，没有顾客就没有生意。建立商务关系是国际贸易的第一步，也是最基本的一步，因为没有建立商务关系就不可能达成任何交易。

To seek prospective clients and establish business relations is one of the most important measures for a newly-established firm or an old one that wishes to expand its market and enlarge its business scope and turnover. Usually a firm may approach its new business counterparts abroad and obtain necessary information through the following channels:

(1) Banks

(2) Chambers of commerce

(3) Trade directories

(4) Business associates of the same trade

(5) Commercial counselor's offices

(6) Commercial office of a foreign embassy

(7) Advertisements

(8) Exhibitions and trade fairs

(9) Market surveys

(10) Recommendation by a business friend or a client

(11) SNS marketing on Facebook, Twitter and so on

(12) Other sources

寻找潜在客户，建立业务关系，是新老公司拓展市场、扩大业务范围和营业额的重要举措之一。通常，一家公司可以通过以下渠道与其在国外的新业务同行接洽，并获得必要的信息：① 银行，② 商会，③ 贸易名录，④ 同行业商业协会，⑤ 商务参赞办公室，⑥ 外国大使馆商务处，⑦ 广告，⑧ 展览和交易会，⑨ 市场调查，⑩ 商业朋友或客户的推荐，⑪ Facebook、Twitter 等上的 SNS 营销，⑫ 其他来源。

To contact potential customers, there are many different ways. We can approach them by way of making telephone calls, making face-to-face talks, sending faxes or E-mails. Of all these methods, communication in writing is the most commonly used means to build up business relations.

联系潜在客户有很多不同的方式。我们可以通过打电话、面谈、发传真或发电子邮件等方式与他们沟通。在所有这些方法中，书面交流是最常用的建立商业关系的手段。

3.1.2　Writing Tips 写作技巧

(1) State the source (the channels) of information about the company.

(2) Briefly introduce your own company.

(3) Demonstrate the intention of writing the E-mail.

(4) State the wish of cooperation and the anticipation of an early reply.

（1）述明有关公司的资料来源（渠道）。

（2）简要介绍你自己的公司。

（3）表明写电子邮件的意图。

（4）表明合作意愿，期待早日答复。

3.1.3　Sample E-mails 电子邮件模板

1. Self-introduction by an Importer 进口商的自我介绍

Dear Sir or Madam,

Your company was recommended as a manufacturer of quality garments. TradeExpo LLC is a privately-held company, established in 1996 with current annual imports of approximately 150,000 men's suits and 100,000 sports coats. We are looking to establish a long term relationship with a manufacturer in the region capable of meeting the tailored clothing industry quality levels prevailing on the US market.

If you would be interested in exploring this opportunity any further, please provide the following initial information:

Plant and product description

Annual capacity available for new customers

Annual exports-Europe/USA/Others

Acceptable production arrangements-complete garment, CMT, CM

For craftsmanship evaluation purpose, later on, we would need production samples as well—preferably a suit or the item best describing your line.

Look forward to your comment. For improved communications, a preferred method of communications would be E-mail at: tradeexpo@pacell net.

Please advise whether your company has authority to export directly or you need a licensed export intermediary.

We plan on visiting the fairs in Shanghai and Guangzhou in October, please advise whether your company will be represented on any of these venues.

Sincerely yours,

Richard

尊敬的先生或女士：

您的公司被推荐为优质服装制造商。TradeExpo LLC 是一家私人持股公司，成立于 1996 年，目前每年进口约 15 万套男式西装和 10 万件运动外套。我们正在寻求与该地区的一家制造商建立长期的合作关系，该制造商能够满足美国市场上流行的裁剪服装业的质量要求。

如果您有兴趣进一步探索此机会，请提供以下初始信息：

工厂和产品说明

可供新客户使用的年产能

年出口——欧洲/美国/其他

可接受的生产安排——成衣、CMT、CM

出于工艺评估的目的，稍后我们还需要生产样品——最好是一套西装或最能描述您产品系列的产品。

期待您的意见。为了改善沟通，首选的通信方式是发送电子邮件至 tradeexpo@pacell.net。

请告知贵公司是否有权直接出口或您是否需要获得许可证的出口中介。

我们计划于 10 月份参观上海和广州的展会，请告知贵公司是否将派代表参加这些展会。

谨上，

理查德

2. Self-introduction by an Exporter 出口商的自我介绍

Dear Sir or Madam，

We learn from http://www.alibaba.com that you are looking for suppliers of electronic connectors. We are one of the leading manufacturers of electronic connectors in China, and we have many years' experience in this particular line of business. We'd like to enter into direct business relations with you on the basis of equality and mutual benefits.

To give you a general idea about the main products of our company, we have attached an electronic version of our latest catalogue for your information.

If any of our products interests you, please do not hesitate to let us know.

We are looking forward to receiving your early inquiry, and assure you that your requirements will have our very best and prompt attention.

Best wishes，

Lucy Li

尊敬的先生或女士：

我们从阿里巴巴网站上得知您正在寻找电子连接器的供应商。我们是中国领先的电子连接器制造商之一，我们在这一行有多年的经验。我们愿意在平等互利的基础上与你们建立直接的业务关系。

为了使您对我们公司的主要产品有一个大概的了解，我们附上了我们最新产品目录的电子版供您参考。

如果您对我们的任何产品感兴趣，请不要犹豫让我们知道。

我们期待着早日收到您的询价，并向您保证，我们将及时处理您的要求。

最好的祝福，

露西·李

3. Accepting to Establish Business Relations 接受建立业务关系

Dear Mr. Smith，

With reference to your E-mail dated 1st July, we are delighted to learn that you wish to establish trade relations with us in the line of light industrial products. This happens to coincide with our desire.

We specialize in exporting Chinese light industrial products which have enjoyed great popularity in the world markets. In compliance with your request, we attached a copy of our latest catalogue for your reference.

If any of the items listed in the catalogue meets your interest, please let us have your specific enquiries, and our quotation will be sent to you without delay. In the meantime, could you please provide us with the name of your bank prior to the conclusion of the first transaction between us?

Yours sincerely,

Jane Yang

尊敬的史密斯先生：

关于您 7 月 1 日的电子邮件，我们很高兴得知您希望与我们建立轻工业品贸易关系。这与我们的愿望不谋而合。

我们专门出口在世界市场上很受欢迎的中国轻工业产品。应贵方要求，随函附上我方最新目录一份，供贵方参考。

如果目录所列项目中有贵方感兴趣的，请告知具体询价，我方报价单将立即寄给贵方。同时，在我们达成第一笔交易之前，请您提供贵银行的名称，好吗？

您诚挚的，

杨珍

4. Refusing to Establish Business Relations 拒绝建立业务关系

Dear Sir or Madam，

Thank you for your E-mail dated Sept. 17, 2019 and your interest in our products.

As an exporter, we are willing to do business with you. However, we regret very much that we are not in a position to supply you with chinaware directly, as we have already been represented by Monkking International Enterprise for the sale of this commodity at your end. Therefore, we would kindly advise you to get in touch with them for your requirements.

However, if you are interested in other items of our products, please kindly let us know and we shall be only too pleased to make you the best offers.

Best wishes,

Jane Yang

尊敬的先生或女士：

感谢您 9 月 9 日的电子邮件。以及您对我们产品的兴趣。

作为出口商，我们愿意与您做生意。然而，很遗憾，我们不能直接供应贵方瓷器，因为蒙金国际公司已经代表我们在贵方销售这种商品。因此，我们诚挚地建议您就您的要求与蒙金国际联系。

不过，如果您对我们的其他产品感兴趣，请告知我们，我们将非常乐意为您提供最优惠的报价。

祝您幸福，

杨珍

Section 3.2　Replying to E-mail Regarding Business Contacts 回复商务往来的电子邮件

New Words

convenient	*adj.*	实用的；便利的；方便的；省事的
inform	*v.*	通知；通告；知会；了解
bathrobes	*n.*	〈美〉浴衣
cotton	*n.*	棉；棉布；棉纱；棉织物
mutual	*adj.*	相互的；彼此的；共有的；共同的
lamp	*n.*	灯；（理疗用的）发热灯；（科学上用的）射线照射器
	v.	重击；狂殴
enclose	*v.*	附入；随函（或包裹等）附上
long-term	*adj.*	长期的；长远的；长期有效的；近期不大可能改变的
previous	*adv.*	在先
	adj.	先前的；以往的；（时间上）稍前的
quotation	*n.*	报价；引用；引文；引语
patterns	*n.*	模式；方式；格局；型
	v.	给……加花样；照图样做；仿造；形成图案
satisfactory	*adj.*	令人满意的；够好的；可以的
mutually	*adv.*	彼此；相互地；共同地
straw	*n.*	稻草；一根禾秆（或麦秆、稻草）；（喝饮料用的）吸管
notification	*n.*	通知；通告；告示
fax	*n.*	传真（照片、文件）；电视（传真）画面；复印本
	v.	给（某人）发传真
reminders	*n.*	提示；使人回想起某人（事）的东西；提醒者；【商】催询单
defective	*adj.*	有缺点的；有缺陷的；有毛病的
	n.	身心有缺陷的人；变化不全的词
lodge	*n.*	传达室；（供户外运动者暂住的）乡间小屋；门房；管理员室
	v.	（向公共机构或当局）正式提出（声明等）；借宿；租住
prompt	*n.*	提示；提示符
	v.	提示；促使；激起；导致
	adj.	迅速；敏捷；准时；立即的
	adv.	准时地
sincerely	*adv.*	真诚地；诚实地
compensate	*v.*	补偿；弥补；给（某人）赔偿（或赔款）

Phrases

electric bicycles	电动自行车
to compare with	和……比起来
international market	国际市场
to look forward to	盼望

Sentences

1. They now need to put some real elbow grease into promoting the products.
   他们现在推销产品确实需要花大力气。

2. We are doing a special promotion of our paperback list.
   我们正在搞推销平装书的特别宣传活动。

3. How can we promote the sales of this product?
   我们应该如何推销这种产品？

4. I'm in charge of the new sales promotion campaign.
   我负责新的促销活动。

5. We decided to start a large-scale promotion.
   我们决定发起一次大规模的促销活动。

6. The company is trying to promote a new product.
   这家公司在尽力推销一种新产品。

7. How do you promote the brand?
   你怎样推广品牌？

8. The firm is big on extravagant promotion drives.
   这家公司正在大搞促销活动。

9. She is responsible for sales promotion.
   她负责促销工作。

10. They're planning a big promotion for their new washing powder.
    他们正筹划举办一次新款洗衣粉的大促销活动。

11. At the sales promotion stage, we're going to allow you 5% discount.
    在促销阶段，我们打算给贵公司 5%的折扣。

12. For us to stay competitive, our company has to increase retail sales for this important sales cycle.
    出于竞争需要，我们公司要在这个重要的销售周期中提高我们的零售销量。

13. We should like to know your plan to push the sale of our products.
    我们很想了解你方推销我们产品的计划。

14. I was trying to get some ideas for our sales promotion.
    我们在努力为我们的促销活动搞出一些创意。

15. We're spending a fortune on marketing and sales promotion these days.
    我们近来在营销和促销方面花了不少钱。

16. We regret our inability to comply with your request.

我方无法满足你方需求，非常遗憾。

17. We are not in a position to accept new orders because we have already been heavily committed.

由于当前承约量很大，无法接受新订单。

18. We will try our best to supply you with any information you need.

我们将竭尽所能为你方提供所需信息。

19. We would advise you to accept our offer without delay to take advantage of the advancing market.

我方建议贵方立即接受报盘以便赶上销售旺季。

20. Please advise us of the shipment date the soonest possible.

烦请尽快告知装运日期。

21. The most valuable item on show will be a Picasso drawing.

展览会上最贵重的物品是毕加索的一幅素描。

22. We are willing to make you an offer for the following item.

我方很乐意对下列商品做出报盘。

Conversations

1. Developing Brand

A: What are our areas for growth? What sectors do you see the most potential in? If we are going to pull our sales numbers up and develop the brand, we got to work across the board.

B: It's not just spreading out to new markets that we have to address. I think we'd better first pay attention to developing our brand in the markets we already have. We've reached the awareness level, but we haven't established customer loyalty. People know who we are, but they still don't trust in our brand.

A: I don't see why we can't work on opening new markets and developing the markets we've already penetrated at the sometime... It is very important to develop both the aspects of our customer base and our brand.

1. 发展品牌

A：我们的发展空间是什么？你看我们最有潜力的部分是什么？如果我们要提高销售额并开发品牌，我们大家一定要一起努力。

B：我们要做的不仅仅是拓展新市场。我认为我们最好首先重视开发我们在市场上已经拥有的品牌。我们已经让大家知道了我们的品牌，但还没有建立起顾客的品牌忠实度。人们知道我们是谁，但他们还不信任我们的品牌。

A：我不明白我们为什么不能同时既开发新市场，又开发我们已经渗透的市场……发展顾客基础和发展我们的品牌两方面同样重要。

2. Scheduling Program

Manager: What is on the agenda for today?

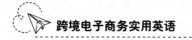

Secretary: It's a tight schedule.

Manager: Is it another busy day?

Secretary: Yes. You have a meeting with Mr. Green at 10:00 p.m.

Manager: What does it pertain to?

Secretary: It's about the overseas market.

Manager: OK.

Secretary: Then you have made a lunch appointment with Mrs.Foster.

Manager: Mmm.

Secretary: This afternoon at 3:00 you will attend a press conference.

Manager: Please cancel the reservation of attending the press conference. I have an urgent meeting this afternoon.

Secretary: All right.

Manager: Anything else?

Secretary: The last one is that you have a flight to Paris this evening.

Manager: I almost forgot.

2. 日程安排

经理：我今天的日程是如何安排的？

秘书：安排得很紧。

经理：又是很忙的一天吗？

秘书：是的。上午 10:00 你要与格林先生见个面。

经理：是有关哪方面的？

秘书：是关于海外市场的问题。

经理：好的。

秘书：然后，您与福斯特女士约定共进午餐。

经理：嗯。

秘书：下午三点您要出席一个新闻发布会。

经理：帮我把新闻发布会的预定取消了吧。下午 4:00 我要开一个紧急会议。

秘书：好的。

经理：还有其他事吗？

秘书：最后一件就是您今天晚上要飞往巴黎。

经理：我差点忘了。

Text

3.2.1 Pre-sale E-mail 售前邮件

1. Making an Appointment 预约

Dear Mr. Cole,

Our sales manager will be in New York for five days from June 12-17, and would like to come and see you to discuss our contract dispute on June 14 at 10:00 a.m.

Please let us know if you are convenient. If not, what time would you suggest?

Yours sincerely,

CH Co

亲爱的科尔先生：

我们的销售经理 6 月 12 日到 17 日将在纽约，想在 6 月 14 日上午 10 点拜访您，讨论有关我们合约的纠纷事宜。

请告知这个时间对您是否方便。如不方便，请建议具体的时间。

您诚挚的，

CH 公司

2. Introducing New Products 介绍新产品

Dear Mr. Liu,

We are pleased to inform you that we have introduced our new products to the market. Our new brand bathrobes are made of pure cotton. Owing to the carefully selected materials used and the great attention paid to weaving and printing, they possess a very attractive appearance as well as novel designs. They have been generally well-received by customers.

As we guess, you might be interested in our new products, so we attach the latest catalogue and price list. We hope you will take this opportunity for our mutual benefits.

Look forward to hearing from you.

Yours sincerely,

Jim Green

ABC Corporate

亲爱的刘先生：

很高兴通知贵方，我方已经向市场推出了新产品。我们的新品浴袍是纯棉制品，选料考究，纺织和印花工艺严格，款式美观新颖，广受消费者好评。

我方猜想，贵公司应该会对我们的新产品感兴趣，特此附上我方最新的产品目录和价格表。希望贵方能够抓住此次机会促成双方互惠互利的合作。

期待收到您的来信。

您诚挚的，

吉姆•格林

ABC 公司

3. Inquiry 买方询盘

Dear Mr. Smith,

We were deeply impressed by your new energy-saving lamp exhibited in your stand at the trade fair on July 8, 2013. So we would like to import large quantities of this kind of products from your company.

Would you please send us your price list and catalogues of your updated energy-saving lamp, with your earliest delivery date, your terms of payment? It would help us the most if you could also supply some samples.

Look forward to hearing from you.

Yours sincerely,

Chuck Thomas

AE Company

亲爱的史密斯先生：

贵公司在 2013 年 7 月 8 日的交易会上展示的新式节能灯给我方留下了深刻的印象。因此，我方想从贵方那里大批进口此产品。

请贵公司向我方发送一份最新款节能灯的价目表、目录，贵方最早的交货期和付款条件。如果贵公司能够提供一些样品，对我方是最有帮助的。

期待您的回复。

您诚挚的，

查克·托马斯

AE 公司

Dear Sir or Madam,

Our company specializes in electronic products trade. In the eastern United States, we have a big market. We are very interested in the BE40 mini bluetooth earphone and would like to order your products. Please give us detailed information on MOQ, discount information and FOB price, we are expecting your samples.

We are sincerely want to establish business relations with you.

Sincerely yours,

Richard

尊敬的先生或女士：

我们是一家专门做电子产品贸易的公司，在美国东部有很大的市场，我们对型号为 BE40 的迷你蓝牙耳机很感兴趣，想订购你们的产品。我们想了解你们的最小起订量、折扣信息以及 FOB 价，希望你方能寄上样品。

我们真诚地希望能与你们建立业务关系。

谨上，

理查德

Dear Richard,

Many thanks for your inquiry dated of august 11 from Alibaba.com. As the quantity of your order is too vague to enable us to reply you the discount. Will you please tell the quantity you require so as to enable us to make an offer? Please reply as soon as possible.

Sincerely yours,

Mary

亲爱的理查德：

非常感谢你方在 8 月 11 日从阿里巴巴网站发来的询价。但由于您的订购数量不明确，我们无法答复您相关折扣信息。为了方便我方报价，你方能告知所需产品数量吗？请尽快回复。

谨上，
玛丽

4. Asking Price 卖方报价

Dear Mr. Blair,

Thank you very much for your inquiry dated July 7, 2020. We are very grateful to you for your interested in our electric bicycles.

Now we send you our price list, catalogue and enclose some samples.

Commodity: electric bicycle

Price: US $430 per unit CIF London

Payment: L/C at sight

Our prices are reasonable as compared with those in the international market. We insure that we can ship the goods within two weeks after receipt your orders.

Look forward to your order and long-term cooperation with you.

Sincerely yours,
Dong Bo
QC Corporation

亲爱的布莱尔先生：

十分感谢贵方 2020 年 7 月 7 日的询盘，感谢对我公司电动自行车的浓厚兴趣。

我公司现在向贵方寄送价格清单、产品目录，并寄送一些样品。

商品：电动自行车

价格：伦敦到岸价每辆 430 美元

支付方式：即期信用证

与国际市场相比，我方的价格是很合理的。我方保证在收到贵方订单两个星期内为贵方发货。

期待您的订单，并希望能与您长期合作。

谨上，
董博
QC 公司

Dear Sir,

Thank you for your inquiry dated July 15, showing interest in our men's shirt. At your request, we are making you the following offer.

Commodity: Men's shirt

Quantity: 2000 dozens

Specification: S/M/L

Price: $20 per item, FOB Guangzhou

Shipment: Within August

Payment: by PayPal

As you know, our stock is limited, and the prices of these items are still on the rise. We therefore suggest that you make an early decision.

We look forward to receiving your order soon.

Sincerely yours,

Mary

QC Corporation

亲爱的先生：

感谢你方 7 月 15 日的询价，对我们的男士衬衫感兴趣。应你方要求，我方现向你方报盘如下。

商品：男士衬衫

数量：2000 打

规格：S/M/L

价格：每件 20 美元，FOB 广州

装运：8 月内

付款方式：贝宝

如您所知，我们的存货有限，这些商品的价格仍在上涨，因此我们建议你方尽早做出决定。

我们期待尽快收到你方订单。

谨上，

玛丽

QC 公司

Dear Sir,

Thanks for your letter of inquiring about our sleeveless silk dress on June 3. As requested, we take pleasure in offering you, 400 dozen sleeveless silk dress at $200.00 per dozen FOB Tianjin. Shipment will be effected within 15 days after receipt of T/T from your bank in London.

We are manufacturing various kinds of ladies fashion for exportation, and enclosed brochure of products for your reference.

If we can be of any further help, please feel free to let us know.

Sincerely yours,

Mary

QC Corporation

亲爱的先生：

感谢您 6 月 3 日来函询问我们的无袖丝绸连衣裙。根据你方要求，我们很高兴向你方提供 400 打无袖丝绸连衣裙，每打天津离岸价 200 美元。收到你方伦敦银行的电汇后 15 天内装运。

我们生产并出口各种时尚女装，顺便附上产品说明书供您参考。

如果我们能提供任何进一步的帮助，请尽管告诉我们。

谨上，
玛丽
QC 公司

5. Refusing Counter Offer 拒绝还盘

Dear Mr. Brook,

Thank you for your letter of June 29. We are very sorry to hear that the price for our products is still too high for you. However, that is the best offer we can give. We cannot make a better offer than the one we suggested to you.

We have done business for such a long time and our products are very popular in your market. We are always ready to offer you a reasonable and competitive price. We have already reduced our previous quotation by 4%. If we lower the price again, our profit will be negative.

We hope that you can agree on the price we offered after you think twice.

Yours sincerely,
Wang Xudong
LT Corporation

亲爱的布鲁克先生：

感谢贵公司 6 月 29 日的来信。很遗憾得知贵公司认为我方的报价仍然过高。然而，这是我方能够提供的最好报盘。我方不可能报出比那更低的价格了。

我们双方做贸易这么长时间以来，我方的产品在贵方市场上一直很畅销。我方一直以来都为贵方提供合理的且具有竞争力的价格。我方已经在之前报价的基础上降价 4%。如果再降价，将会亏损。

希望贵方再三考虑之后能够同意我方提出的价格。

您诚挚的，
王旭东
LT 公司

Dear Sir,

Thank you for your letter of March 5th, requesting us to provide you a more favorable term for the goods. We appreciate your position and we regret to say that the price we quoted has reflected the furthest we could go. As the price of the raw materials has almost doubled, we want to control inventory costs.

Nevertheless, if you are willing to increase the quantity the order, we promise to offer some discounts. Now enclosed is a catalogue of the goods. You will see detailed information about the discounts that could be given.

We hope you can make your final decision as soon as possible.

Sincerely yours,
Mary
QC Corporation

亲爱的先生：

贵方 3 月 5 日的来函已收到，要求我们提供更优惠的条款。我们完全明白你方的立场，不过很遗憾，目前该报价已经是我们所能做到的最大限度。原因在于原材料的价格几乎涨了一倍，我们希望控制库存成本。

尽管如此，如果你方愿意增加订货数量，我方承诺会提供一些折扣。现随函附上有关商品清单，清单上列明了每种商品的折扣。

我们希望你方能尽快做出最后决定。

谨上，

玛丽

QC 公司

3.2.2　On-sale E-mail 售中邮件

1. Ordering 订购

Dear Mr. White,

Thank you for your letter of sending us patterns of coals on June 4. We find that both prices and quality are satisfactory. So we are pleased to write to you to order 5 tons of coals on the understanding that they will be supplied from current stock at the price named. We hope that we can succeed in cooperating and benefit mutually, and will establish a good relationship with you in the future.

If you would like to make inquiries concerning our company, please let us know.

Please send us your confirmation of sales in duplicate.

Yours sincerely,

David

亲爱的怀特先生：

非常感谢您 6 月 4 日寄给我方的煤炭样品。经过研究，我方觉得你方产品的价格和质量都很合适，所以我方很高兴向你方订购 5 吨煤炭，并且希望你方从现有库存中取出，价格不变。希望我们合作成功，互惠互利，并且以后能够长期合作。

如果你方还有任何疑问，请告知我方。

如果确认销售，请告知我方。

您诚挚的，

大卫

Dear Sir,

Please dispatch to us 3000 efficient bulbs as per the terms started in your offer of October 9.

Enclosed please find our order No.05 in duplicate. Please sign on one of the copies and return for our file. As we are in urgent need of this goods, you are requested to effect shipment during November promised in your offer.

The relative letter of credit will be opened in your favor soon. Please arrange shipment without any delay upon receipt of the credit. If the quality is up to our expectation, we shall give further orders in the near future.

Sincerely yours,

Mary

QC Corporation

亲爱的先生：

请按照贵方 10 月 9 日的报价条款，向我方发运 3000 只节能灯泡。随函附上我们第 05 号订单，一式两份，请签退一份供我方存档。由于我们急需该批货物，请在你方报价所承诺的 11 月装运。

以你方为受益人的相关信用证会尽快开出，请收到信用证后立即安排装运。如果质量符合我方要求，我们将在不久的将来再次订货。

谨上，

玛丽

QC 公司

2. Packing 包装要求

Dear Mr. Jia,

Before the shipment, I'd like to write this letter to put forward some packaging requirements.

As your products are easily damaged, it is quite necessary to pay special attention to packaging.

(1) Packing in strong wooden cases is essential.

(2) The products are to be wrapped in straw board before being packed in wooden cases.

(3) All cargoes are required to be marked and numbered on the outside.

We believe that you will pay high attention to the packing to avoid any possible loss.

Yours sincerely,

Robert Tuner

ABC Company

亲爱的贾先生：

在贵公司发货之前，我想提出一些包装的要求，特写此信。

由于贵方货物容易损坏，因此在包装时需特别注意：

（1）有必要使用结实的木箱。

（2）装入木箱之前，用草纸板把货物包好。

（3）所有货物都应该在外面做好标记，写好编号。

我方相信贵公司定会高度重视货物的包装，避免任何可能的损失。

您诚挚的，

罗伯特·特纳

ABC 公司

Dear Sir,

We refer to our order No. 123 for 800 wine glasses to be shipped to us in June. As the goods are highly fragile, we have put forward a number of requirements with regard to packaging:

(1) We would like to have them packed half dozen in a box, 6 boxes in a carton, 4 cartons in a wooden case. The boxes are to be padded with foamed plastics.

(2) We hope that the inner packing will be attractive and helpful to the sales, and that the outer packing is strong enough to withstand the sea transportation.

We hope that the goods will arrive in perfect condition.

Sincerely yours,
Mary
QC Corporation

亲爱的先生：

根据我方第 123 号订单，我方所订购的 800 只酒杯应该在 6 月份装运给我方。由于货物易碎，我方就包装问题提出一些要求：

（1）我方希望每盒装半打，每 6 盒用一个纸箱包装，每 4 个纸箱用一个大木箱包装。而且这些箱子要用泡沫塑料填充。

（2）我方希望内包装卖相好，而外包装足够坚固，可以经受海运。

我方希望货物能够完好无损地抵达。

谨上，
玛丽
QC 公司

3. Informing the Shipment 出货通知

Dear Mr. Blair,

This is a notification of shipment.

We have shipped your order NO. 22 as of June 5, 2020. And I have faxed you the relevant shipping documents. Please check.

You should receive the goods you ordered by June 15, 2020, if there is no accident.

Please let us know when they arrive. Thank you very much!

Yours sincerely,
WM Co.

亲爱的布莱尔先生：

这是我们的出货通知。

您订单号为 22 号的货物已于 2020 年 6 月 5 日出货。相关出货资料也已经传真给您了，请注意查收。

如无任何意外，您的货物在 2020 年 6 月 15 日之前就能到达。

如果货物到达，请通知我们。谢谢！

您诚挚的，
WM 公司

4. Prompting the Payment 催促付款

Dear Mr. Parker,

This is about your account No.100. We have sent you many reminders before, but you have not pay off the bill until today. We are wondering whether there is any special reason for it. Anyhow, you are expected to make payments within the limits stated in our contract.

Your early attention would be highly appreciated.

Yours truly,

MP Corporation

亲爱的帕克先生:

此信是关于您的第 100 号账单的。我方已多次提醒您付款,但您至今都未做出偿付。不知是否有其他特殊原因。然而无论如何都希望贵方能够在合同规定的日期内付款。

如能及时处理,我方不胜感激。

MP 公司

5. Postponing the Payment 延期付款

Dear Mr. Black,

I am terribly sorry for the overdue balance on our account. I know that payment for our order is due this Thursday. But something wrong happened to our finance. I was wondering if it is possible to grant us a week payment extension. I can ensure that you will receive the outstanding balance on time.

I appreciate it very much for your understanding.

Yours sincerely,

Lucy

亲爱的布莱克先生:

非常抱歉我们逾期未能付清账款。我知道我们的订单应于本周四付款,但是我们的财务突然出了些问题。能否再延长一周的支付期限呢?我保证您可以准时收到未付账款。

非常感谢您的谅解。

您诚挚的,

露西

3.2.3 After-sale E-mail 售后邮件

1. Returning the Goods 退货

Dear Mr. Brown,

We are so sorry for delivering the defective goods in our shipment. We will, of course, accept the return of these items and send you replacements immediately. Please accept our apologies for inconvenience our mistake have caused to you. We guarantee that this will not happen again.

Sincerely yours,

AB Company

亲爱的布朗先生：

关于发给您的货物中出现了瑕疵品这一事情，我们深表歉意。我们当然会接受退货，并且会立即寄出新的货品。由于我们的失误给您带来不便，请接受我们的道歉。在此，我们向您保证，不会再发生此类事情。

谨上，

AB 公司

2. Claiming 索赔

Dear Mr. Blair,

Thank you for your prompt delivery and the goods arrived yesterday. The 400 boxes appeared to be in good condition. However, when we unpacked the boxes with great care, we were disappointed to find that 50 boxes of tea were totally wetted, which made our goods be in short supply.

We hope that you can understand that we have to lodge a claim against you for the damaged goods.

Your prompt cooperation will be beneficial to both of us.

Yours sincerely,

Eric Lynch

PT Corporation

亲爱的布莱尔先生：

感谢贵方及时发货，货物已于昨日运抵。装货物的 400 个箱子完好无损，但当我们小心地打开箱子后，有 50 箱茶叶完全受潮，这令我们很失望，而且导致了供不应求的后果。

对于受损货物，我方不得不向贵方提出索赔，希望贵方能够理解。

期待您的及时回复，这对双方都有好处。

您诚挚的，

艾瑞克·林奇

PT 公司

Dear Sir,

With reference to our order No.56, upon examination, we found that many of the goods were severely damaged, though the cases themselves show no trace of damage. The surveyor maintains that the damage was due to insecure packing and not to any unduly rough handling. We are compelled to claim on you to compensate us for the loss, $10,000, which we have sustained by the damage to the goods. We will appreciate your expeditious handling of this matter.

Sincerely yours,

Mary

QC Corporation

亲爱的先生：

关于我们的第 56 号订单，经检验，我们发现虽然箱子本身并无损坏迹象，但很多货物已严重损坏。鉴定员认为损失是由包装不牢固造成的，而非搬运不当所致。我方不得不向你方提出索赔，要求你方赔偿我方因货物损坏蒙受的损失，共计 10 000 美元。我方希望你方迅速处理此事。

谨上，
玛丽
QC 公司

3. Making up the Loss 弥补对方损失

Dear Mr. Wang,

We have received your letter about the claim for the wetted tea. We apologize sincerely for the trouble caused to you, and will take all possible steps to ensure that such a mistake will not be made again.

Although every possible attention has been paid to all your orders, we still made a mistake in packing. We will send 40 boxes of tea by air-mail as soon as possible and we will make payment by cash to compensate you for your loss.

We hope this matter will not influence our good relations.

Yours truly,
Mike Roberts

亲爱的王先生：

我方已收到贵方要求赔偿受潮茶叶的来信。我们为给贵方带来的麻烦表示诚挚的歉意，并将采取一切措施避免再次发生同样的错误。

尽管我们对您的订单万分重视，但还是在包装中出现了失误。我们会尽快向贵方空运 40 箱茶叶，并将支付现金作为赔偿。

希望这次事件不会影响到双方的友好合作。

迈克·罗伯茨谨启

Dear Sir,

We have received your letter of 15 March, we looked into the situation and found that the damage was due to negligence in our shipment. We apologize for our mistake and the inconvenient caused by this change. We learn from your letter that you want to callback the products and ask for 5000 in US dollars in compensation. As regards to compensation, it is difficult for us to pay you 5000 dollars, but we can call back the broken ones and deliver a new lot to replace them. Of course, we'll pay the freight. We also can give you 10% discount in our following business deal.

Sorry again for the inconvenience caused by us. Look forward to your reply.

Sincerely yours,
Mary
QC Corporation

亲爱的先生：

我方已收到你方 3 月 15 日的来信，调查相关情况后，发现是由于我方装运的疏忽造成了货物损毁。我们对由于工作疏漏导致的不便表示歉意。我方从你方来信中得知，你方想召回产品并要求 5000 美元的赔偿。关于赔偿问题，我方很难支付你方 5000 美元，但我方可以收回损坏货物，并提供一批新的替换。当然，运费由我方支付。我方还可以在以后的交易中给你方 10% 的折扣。

对此事造成的不便我方再次深表歉意，期待你方的答复。

谨上，

玛丽

QC 公司

4. Infringing the Contract 违反合同

Dear Mr. Black,

We're very sorry for failure to deliver your ordered goods at scheduled time in accordance with the contract we have reached.

Unfortunately, owing to some technology problems, we have to delay the time we have reached. We sincerely apologize for the violation of the contract. However, we will compensate all your financial loss. And we guarantee that your ordered goods will arrive next Monday.

Thanks very much for your understanding.

Sincerely yours,

PP Corporation

亲爱的布莱克先生：

我们未能按合同约定的时间交货，十分抱歉。

很不幸，由于某些技术问题，我们不得不推迟交易日期。我方对于违反合同一事致以真诚的歉意。不过，我们会赔偿您所有的经济损失。并且我方向您保证，下周一你方一定可以收到货物。

非常感谢您的谅解。

谨上，

PP 公司

Section 3.3　Build Your Online Store 建立你的网上店铺

New Words

establish	*vt.*	建立，设立，安置
guide	*n.*	指南；指导
register	*n & v.*	登记，注册
registry	*v.*	获得，赢得，取得
secure	*v.*	保护；取得；保卫；抵押
	adj.	安心的；有把握的；可靠的；牢靠的
expect	*v.*	期望；预计；期待；指望
intuitive	*adj.*	直觉的；直观的
complicated	*adj.*	复杂的；难懂的

feedback	*n.*	反馈；反馈意见；回授；【电子】反馈
hire	*v.*	雇用；聘用；租用；录用
	n.	租用；租赁；租借；新雇员
temp	*abbr.*	温度
	v.	打临时工；做临时工作；打零工
	n.	临时雇员；临时工
assemble	*v.*	装配；组装；集合；聚集
numerous	*adj.*	许多；数量庞大的；数不清的
handle	*v.*	处理；控制；操纵；拿
	n.	柄；把手；拉手；提梁
template	*n.*	模板；样板；型板；模框
assortment	*n.*	各种各样
shopping-cart	*n.*	购物车
assistance	*n.*	帮助；援助；支持
merchandise	*n.*	商品；货品；相关商品；指定商品
	v.	推销；（运用广告等进行）销售
extremely	*adv.*	非常；极其；极端
pitch	*n.*	沥青；球场；柏油；（体育比赛的）场地
	v.	投；推销；抛；颠簸
outright	*adj.*	完全的；彻底的；绝对的；公开的
	adv.	公开地；直率地；毫无保留地；完全彻底
waive	*v.*	放弃（权利、要求等）
presence	*n.*	存在；出现；在场；出席
range	*n.*	区间；一系列
	v.	徘徊；变动；包括（从……到……）之间的各类事物
prepackage	*n.*	（食品等出售前用透明纸等）预先做好的包装
	v.	（出售前）将（食品或其他商品）按标准重量或单位包装
alternative	*adj.*	可供替代的；非传统的；另类的
	n.	可供选择的事物
differentiate	*v.*	区分；区别；使分化
normally	*adv.*	通常；正常地；正常情况下；平常地
application	*n.*	应用程序；运用；申请；施用
server	*n.*	服务器
connectivity	*n.*	连通性；结合性；接合性；连通图
theoretically	*adv.*	从理论上讲
flock	*v.*	聚集；群集；蜂拥
	n.	（羊或鸟）群；（尤指同类人的）一大群

fuss	*n.*	大惊小怪；无谓的激动（或忧虑、活动）；（为小事）大吵大闹
	v.	瞎忙一气；过分关心（枝节小事）；（为小事）烦恼
represent	*v.*	代表；表现；体现；描绘
interior	*n.*	内部；内陆；内地；里面
	adj.	内部的；里面的
artistic	*adj.*	艺术的；艺术家的；有艺术天赋的；（尤指）有美术才能的
professional	*n.*	专家；专业人士；内行；职业运动员
	adj.	职业的；专业的；有职业的；娴熟的
usability	*n.*	可用；有用；适用
emphasize	*v.*	强调；重视；着重；使突出
seamless	*adj.*	无（接）缝的；（两部分之间）无空隙的
escrow	*n.*	【法】（暂由第三者保存、待某种条件完成后即交付受让人或权利人的）契据（契约、合同、证书等）；第三方托管
authentication	*n.*	认证；鉴定
terminal	*n.*	终端；航站楼；终端机；航空终点站
ponder	*v.*	〈正式〉深思；仔细考虑
boost	*n.*	提高；增长；帮助；激励
	v.	使增长；使兴旺；偷窃
originality	*n.*	创意；独创性；独特构思
malicious	*adj.*	怀有恶意的；恶毒的
attack	*v.*	攻击；袭击；进攻；抨击
	n.	攻击；袭击；打击；侵袭
dismiss	*v.*	解雇；开除；驳回；解散
dial-up	*n.*	〔计〕拨号；拨号上网；拨号
	adj.	拨号上网的
emergency	*n.*	突发事件；紧急情况
broadband	*adj.*	宽带的；宽频的
	n.	宽带
spyware	*n.*	间谍软件；间谍程序
firewall	*n.*	【计】防火墙；风火墙；马头墙
guardian	*n.*	守卫者；保护者；保卫者；（尤指双亲已故孩子的）监护人
	adj.	守护的
replicate	*v.*	复制；（精确地）仿制；再造；再生
	adj.	【植】折转的
	n.	【统】重复实验中的一次
rampant	*adj.*	泛滥的；猖獗的；疯长的
freeware	*n.*	免费软件

threat	*n.*	威胁，恐吓；凶兆；隐患
dub	*v.*	刺；撞；为（影片、广播节目等）配音；译制（影片）
	n.	（西印度群岛的）强节奏音乐
fight	*v.*	战斗；打架；作战；打斗
	n.	斗争；打架；打斗；搏斗
frustrate	*v.*	挫败；使懊丧；使懊恼；使沮丧
	adj.	无效的；受挫折的；被破坏的；失败了的
parcel	*n.*	包裹；小包；一块地；一片地
	v.	包；裹好；打包
	adj.	部分（时间）的
	adv.	局部地
fundamental	*n.*	基础；基本原理；基本规律；根本法则
	adj.	十分重大的；根本的；基础的；基本的
execution	*n.*	执行；实施；实行；处决
spinner	*n.*	纺纱工；投旋转球的投球手；纺线者；（钓鱼用的）旋式诱饵
sponsor	*n.*	赞助商；发起人；保证人；为慈善活动捐资的人
	v.	主办；举办；赞助（活动、节目等）；促成
headline	*n.*	（报纸的）大字标题；（电台或电视的）新闻摘要
	v.	给（报道、文章）加标题
organic	*adj.*	有机的；不使用化肥的；绿色的；有机物的
	n.	分子有机体
approach	*n.*	方法；接近；路径；道路
	v.	接近；建议；接洽；着手处理
myth	*n.*	神话；神话故事；虚构的东西；荒诞的说法
	v.	使神化
revenue	*n.*	收益；营业额；税务署
household	*n.*	家庭；一家人；同住一所（或一套）房子的人
	adj.	家庭的；家常的；王室的
solid	*n.*	固体；立体图形
	adj.	固体的；坚硬的；无空隙的；非中空的
	adv.	一致
credibility	*n.*	可信性；可靠性
essentially	*adv.*	基本上；本质上；根本上
account	*n.*	账户；说明；账号；叙述
	v.	认为是；视为
rejection	*n.*	拒绝；否决；抛弃；拒斥
prohibit	*v.*	阻止；（尤指以法令）禁止；使不可能

restrict	*v.*	限制；约束；阻碍；束缚
approval	*n.*	批准；同意；赞成；（商品）试用
mess	*n.*	混乱；餐厅；杂乱；肮脏
categorization	*n.*	加以分类
demonstrate	*v.*	演示；证明；说明；示范
catalog	*n.*	目录册；产品样本；学校便览；一览表
	v.	（为……）编目录；（把……）按目录分类
assign	*v.*	指定；指派；转让；分派
	n.	【法】受让人
latency	*n.*	潜伏；潜在因素
regularly	*adv.*	经常地；有规律地；定期地；均匀地
shortage	*n.*	短缺；不足；缺少
uphold	*v.*	支持；维持（原判）；受理（申诉）
empire	*n.*	帝国；大企业；企业集团
inaccurate	*adj.*	不精确的；不准确的；有错误的
disapprove	*v.*	不赞成；反对；不同意
highly-competitive	*adj.*	高度竞争的；富有竞争力的；竞争多元化的
anticipated	*v.*	预期；期待；预测；促进
participate	*v.*	参与；参加
monitor	*v.*	监控；监视；监听；检查
	n.	监测仪；屏幕；显示屏
acknowledge	*v.*	承认；认识；感谢；致谢
capture	*v.*	捕获；采集；俘获；拍摄
	n.	（被）捕获；（被）俘获
negotiation	*n.*	谈判；协商；磋商
extinct	*adj.*	（动植物、语言）灭绝的；（习俗、工作等）消失的；指死火山
transact	*v.*	（与人或组织）做业务
hands-off	*adj.*	不干涉的
storefront	*n.*	店面；铺面；商店门面；铺面房
	adj.	沿街的
insight	*n.*	洞察力；了解；洞悉；领悟
unauthorized	*adj.*	未经许可（或批准）的
abide	*v.*	容忍；等候；逗留；居留
stamp	*n.*	邮票；戳；印花；章
	v.	冲压；跺（脚）；重踩；重踏
display	*v.*	显示；展示；陈列；展出
	n.	展示；陈列；表现；展览

awareness	*n.*	意识；认识；了解；觉察
module	*n.*	模块；组件；功能块
minimal	*adj.*	极小的；极少的；最小的
	n.	最简单派艺术作品
personalize	*v.*	个人化；在……上标明主人姓名；为个人特制（或专设）；针对个人
button	*n.*	纽扣；扣子；（机器的）按钮；（电脑屏幕上的）按键
	v.	扣……的纽扣；用纽扣扣上
scenarios	*n.*	方案；（可能发生的）情况；前景；【戏、影视】脚本
suspend	*v.*	暂停；悬浮；中止；挂
syndication	*n.*	企业联合组织；辛迪加组织

Phrases

to set up	建立，设立
to serve as	作为
sales channel	销售渠道
above all	最重要，首先
communications channel	通信渠道
to break the bank	耗尽资源
to eat up	吃光，耗尽
domain name	域名
in general	通常，大体上，一般而言
annual fee	年费
be inclined to	倾向于
comparison shop	比价商店
in earnest	认真地，诚挚地
an assortment of	多种多样
individual merchant	个体商人
off the shelf	现货供应，不用定制的
partner with...	做……伙伴
transaction fee	交易费
keep... in mind	牢记
URL(uniform resource locator)	统一资源定位符
local web	本地网
go for	适用于，应用于
bear with	容忍；忍耐
target market	目标市场
discount rate	折扣率

computer virus	计算机病毒
a.k.a.(also known as)	又名……，也叫作……
B.A.M.(brick and mortar)	砖头和水泥
SSL (secure socket layer)	加密套接字协议层
IP(Internet protocol)	网际协议
OEM(original equipment manufacturer)	原始设备制造商、代工、贴牌
third-party seller	第三方卖方
starting point	出发点，起始点
fulfillment center	订单履行中心，物流中心，运营中心
to speed up	加速，增速
to be well within reach	近在咫尺，触手可及
to one-stop shop	一站式商店
to sign up	（和……）签约；报名
volume selling	批量销售
subscription fee	会员费
a ton of	大量的，许多
restricted brand	常限制品牌
product description	产品描述，产品说明
mandatory field	必备字段，必填字段
keep track of	跟上……的进展；掌握……的最新消息
feedback message	反馈信息，反馈消息
stand out	脱颖而出
ISBN(International Standard Book Number)	国际标准书号
UPC(Universal Product Code)	通用产品码
EAN(European Article Number)	欧洲商品编号（代码）
JAN(Japanese Article Number)	日本商品编号（代码）
GTN(Global Trade Item Number)	全球贸易项目代码
HTML(hyper text markup language)	超文本标识语言
CSS(cascading style sheet)	层叠样式表
Amazon Vendor Central	亚马逊供应商中心
first-party seller	第一方卖家，第一手卖家
invite-only portal	只邀请门户
in bulk	大量；整批，不加包装
pricing strategy	定价策略
storage fee	寄存费，仓储费
take care of	照顾好
product details page	产品详细信息页面
be made up of	由……构成；由……组成

profit margin	利润率
world-recognized brand	世界公认的品牌
retail channel	零售渠道
product type	产品类型
end up	最终成为；最后处于
price war	价格战
ASC(Amazon Seller Central)	亚马逊卖家中心
FBA(fulfillment by amazon)	由亚马逊完成，亚马逊提供的代发货业务
SVS(strategic vendor services)	战略供应商服务
VSP(vendor success program)	供应商成功计划
CRaP(can't realize any profit)	无法实现利润
SC(Seller Central)	卖家中心

Sentences

1. They scheduled the negotiation at nine tomorrow morning.
   他们把谈判安排在明天上午九点。

2. We've arranged our schedule without any trouble.
   我们已经很顺利地把活动日程安排好了。

3. Is there enough time for us to discuss this issue?
   我们是否有充足的时间讨论这个议题？

4 .Can you arrange a meeting with your boss?
   可以安排和你们老板见个面吗？

5. You are fully booked up in the morning.
   您上午的时间都安排满了。

6. How about next Wednesday instead?
   改在下周三，可以吗？

7. Choosing the proper site for negotiations is also very important.
   选择适当的谈判地点也非常重要。

8. The two schedules dovetailed together without friction.
   这两个日程安排相吻合，没冲突。

9. This is the schedule for tomorrow.
   这是明天的日程安排。

10. Let me check my schedule.
    让我看看我的日程安排。

11. Lighten your schedule by cutting back on the assignment in your calendar.
    通过减少日历上的任务来减轻你的日程安排。

12. Don't let it seep into other items on my Tuesday's schedule.
    不要让其他项目打乱我周二的日程。

13. Please again confirm the date of the negotiation.

请再次确认谈判日期。

14. I'm here to ask your opinion about the time schedule of the next five days.

我来这儿想征求一下您对以后五天日程安排的意见。

15. Sorry, I have another appointment that day.

对不起，那天我有另外一个预约。

Conversations

1. Forming a Joint Venture

White: My purpose of coming here is to set up a joint venture with you.

Brown: What's your joint venture strategy?

White: We will provide cash and technology and you provide market.

Brown: Then how much will the total amount of investment be?

White: A total amount of $8,000,000 would be large enough for the construction and circulation.

Brown: Will you provide technical support?

White: Sure. We will send experts and technicians to provide technical guidance.

Brown: But it's not easy to open up a new market.

White: Yes. So it will take us much more efforts to be successful.

1. 组建合资公司

怀特：我此行的目的是希望与贵公司建立一家合资企业。

布朗：贵方的合资战略是什么？

怀特：我们提供资金和技术，贵方提供市场。

布朗：那么投资总额是多少？

怀特：投资总额 800 万美元，这足够用于建设和流通了。

布朗：你们提供技术支持吗？

怀特：当然。我们会派专业人员和技术人员提供技术指导。

布朗：但开拓新市场可不是件容易的事。

怀特：是啊。所以我们需要付出更多的努力才能获得成功。

2. Transfer the Trademark

Green: Good afternoon, Mr. Smith. I am here today to discuss the trademark transfer with you.

Smith: Good afternoon. Take a seat, please.

Green: Thanks! Since the plant installation consists of your equipment, we hope to use your trademark.

Smith: As is known to all, our trademark is known all over the world.

Green: Then how much will you ask for it?

Smith: $60,000.

Green: It's too high! Would you please cut it by 20%?

Smith: I am afraid I can't, Mr. Green.

Green: But the price you asked for is too high. We have been keeping a good partnership for such a long time, so would you like to cut it a little bit?

Smith: In that case, the lowest price we can accept is $55,000.

Green: OK, we'll discuss about the price and let you know when we make a decision.

2. 转让商标

格林：下午好，史密斯先生。我今天来是和你商讨商标转让的事的。

史密斯：下午好，坐这里吧。

格林：谢谢！由于我们工厂是用你们的设备装备起来的，所以我们希望用你们的商标。

史密斯：众所周知，我们的商标在世界上声誉很好。

格林：那么你们要价多少？

史密斯：6 万美元。

格林：太高了。能降低 20%吗？

史密斯：恐怕不能了，格林先生。

格林：但是你要的价实在太高了。长期以来我们一直保持着良好的合作关系，你能再稍微降点价吗？

史密斯：那样的话，我们能接受的最低价格就是 5.5 万美元了。

格林：好吧，我回去再讨论一下这个价位，决定了就通知您。

Text

3.3.1   Introduction of Online Store 线上商店简介

At some point, every small business must set up a shop online. A website can serve as another sales channel, a place to feature products, or just a resource for more information about your business. But above all, it serves as communications channel with your customer. Establishing an online presence doesn't have to break the bank or eat up your time. Here's a guide to help get you on your way.

从某种意义上来说，每个小公司都必须建立在线商店。网站可以作为另外一个服务渠道，一个说明产品特性的地方，或者仅仅提供公司的相关更多信息。但是，它首先是与客户沟通的渠道。建立在线商店不必耗尽资源或时间。下面的指南可以帮助你建立自己的虚拟商店。

1. The Basic Preparations of Online Store 线上商店的基础准备

1) Register a Domain Name 注册一个域名

Dozens of online registry sites allow you to secure a domain name. Some of the most popular include Register.com, NetworkSolutions.com and GoDaddy.com. They're all fairly similar, and which one you, choose won't really affect anything else about your site, so the main difference is price. In general you can expect to pay an annual fee of about $15. Try to pick a domain name that's as simple and intuitive as possible complicated URLs just make it harder for customers to find you. Most companies simply drop their name in the middle of www and com, such as www.×××.com.

许多在线注册网站允许你获得一个域名。其中最流行的有 Register.com、Network-Solutions.com 及 GoDaddy.com。它们十分相似，选择哪一个都可以，效果不会有什么不同，因此主要区别是价格。一般来说，年费大约 15 美元。尽量选简单且直观的域名——复杂的 URLs 只能使客户更难找到你。大部分公司干脆把它们的名字放在 www 与 com 中间，例如 www.×××.com。

2) Set up an E-mail Account to Receive Customer Feedback 建立一个电子邮件账号接受用户的反馈

One of the keys to your Web success is making sure that your customers can always reach you. Once you have your domain set up, be sure to create an active E-mail address and post it on your site right away. As your platform grows, this will become key contact point for your customers, and it will allow you to get feedback on your business.

网站成功的关键之一是确保客户方便登录。一旦建立了你的域，一定要建立一个有效的电子邮件地址并马上把信息放到网站上。随着网站的成长这会成为客户的主要联络点，也可让你得到业务反馈。

3) Hire a Temp 雇用临时雇员

You probably have better things to do than spend all day entering data for every item you intend to sell online. As you start assembling your site in earnest, hire someone else to help with the setup work.

相较于花费整天时间输入要在网站销售货物的数据，也许你有更重要的事情要做。在你忙于编排网站时，可雇用他人帮助你工作。

2. Sources to Turn to for Easy Solutions 寻找简单解决方案的提供者

Numerous Internet service providers(ISPs) offer E-commerce solutions that require little work on your part. Some of the most basic solutions can handle your Web hosting needs and provide standardized storefront templates. These companies can provide basic design templates and technology to process transactions, too.

许多互联网服务提供商提供你只需做很少工作的电子商务方案。一些最基本的方案都能够满足你的需求，并提供标准的店面模板。这些公司也能够提供处理业务的基本设计模板和技术。

Telecommunications company SBC offers an assortment of off-the-shelf set-up packages for individual merchants. Some key components included in such packages are shopping-cart software (allowing your customers to drop in items as they go through your site) and assistance with Web design. This last part is extremely important, as deciding how customers will flow your site is the same as directing them to merchandise. You have to get this part right.

SBC 电讯公司为个体商提供多种多样现成的建店软件包。其中一些主要的部件包括购物车软件（允许客户在网站浏览时把货物放进去）和网站设计助手。最后一部分极其重要，因为决定客户如何在网站流动，与引导他们购买商品一样重要，必须把这部分做好。

You may have to go through your bank or through services like Verisign to set up secure system to accept online payment for orders. For smaller operations, you can also use services like PayPal, which make it easy to accept customer payments with an easily downloadable software package.

你也许不得不通过银行或者 Verisign 之类的服务建立一个接受订单的在线支付的安全系统。对一些较小的运作，也可以使用 PayPal 之类的服务，用一个容易下载的软件包轻松地接受客户支付。

3. Think about Affiliating with Another Site 考虑加入其他网站

Is it better to go it alone or join an existing online community? If you really need to differentiate your product or brand, particularly through site design, you may be better off building your own site. But if your needs are more basic and you want to keep costs down, it's probably to your benefit to pitch your tent in an existing online marketplace, which can provide more traffic than if you just open a shop and wait for customers to blow by. Sites like eBay, Yahoo, and Amazon offer prepackaged storefront services with a variety of options for individual merchants, often including free registration of your domain name.

是独自建站好还是加入现有的在线团体好？如果确实需要使你的产品或品牌与众不同，尤其是通过网站设计达到这一目的，那么最好建立自己的网站。但是如果你的要求较基本而且想降低成本，那么最好把你的网店建在现有的在线市场上，这样比开一个商店等顾客上门的客流量更大，像 eBay、Yahoo 和 Amazon 这样的网站，可以为个体商提供有多种选择的打包好的店面服务，通常包括域名的免费注册。

eBay offers your customers the chance to bid on items or buy them outright at a set price. The eBay package also includes flexible listing options, limited customization tools, monthly sales reports inventory search options, and the ability to cross-promote other items with ones you are selling. A mid-level eBay store costs $49.95 per month but options rage from $9.95 a month for a bare-bones storefront to $499.95 for full-service store complete with marketing support.

eBay 为你的客户提供了竞价或即刻以固定价格购买的机会。eBay 软件包也包括弹性的清单选项、有限的定制工具、月度销售报表、库存检索选项以及与你正在出售的商品进行交叉促销的能力。一个中级的 eBay 商店每月需要花费 49.95 美元，但是价格范围从一个空骨架店面的 9.95 美元到具有市场支持全方位服务功能的 499.95 美元。

Yahoo offers three basic levels of services, ranging from $39.95 month to $299.95 a month. plus a $50 setup fee (sometimes the setup fee is waived during promotions) and transaction fees that range from 0.75 percent to 1.5 percent. It, too, offers a selection of services as well as simple step-by-step methods for listing your products online and software for accepting payment.

Yahoo 提供 3 个基本等级的服务，费用从每月 39.95 美元到每月 299.95 美元不等，外加 50 美元的开办费（促销时有时会免去开办费）以及从 0.75%到 1.5%的交易费。它也提供许多服务和产品上网的简要步骤，还有接受支付的软件。

Depending on what kind of products you're selling, Amazon also offers several online options for third-party sellers. Amazon's marketplace program charges a 15 percent commission, on top of a $39.99 monthly subscription cost (or $0.99 per item if you prefer), but leaves shipping and customer service to you. As another alternative, you can partner with Amazon and sell its goods on your own site for a commission.

根据所销售产品的种类，Amazon 也为第三方商家提供一些在线选择。Amazon 的市场项目收取 15%的佣金，最多每月 39.99 美元的签约费（如果你愿意，也可以按每项 0.99 美元收费），但是不包括货物运输和客户服务。另外也可以加盟 Amazon，在你的网站销售它的货物，以收取佣金。

4. The Bottom line: Always Focus on the Benefits to Your Business 底线：总是要关注自己的利益

Be sure to keep your customers and your business goals in mind as you set up your site. Getting online is the easy part. Creating an online presence that adds value to your core business is what really matters.

建立网站时牢记你的客户和商业目标。建立在线商店很容易。建立一个能够增加你的核心商务价值的在线商店才是至关重要的。

3.3.2　Tings You Need to Do While Selling Online 网上卖货需要做的事情

Have you decided to take your business online? There are a few things you will need before venturing into the world of E-commerce. Internet is a powerful channel to reach out and better serve your customers. Below are the 10 things you will need to give yourself a head start.

你决定把你的生意放在网上了吗？在冒险进入电子商务世界之前，你需要一些东西。互联网是联系和更好地为客户服务的强大渠道，下面是你需要做的 10 件事，它们可以让你领先一步。

1. Domain Name 域名

A unique address on the Internet, like www.neowave.com.my, where clients or potential customers can find your business. This is the first step to get your business online. Normally a business will either register for a.com/.net./.org domain or a top level country coded domain e.g..com. my/.net.my./.org.my.

互联网上的唯一地址，如 www.neowave.com.my，客户或潜在客户可以在这里找到您的企业。这是让您的企业上线的第一步。通常情况下，企业要么注册.com/.net./.org 域名，要么注册顶级国家编码域名，例如.com. my/.net.my./.org.my。

2. Web & E-mail Hosting 网站/电子邮件托管

Just like a warehouse that keeps your stocks, you will need a place that keeps your web site files and web applications. It is a service that provides server space (a.k.a. hard disk space), tools, always-on network connectivity, E-mail services and more so that you can publish your website on the Internet and millions of potential buyers from any corners of the world (theoretically, of course) will flock to your website and buy your products!

就像存放库存的仓库一样，您需要一个存放网站文件和 Web 应用程序的地方。它可提供服务器空间（也称为硬盘空间）、工具、始终在线的网络连接、电子邮件服务等，这样您就可以在互联网上发布您的网站，来自世界任何角落的数以百万计的潜在买家（当然是理论上的）会蜂拥到您的网站购买您的产品！

3. Web Design 网页设计

A great design speaks a thousand words. It is the front-end which represents the ultimate image of your company. If you are running B.A.M. (brick and mortar) store, you hire the best interior designer to put up the best renovation for your store. The same should go for your E-commerce website. Designing an E-commerce store takes more than just artistic skills. You will need a professional web designer who possesses in-depth knowledge about usability, shopping cart buying process, web technologies, E-commerce software, and most of all, your business. The good news is that it costs much lesser compared to your burn-a-hole-in-pocket renovation, and good web design service probably will cost you only 20% of your renovation cost or less. We cannot emphasize more on the importance of a good Web design; it can make or break your online business.

说一千道一万，伟大的设计是代表贵公司终极形象的前端。就像如果你在经营 B.A.M（实体店），你聘请最好的室内设计师为你的店铺进行最好的装修，你的电子商务网站也应该如此。设计一家电子商务商店需要的不仅仅是艺术技能，你还需要一位专业的网页设计师，他拥有关于可用性、购物车购买流程、网络技术、电子商务软件的深度知识，最重要的是，你的业务也是如此。好消息是，它的成本比你的一次性装修要便宜得多，而且好的网页设计服务可能只会花费你装修成本的 20%，甚至更少。我们再怎么强调一个好的网页设计的重要性也不为过，它可以决定你的在线业务的成败。

4. Online Storefront (E-commerce) Software　网上店面（电子商务）软件

Online storefront (E-commerce) software, also known as shopping cart software or online storefront, allows you to build an electronic catalog of your products which allows online ordering and seamlessly integrates with modules like order management, shipping management, tax and payment gateway. There are lots of applications to choose from, so make sure the one you choose is easy to install and use.

网上店面（电子商务）软件也称为购物车软件或在线店面。它允许您建立产品的电子目录，允许在线订购，并与订单管理、发货管理、税务和支付网关等模块无缝集成。有很多应用程序可供选择，因此请确保您选择的应用程序易于安装和使用。

5. Payment Gateway 支付网关

The payment gateway serves as a "secure hosting agent" between online storefront software and credit card processing network. It is used in real-time authentication and charging of your customers credit cards. You can think of it as a digital equivalent of a credit card processing terminal. Before you decide on which payment gateway to use, please ponder through your target market, convenience and popularity of payment gateway, how and when money is deposited to your account, and etc. Typical types of charges by payment gateway are setup fees, deposits, monthly rental charges transaction charges (also known as discount rate) & chargeback fees. There is no one-size which fits all solutions, and decision should be made based on which (or combination) payment gateway best suits your business needs.

支付网关在在线店面软件和信用卡处理网络之间充当"安全托管代理"的角色。它用于您的客户信用卡的实时认证和充值。您可以将其视为信用卡处理终端的数字等价物。在您决定使用哪个支付网关之前，请仔细考虑您的目标市场、支付网关的便利性和受欢迎程度、将钱存入您的账户的方式和时间等。支付网关的典型收费类型包括设置费、押金、月租费、交易费（也称折扣率）和退款费用。没有适用于所有解决方案的单一形式，应根据最适合您的业务需求的支付网关（或组合）做出决定。

6. Merchant Accounts 商户账户

Merchant accounts are commercial bank accounts set up between a retail business and financial institution to allow a business to accept credit card transactions. In short, it's just an account to receive funds from credit card sales. Please take note that it is NOT a must to apply for a merchant account locally as most foreign payment gateways providers like Worldpay or PayPal will have a merchant account setup for you. But if you opt for local payment gateway providers, you will need local merchant account.

商户账户是在零售企业和金融机构之间设立的商业银行账户，允许企业接受信用卡交易。简而言之，它只是一个从信用卡销售中获得资金的账户。请注意，不是必须在当地申请商家账户，因为大多数外国支付网关提供商，如 Worldpay 或 PayPal，都会为您设置商家账户。但如果你选择当地的支付网关提供商，你将需要当地的商家账户。

7. SSL(Secure Socket Layer) Certificate SSL（安全套接字层）证书

SSL(secure socket layer) certificate is not a must. But in order to build trust and credibility for your customers, we strongly recommend that you consider spending some cash to obtain an SSL certificate. So, what does SSL do? It enables a secure connection between your website and your customers' browsers and it can help you to boost your customers' confidence levels. Besides that, most of the SSL providers also provide trusted site seal which validates the originality of your website. It helps lower down the risk of exposure to a malicious attack like phishing and identity theft! Last but not least, an SSL certificate will need a fixed IP address (a dedicated IP to your domain) to work properly, and it can be obtained at around RMB 100/year from the web hosting companies.

SSL（安全套接字层）证书不是必需的。但是，为了为您的客户建立信任和信誉，我们强烈建议您考虑支付一定费用来获得 SSL 证书。那么，SSL 是做什么的呢？它可以在您的网站和客户的浏览器之间实现安全连接，并且可以帮助您提升客户的信心水平。除此之外，大多数 SSL 提供商还提供可信站点印章来验证您网站的原创性。它有助于降低暴露于恶意攻击（如网络钓鱼和身份盗窃）的风险！最后，同样重要的一点是，SSL 证书需要一个固定的 IP 地址（您的域的专用 IP）才能正常工作，它可以通过每年支付人民币 100 元左右从网络托管公司获得。

8. Broadband 宽频

Can you bear with the speed of 56Kbps download? Forget about it by the time you came back from YOGA class. It still has YET to finish downloading all your SPAMS. Not to mention login to your storefront software to actively update your E-commerce website and process the orders. But, please don't dismiss dial-up entirely. We actually recommend to have one dial-up account for emergency purpose considering the "stability" of broadband services by local service providers.

你能忍受 56Kbps 的下载速度吗？当你上完瑜伽课回来的时候忘了它吧，因为它还没有下载完你所有的垃圾邮件。更不用说登录您的店面软件来主动更新您的电子商务网站并处理订单了。但是，请不要完全拒绝拨号，考虑到本地服务提供商提供的宽带服务的"稳定性"，我们实际上建议使用一个拨号账户以备不时之需。

9. Security Tools: Antivirus, Antispyware & Firewall Software 安全工具：防病毒、反间谍软件和防火墙软件

Computer viruses and malicious software are the "bad things" living on the Internet that can cause you to lose a lot of time and money (even sleep). The security software is the guardian to protect you against various attacks.

电脑病毒和恶意软件是生活在互联网上的"坏东西"，会让你损失大量的时间和金钱（甚至睡眠）。安全软件是保护您免受各种攻击的守护者。

A computer virus is a malicious piece of software that replicates itself and most likely will cause harm to your computer. It is rampant nowadays and you need to protect your computer and always connect it to the Internet via a broadband connection. You can buy the antivirus software from the established security software vendors like Trend Micro, Symantec, or McAfee at a very affordable price. If you were looking for cheaper version of the same software, a.k.a. OEM package, you can try our local computer stores. Don't feel like paying? Check out some antivirus freeware (for home use only !) like AVG or AntiVir.

计算机病毒是一种自我复制的恶意软件，很可能会对您的计算机造成损害。它现在很猖獗，你需要保护你的电脑，并始终通过宽带连接到互联网。您可以从趋势科技、赛门铁克或 McAfee 等知名安全软件供应商那里以非常实惠的价格购买防病毒软件。如果您正在寻找相同软件的更便宜版本（又称 OEM 包），您可以尝试我们当地的电脑商店。不想付钱吗？可检查一些防病毒免费软件（仅限家庭使用），比如 AVG 或 AntiVir。

Spyware is a broad category of malicious software that is secretly installed on your computer without your consent. It has become a serious security threat that Microsoft is releasing a beta program dubbed Microsoft AntiSpyware to fight the entire malicious program installed on your Windows-powered PC.

间谍软件是一大类恶意软件，它们在未经您同意的情况下被秘密安装在您的计算机上。微软发布名为微软反间谍软件（Microsoft AntiSpyware）的测试版程序，以对抗安装在你的个人电脑上的 Windows 系统的整个恶意程序，这已经成为一种严重的安全威胁。

Firewall is a system designed to prevent unauthorized access to your computer (or network) which is connected to the Internet. It can be implemented in either hardware or software, or combination of both.

防火墙是一种旨在防止对连接到 Internet 的计算机（或网络）进行未经授权的访问的系统。它可以通过硬件或软件或两者的组合实现。

10. Delivery 送货

Delivery of goods is important, especially when your orders could be coming in from all over the world. Nothing is more frustrating to a customer than not being able to receive the goods they pay for in good condition and timely manner. An online order doesn't end until the parcel is delivered to the customer's doorstep. To do it right, and you can start by picking the right courier services company.

送货很重要，特别是当你的订单可能来自世界各地的时候。没有什么比顾客不能及时完好地收到他们购买的货物更令其沮丧的了。直到包裹送到客户的家门口，在线订单才会结束。要做到这一点，你可以从选择正确的快递服务公司开始。

If you are delivering the goods locally, check out some local courier service. If you are delivering the goods worldwide and won't mind paying extra for reliable and fast services, you might want to consider the BIG 3 — FedEX, UPS, and DHL.

如果你在当地送货，可以咨询一下当地的快递服务。如果你在全球范围内送货，并且不介意为可靠快捷的服务支付额外费用，你可能会考虑三大快递公司——联邦快递（FedEx）、UPS 和 DHL。

In summary, these are the basic fundamentals that form your E-commerce website. This is only the first step towards E-commerce venture. Remember, E-commerce is no magic. Just like running the brick and mortar stores, you need a SOUND business plan and very good execution to make it a money spinner.

总而言之，这些是构成您的电子商务网站的基本原则。这只是迈向电子商务创业的第一步。记住，电子商务不是魔术，就像经营实体店一样，你需要一个健全的商业计划和非常好的执行力才能让它成为摇钱树。

3.3.3　Selling on Amazon 在亚马逊上卖货

1. The Benefits and Possibilities Selling on Amazon 在亚马逊上卖货的好处与可能性

Amazon is a crucial selling platform for online merchants and brands. Here are a few possibilities of what you can expect when you sell your products on Amazon.

亚马逊是在线商家和品牌商的重要销售平台。以下是你在亚马逊上销售产品时可以期待的：

(1) Increased sales opportunities. A common myth about selling on Amazon is that third-party sellers (i.e. brands and retailers) don't account for much of the channel's total sales. The truth? According to Amazon, 50% of all items sold on the channel are by third-party sellers. Given the number of transactions that take place on the platform each year, that is a huge amount of business going directly to third-parties.

增加销售机会。关于在亚马逊上销售的一个常见神话是，第三方卖家（即品牌商和零售商）并不占渠道总销售额的大部分。真相呢？亚马逊称，在该渠道销售的所有商品中有 50%来自第三方卖家。鉴于每年在平台上发生的交易数量，第三方直接交易有巨大的业务量。

　　Moreover, with 64% of households having an Amazon prime account in the US alone, the opportunities for new customers, new markets, and an increase in overall revenue is huge.

　　此外，仅 64%的家庭在美国拥有亚马逊金牌账户，新客户、新市场和整体收入增加的机会还很巨大。

　　(2) International expansion being simple. With global marketplaces and customers from 180 different countries, Amazon is the perfect starting point for brands and retailers looking to sell their products internationally. In fact, one-fifth of third-party sales have already occured outside the seller's home country!

　　国际扩张变得简单。亚马逊拥有 11 个全球市场和来自 180 个不同国家和地区的客户，是寻求在国际上销售产品的品牌商和零售商的完美起点。事实上，已经有 1/5 的第三方销售发生在卖方的本国之外！

　　On top of Amazon's global reach, the E-commerce king also has 109 product warehouses or "fulfillment centers" across the world. An Amazon fulfillment center is basically where you can send and store your products until they are sold. This not only speeds up delivery times but also means that Amazon can handle everything from the shipping and delivery of your products all the way to returns, refunds, and exchanges.

　　除了亚马逊的全球影响力，这个电子商务大王还在全球拥有 109 个产品仓库或"履行中心"。你可以在产品售出之前把它们发送和存储在亚马逊配送中心。这不仅加快了交货时间，还意味着亚马逊可以处理从产品的运输和交付到退货、退款和换货的所有事情。

　　With all of the logistics and a positive reputation already set in place, the global market is well within reach.

　　鉴于所有物流和良好的声誉已经建立，全球市场已经触手可及。

　　(3) Strong brand trust. Above all else, one of the most powerful benefits of being an Amazon seller is its solid reputation as a trusted brand. Shoppers on the marketplace trust what they are buying and have no questions or concerns about the process. Amazon has perfectly positioned itself in the E-commerce playing field to be the "one-stop shop" for its users, and because of its credibility, it is working. For sellers and smaller retailers, this means less work getting their name out there, because they are essentially already trusted and a part of Amazon's great reputation.

　　强大的品牌信任。最重要的是，成为亚马逊卖家最大的好处之一就是其作为值得信赖的品牌商的良好声誉。市场上的购物者相信他们正在购买货物，并且对该过程没有任何问题或担忧。亚马逊已经完全将自己深植于电子商务领域，为用户提供"一站式服务"，并且其因为信誉良好，确实也做到了这一点。对于卖家和小型零售商而言，这意味着只要做很少的事情就能获得知名度，因为它们已经赢得了基本的信任并且分享了亚马逊的卓越声誉。

2. How to Start to Build an Online Store 如何开始创建网上店铺

Wondering how to get started? Here are a few key things you'll need to do.

想知道如何开始？以下是你需要做的一些关键事项。

1) Create an Amazon Seller Central Account 创建亚马逊卖家中央账户

If you don't already have one, you'll need to create your Amazon Seller Central account. If you plan to sell more than 40 products per month, it makes financial sense to sign up for the professional plan, which is fit for volume selling. With this plan, the $0.99 fee per item sold is waived and you'll only need to pay a $39.99 monthly subscription fee instead.

如果你还没有亚马逊卖家中央账户，则需要创建一个。如果你计划每月销售超过40个产品，那么签订适合批量销售的专业计划是有经济意义的。有了这个计划，可以免除每售出一件的0.99美元的费用，只需支付每月39.99美元的会员费。

2) Access the Correct Feed Template 访问正确的推送模板

Amazon provides a unique template for each type of product sold on its marketplace. With varying regulations and requirements, it is important that you use the correct one. Try to avoid the common mistake of choosing the wrong template to prevent your feeds rejection and a ton of wasted time.

亚马逊为其市场上销售的每种产品提供独特的模板。由于规则和要求各不相同，正确使用非常重要。尽量避免选择错误模板这一常见错误，以免你的推送被拒绝并浪费大量时间。

3) Prepare Your Product Feed 准备产品推送

As with any large online marketplace, there are several rules and regulations that you'll need to follow for both the structure and content of your product feed. Here are a few key things to keep in mind when creating an Amazon feed.

与任何大型在线市场一样，你需要遵循一些规则和规定，以满足产品推送的结构和内容要求。在创建亚马逊推送时，请注意以下几个关键事项。

(1) The sale of many brands is prohibited: Since Amazon hasn't released a master list of restricted brands, it is recommended that you contact them directly with any questions.

禁止销售许多品牌：由于亚马逊尚未发布限制品牌的主要清单，因此建议你直接与其联系以解决遇到的任何问题。

(2) Certain categories need approval: Amazon doesn't mess around with categorization. Depending on which types of categories you want to use, you may need to seek Amazon approval before being able to list your product.

某些类别需要批准：亚马逊不会搞乱分类。根据你要使用的类别类型，可能需要先获得亚马逊批准才能列出你的产品。

(3) All products need accurate and complete product IDs:

Any of the following format types are accepted: ISBN (International Standard Book Number), UPC (Universal Product Code), EAN (European Article Number), JAN (Japanese Article Number), and GTIN (Global Trade Item Number).

所有产品都需要准确完整的产品标识：

接受以下任何格式类型：ISBN（国际标准书号）、UPC（通用产品代码）、EAN（欧洲商品编号）、JAN（日本商品编号）和 GTN（全球贸易项目编号）。

(4) Understand variations and parent/child product relationships: This is crucial for Amazon to be able to display your items correctly to their users and for customers to understand what variations (colors, sizes, scents, etc.) of your products you offer.

了解变体和父/子产品关系：这对于亚马逊能够正确地向用户展示你的产品以及让客户了解提供的产品的变化（颜色、尺寸、气味等）至关重要。

(5) Some HTML and CSS is allowed: A common myth is that no code is allowed in Amazon product descriptions; however, this is false.

允许使用某些 HTML 和 CSS：一个常见的误解是亚马逊产品说明中不允许出现任何代码；然而，并非如此。

(6) All products need an ASIN: Every product in the Amazon catalog must have an ASIN (Amazon Standard Identification Numbers). If your product is already being sold on Amazon, it's already been assigned an ASIN that you need to locate. If your product is not already being sold, Amazon will create an ASIN for it. For volume sellers, this can be an extremely time-consuming process.

所有产品都需要 ASIN：亚马逊目录中的每个产品都必须具有 ASIN（亚马逊标准识别码）。如果你的产品已在亚马逊上销售，则已经为其分配了一个方便你定位的 ASIN。如果你的产品尚未销售，亚马逊将为其创建一个 ASIN。对于批量销售商来说，这可能是一个非常耗时的过程。

(7) Fulfillment latency is essential: Basically, Amazon wants to know how quickly you can get the product to a customer once they've purchased. They have a high standard of service and speed and expect their sellers to have the same.

配送延迟至关重要：基本上，亚马逊想知道一旦购买产品，你可以多快地将产品送到客户手中。亚马逊有高标准的服务和速度，并期望其卖家也一样。

Note: Amazon is well-known for changing specifications regularly. Therefore, you will need to keep track of any changes or updates they make at all times.

注意：亚马逊以定期更改规格闻名。因此，你需要及时掌握其所做的任何更改或更新。

Sound like a lot to take into consideration? This is why Amazon recommends that volume sellers use a feed management tool for feed preparation and export.

听起来好像要考虑很多事情？这就是为什么亚马逊建议批量销售商使用推送管理工具进行推送准备和发布。

3. The High Standards of Amazon Marketplace 亚马逊商城的高标准

Amazon marketplace has no shortage of buyers or sellers. With some of the strictest feed requirements of any online marketplace, a high-quality feed is not only needed for a high performance but for your listing to be accepted at all. Let's look at a few reasons why your Amazon feed should be perfect.

亚马逊商城不缺少买家或卖家。因为对任何在线市场都有一些最严格的推送要求，所以高品质的推送不仅是高性能所需，也是产品目录被接受的条件。让我们看看亚马逊推送完美的几个原因。

(1) They have a positive, global reputation to uphold. Amazon could not have built an international E-commerce empire without establishing consumer trust and providing excellent service along the way. Because of this, they have set their standard high for brands and merchants looking to sell on their marketplace. If your products are incomplete, inaccurate, or do not abide by their strict rules and regulations, they have no problem disapproving your product. They will, however, provide a feedback message as to why it was rejected, allowing you to correct the issue.

拥有良好的全球声誉。如果没有建立消费者信任并在此过程中提供优质服务，亚马逊就无法建立国际电子商务帝国。正因为如此，亚马逊为希望在其市场上销售的品牌商和商家设定了标准。如果你的产品不完整、不准确或不遵守严格的规章制度，亚马逊就可以不批准你的产品。但是，亚马逊会提供反馈信息，说明拒绝的原因，以便你更正。

(2) Highly-competitive environment. It's no secret that Amazon, being a massive online marketplace, has millions of merchants and brands using it to sell their products. This does, however, make for a highly-competitive sales environment. By providing high-quality product content, you are increasing the chances of your products standing out from the crowd and being seen by users who are ready to buy.

竞争激烈的环境。作为一个庞大的在线市场，已经有数百万商家和品牌商来亚马逊销售产品，这已不是什么秘密。然而这确实构成了竞争激烈的销售环境。通过提供高质量的产品内容，你可以增加产品脱颖而出的机会，让准备购买的用户看到。

4. Amazon Seller Central and Amazon Vendor Central 亚马逊卖家中心和亚马逊供应商中心

1) Amazon Seller Central 亚马逊卖家中心

Amazon Seller Central (ASC) is the program used by third-party sellers. These are brands or merchants selling directly to consumers on Amazon marketplace. Sellers have the option to become either an individual seller or a professional seller, based on their anticipated sales forecast.

亚马逊卖家中心（ASC）是第三方卖家使用的程序。这些是在亚马逊上直接向消费者销售的品牌或商家。卖家可以根据其预期销售预测，选择成为个人卖家或专业卖家。

Sellers have two fulfillment options. Once a purchase is made, they can either handle the fulfillment or distribution themselves or choose to use fulfillment by Amazon (FBA). The latter works by providing stock to an Amazon warehouse before an order is even placed. From here, Amazon handles the shipping, handling, returns, and most of the customer service of your products for you. Amazon FBA can also increase consumer confidence as the product is displayed "Fulfilled by Amazon".

卖家有两个履行选项。购买后，卖家可以自己处理履行或分销，也可以选择使用FBA的履行服务。后者的工作方式是在下订单之前向亚马逊仓库提供库存。从这里开始，亚马逊负责发货、处理、退货，并为您的大部分产品提供客户服务。亚马逊FBA还可以在产品展示时增加消费者信心，因为"由亚马逊履行"。

2) Amazon Vendor Central 亚马逊供应商中心

There is Amazon Vendor Central. This is the portal leveraged by brands and manufacturers to sell wholesale to Amazon through purchase orders. These companies are referred to as first-party sellers or Amazon vendors.

还有亚马逊供应商中心（Amazon Vendor Central），其是品牌和制造商通过采购订单向亚马逊批发销售的门户。这些公司被称为第一方卖家或亚马逊供应商。

Vendor Central is an invite-only portal where participating businesses can monitor their product inventory, add new products, receive and acknowledge purchase orders, and gain a general overview of their Amazon account health. In order to obtain an invite, you will need to capture the attention of an Amazon buyer.

供应商中心是一个仅限邀请的门户，参与的企业可以在其中监控其产品库存、添加新产品、接收和确认采购订单，并获得其亚马逊账户健康状况的总体概述。为了获得邀请，您需要吸引亚马逊买家的注意。

Once a purchase order is placed to the distributor or vendor, the products will need to find their way to an Amazon warehouse or fulfilment center. It is defined during the initial contract negotiations whether it is Amazon that picks the order up or the vendor who ships.

一旦向总代理商或供应商下了采购订单，这些产品就需要找到到达亚马逊仓库或配送中心的方式。无论是由亚马逊提货，还是由供应商发货，都是在最初的合同谈判中定义的。

Going through Vendor Central (similar to the now extinct Amazon Vendor Express) essentially means that Amazon is your retailer and they are buying your products in bulk, which they will then list on their marketplace. In this case, you are not directly transacting to the consumer or handling the customer service and you are able to be a bit more hands-off, while still making sales.

通过供应商中心，本质上就意味着亚马逊是您的零售商，亚马逊批量购买您的产品，然后在其市场上出售。在这种情况下，您不是直接与消费者交易或提供客户服务，您可以稍微放手一些，同时仍然进行销售。

Now that we've introduced each interface, let's take a look at the pros and cons of each. Keep in mind that the impact of each can also depend on your business and what you're looking to get out of selling on Amazon.

现在我们已经介绍了每个接口，让我们看看每个接口的优缺点。请记住，每种方式的影响也可能取决于您的业务以及您希望从亚马逊销售中获得什么。

3) The Pros and Cons of Seller Central 卖家中心的利弊

(1) Pros of Seller Central 卖家中心的优点。

(a) Pricing control 价格控制。

As a seller, you have full control over the pricing of your products. Since customers are buying directly from you, and Amazon is essentially acting just as a storefront, you can set your pricing to whatever suits your business model.

作为卖家，您可以完全控制您产品的定价。由于客户直接从您那里购买，而亚马逊实质上只是充当店面，因此您可以将定价设置为任何适合您的商业模式。

(b) Free access to analytics & seller support 分析和卖家支持的免费访问。

Seller Central gives you free access to insights on customer data and detailed analytics directly in your seller account. These rich statistics can help you understand buying behavior, your target market and help you to optimize your product information and approach. Moreover, support is always readily available within the interface, making it easy to get your questions answered right away.

通过卖家中心，您可以直接在您的卖方账户中免费访问有关客户数据和详细分析。这些丰富的统计数据可以帮助您了解购买行为，了解您的目标市场，并帮助您优化产品信息和方法。此外，在界面中始终可以随时获得支持，这使得您的问题可以很容易地立即得到回答。

(c) Messaging control 信息控制。

Having control over messaging is perhaps one of the biggest advantages of using Seller Central. For sellers, it means they have complete control over what is being sold, how it is being sold, and what is being said about products. Amazon's brand registry program limits and/or eliminates the possibility of any unauthorized product listings.

控制消息传递可能是使用卖家中心的最大优势之一。对于卖家来说，这意味着其完全控制着正在出售的东西，产品是如何销售的，关于产品是怎么说的。亚马逊的品牌注册计划限制和/或消除任何未经授权的产品上市的可能性。

(d) Higher margins 更高的利润率。

Sellers see increased margins compared to vendors. This is mostly because they control their pricing and aren't selling wholesale, which is known for being sold at a discounted rate. Amazon analytics also help sellers to optimize their pricing strategy directly from within their account.

与供应商相比，卖家看到了更高的利润率。这在很大程度上是因为卖家控制了自己的定价，而不是批发。而批发是以折扣率闻名的。亚马逊分析还可以帮助卖家直接从其账户中优化定价策略。

(2) Cons of Seller Central 卖家中心的缺点。

(a) Complex & strict product feed requirements 复杂而严格的产品供给要求。

Sellers have a lot of control over their product listings, but it also means they have a lot of responsibilities. One of these is ensuring the product feed abides by Amazon's strict feed requirements. Although, this actually isn't much of a con when using the right solution provider to help you with your feed.

卖家对其产品列表有很大的控制权，但这也意味着卖家有很多责任，其中之一就是确保产品供应遵守亚马逊严格的供应要求。不过，在提供商使用正确的解决方案帮助您处理供给时，这实际上并不是什么骗局。

(b) Fulfillment costs 履行成本。

While Amazon FBA is a great, efficient option for large retailers, it can cost a pretty penny. Not only do you need to pay the initial FBA fee for them to ship and handle your products, but if they aren't selling fast enough, you'll have to pay additional storage fees to Amazon for storing your goods.

虽然亚马逊的 FBA 对大型零售商来说是一个很好的、高效的选择，但它可能会花费很多钱。你不仅需要支付最初的 FBA 费用，让其运送和处理你的产品，而且如果卖得不够快，你还必须向亚马逊支付额外的仓储费。

4) The Pros and Cons of Amazon Vendor Central 亚马逊供应商中心的利弊

(1) Pros of Amazon Vendor Central 亚马逊供应商中心的优点。

(a) Consumer confidence 消费者信心。

A vendor can essentially get to ride on the back of Amazon's phenomenal reputation. By selling wholesale directly to Amazon, manufacturers are giving the marketplace the right to sell their products for them. In the eyes of the consumer, they are purchasing directly from Amazon — a marketplace they trust and are loyal to. Moreover, each product will carry the Amazon stamp of approval being displayed with "Sold by Amazon".

从本质上讲，供应商可以利用亚马逊非凡的声誉。通过直接向亚马逊批发销售，制造商赋予市场为其销售产品的权利。在消费者看来，他们是直接从亚马逊——一个他们信任并忠诚的市场购买商品。此外，每件产品都将印有亚马逊批准的印章，上面印有"由亚马逊出售"的字样。

(b) Simplified business model 简化的业务模式。

First-party Amazon sellers have much less logistical work to handle. Once the contract is signed and the purchase orders are fulfilled, Amazon takes care of the rest. From pricing and listing all the way to shipping and customer support.

亚马逊的第一方卖家需要处理的物流工作要少得多。一旦签订了合同，完成了购买订单，亚马逊就会处理剩下的事情，从定价和上市一直到发货和客户支持。

(c) Access to A+ content 访问 A+内容。

A massive advantage to those using Amazon Vendor Central is the ability to use A+ content. Essentially, this gives you the opportunity to create an information-rich product details page. This carries many advantages in itself including a more compelling and complete shopping experience, increased sales and brand awareness.

对于使用亚马逊供应商中心的用户来说，一个巨大的优势是能够使用 A+内容。从本质上讲，这使您有机会创建一个信息丰富的产品详细信息页面。这本身就有很多好处，包括更吸引人的、更完整的购物体验，销售额的增加和品牌知名度的提升。

According to Amazon, well-constructed A+ content pages can increase conversion between 3%-10%! The pages can be made up of several individual modules and can be created directly from your Vendor Central account.

根据亚马逊的说法，结构良好的 A+内容页面可以提高 3%～10%的转化率！这些页面可以由几个单独的模块组成，并且可以直接从您的供应商中心账户创建。

Note: Sellers may also be entitled to A+ content, but only if they are the manufacturer of their products sold and upon request.

注意：卖家也可能有权获得 A+内容，但前提是卖家是所售产品的制造商，并应要求提供 A+内容。

(d) Increased revenue 增加收入。

As an Amazon vendor, you'll get a standard price for your items—which means you'll be selling each individual item for less than you would otherwise. However, because you are selling in bulk, you will easily earn more since you're guaranteed to sell more items. Therefore, vendors will see an increased revenue at the end of the day.

作为亚马逊的卖家，你将获得商品的标准价格——这意味着你将以低于其他价格的价格出售每一件商品。然而，因为你是批量销售，你很容易赚到更多钱，因为你"保证会卖出更多的商品"。因此，供应商最终会看到收入增加。

(2) Cons of Amazon Vendor Central 亚马逊供应商中心的缺点。

(a) Minimal pricing control 最低限度的定价控制。

Once you sell your products to Amazon, they control the price of the item. Therefore, first-party sellers aren't able to strongly influence the cost of their items. Although you can set minimum advertised pricing, Amazon doesn't guarantee that it will adhere to your requests. Retail pricing can, therefore, cause a lower profit margin.

一旦你把产品卖给亚马逊，它就会控制商品的价格。因此，第一方卖家不能强烈影响其商品的成本。虽然你可以设置最低广告价格，但亚马逊并不保证它会遵守你的请求。因此，零售定价可能导致较低的利润率。

(b) Wait longer for payment 等待付款的时间更长。

Due to the bulk nature of wholesale, processing products takes longer for vendors than it does sellers. The same goes for payment. If you're a first-party seller, Amazon is technically your client. Therefore, your profit is dependent on your wholesale pricing and your initial contract agreement with Amazon.

由于批发的散装性质，供应商处理产品所需的时间比卖方长。付款也是如此。如果你是第一方卖家，从技术上讲，亚马逊是你的客户。因此，你的利润取决于你的批发价和你与亚马逊的初始合同协议。

(c) Limited support 有限支持。

Unlike on ASC, support is often not readily available for most vendors. Unless you are a world-recognized brand, they aren't likely to offer you personalized vendor support, which means you'll be left with the all too familiar "contact us" button. There are, however, services and programs set in place to offer assistance when you need it depending on the size of your business. Here are two vendor support options: Strategic Vendor Services (SVS) and the Vendor Success Program (VSP).

与 ASC 不同，大多数供应商通常不能随时获得支持。除非你是世界公认的品牌，否则它们不太可能为你提供个性化的供应商支持，这意味着你只会看到熟悉的"联系我们"按钮。但是，有一些服务和计划可以在您需要时提供帮助。这取决于您的业务规模。这里有两个供应商支持选项：战略供应商服务（SVS）和供应商成功计划（VSP）。

5) The Hybrid Approach 混合方法

Some brands and manufacturers may find it beneficial to make use of both Amazon Vendor Central and Seller Central. In this case, they are both selling wholesale to Amazon, while also listing some of their own ducts directly on the marketplace. This can work to your advantage in many scenarios, including.

一些品牌和制造商可能会发现同时使用亚马逊供应商中心和亚马逊卖家中心是有益的。在这种情况下，它们都是向亚马逊批发销售，同时也将自己的一些渠道直接上市。这可以在许多情况下对你有利，包括：

(1) When Amazon doesn't purchase all of your stock.

(2) For listing CRaP (Can't realize any profit), ASINs(products that don't generate enough profit for Amazon to sell on its retail channel).

(3) Products that are out of season.

(4) When Amazon sells more than what they have in stock, so you can fulfill the order yourself.

(5) For product types that Amazon doesn't carry on its retail channel.

(a) Vendors adding Seller Central: Talk to your vendor manager to make sure it is okay with them that you start an SC account. If you don't get the permission required, you may end up having your Seller Central account suspended.

(b) Sellers adding Vendor Central: First, you need to receive an invitation to join from an Amazon buyer. During your initial contract negotiations with vendor manager, let them know that you intend on keeping your SC account active.

(c) Tips: Avoid getting into price wars with Amazon or fighting with them over the buy box. At the end of the day, they are selling your products and it would only be competing against yourself.

（1）当 Amazon 没有购买您所有的库存时。

（2）用于列出 CRaP（无法实现任何利润）、ASIN（没有产生足够利润的产品，Amazon 无法在其零售渠道上销售）。

（3）反季节产品。

（4）当 Amazon 销售的商品超过库存时，你可以自己完成订单。

（5）对于亚马逊不在其零售渠道上经营的产品类型。

（a）添加卖家中心的供应商：与你的供应商经理交谈，以确保其同意你开立 SC 账户。如果你没有获得所需的权限，你可能最终会暂停你的卖方中心账户。

（b）添加供应商中心的卖家：首先，你需要收到亚马逊买家的加入邀请。在你与供应商经理进行初始合同谈判时，让其知道你打算保持你的 SC 账户处于活动状态。

（c）提示：避免与 Amazon 发生价格战或与其争夺购物车。归根结底，亚马逊是在卖你的产品，你这样做等于在和自己竞争。

6) Which is Right for You? 哪个最适合你？

Perhaps the most important factor in choosing to become a vendor or a seller is what type of business you have. It's actually quite difficult to compare the two centrals since they were initially built for different business models.

也许选择成为供应商或卖家的最重要因素是你的业务类型。实际上很难比较这两个中心，因为它们最初是为不同的商业模式构建的。

Amazon Seller Central is more geared towards brands and online merchants that want to get their products listed quickly, whereas Amazon Vendor Central is aimed at brands and manufacturers looking to sell wholesale — with a more hands-off approach.

亚马逊卖家中心更多地面向希望其产品快速上市的品牌和在线商家，而亚马逊供应商中心针对的是希望批发销售的品牌和制造商——采取更不干涉的方式。

If you've already received an invitation from Amazon Vendor Central, consider obtaining product content syndication and optimization software to help you quickly and easily tailor your product catalog to Amazon's unique retail specifications.

如果你已收到亚马逊供应商中心的邀请，请考虑获取产品内容联合和优化软件，以帮助你快速轻松地根据亚马逊独特的零售规格定制产品目录。

【Exercise】

1. Translate the following phrases into Chinese.

general inquiry_____

date of delivery_____

quotation sheet_____

individual merchant_____

transaction fee_____

2. Translate the following phrases into English.

目标市场_____

折扣率_____

计算机病毒_____

网际协议_____

第三方卖方_____

3. Please explain the following terms.

(1) Online storefront (E-commerce) software

(2) Payment gateway

4. Please answer the following questions.

(1) What are the basic preparations of online store?

(2) How do you start to build an online store on Amazon?

(3) What are the cons of Amazon Vendor Central?

Chapter 4　Payment and Settlement of Cross-border E-commerce 跨境电子商务支付与结算

【Ability Objectives】

❑ Be able to introduce the E-commerce in English. 能够用英语介绍电子商务。

❑ Be able to communicate with customers in English. 能够用英语与顾客交流。

❑ Be able to read and comprehend some articles related to cross-border E-commerce.能够阅读和理解与跨境电子商务有关的文章。

【Knowledge Objectives】

❑ Master typical expressions about cross-border E-commerce. 掌握跨境电子商务的经典表达。

❑ Memorize new words and phrases in the texts. 能够记忆文章中的单词与短语。

【Key Words】

electronic payment system（电子支付系统）；PayPal（贝宝支付）；Alipay（阿里支付）；Western Union（西联汇款）；International Settlement（国际结算）

Section 4.1　Overview of Cross-border E-commerce Payment 跨境电子商务支付概述

New Words

objective	*n.*	目标；目的；（望远镜或显微镜的）物镜
	adj.	客观的；就事论事的；不带个人感情的；客观存在的
obstacle	*n.*	阻碍
liquidation	*n.*	清算；（债务的）清偿；（资产的）变现
payee	*n.*	受款人；收款人
monitor	*v.*	监控；监视；监听；检查
	n.	显示屏；屏幕；【计】显示器；监测仪
intercept	*v.*	拦截；【数】（在两点或两线间）截取；窃听；相交
	n.	拦截；【数】截距；侦听

tamper	n.	夯；（爆破孔）填塞人；捣固者；（中子）反射器
	v.	干扰；窜改（遗嘱，稿件等）；贿赂
detail	n.	细节；详情；琐事；细微之处
	v.	详细说明；详述；详细列举；派遣
prevent	v.	阻止；阻碍；阻挠
fraud	n.	骗子；欺诈罪；欺骗罪；行骗的人
protocol	n.	议定书、协议；礼仪；外交礼节；条约草案
	v.	打（草稿）；（把……）记入议定书
dialogue	v.	对话；用对话表达
	n.	对白；（尤指集体或国家间为解决问题、结束争端等进行的）对话
symmetric	adj.	对称的
encryption	n.	〔计〕加密
eavesdrop	n.	檐水
	v.	偷听；窃听；窃取；监听
fraudulent	adj.	欺骗的；欺诈的
authentication	n.	认证；鉴定
anonymity	n.	匿名性
authorization	n.	授权；批准；批准书；授权书
subclass	n.	【生】亚纲；【数】子集（合）；子类
currency	n.	货币；通货；通用；流行
intermediary	n.	中间人；调解人
	adj.	中间人的；媒介的；中间的
versatile	adj.	多才多艺的；有多种技能的；多面手的；多用途的
circulation	n.	循环；流通；血液循环；流传
safeguard	n.	保护；保护措施；装置；防护物
sensitive	adj.	体贴的；体恤的；善解人意的；感觉敏锐的
decode	v.	解（码）；破译（尤指密码）；译解（电子信号）；理解（外文）
logon	n.	登录；注册；构成信息的一个单位
password	n.	密码；口令；暗号；暗语
certificate	n.	证明；证明书；合格证书；文凭
	v.	发给结业证书；（尤指）发给职业培训证书
integrity	n.	完整；诚实正直；完好
non-repudiation	n.	不可否认性；不可抵赖性；非否认
algorithm	n.	【数】算法；规则系统；演段
decrypt	v.	解……的密码（暗号）
state-of-the-art	adj.	最新型的

Phrases

secure socket layer (SSL)	安全套接字层（SSL）
the electronic payment system	电子支付系统
electronic money	电子货币
data exchange	数据交换
electronic check	电子支票
electronic signature	电子签名
legality country	法制化国家
the paper checks	纸质支票
to be based on	以……为基础
the bank clearing system	银行结算系统
to be proposed by	由……提出的
Financial Services Technology Consortium(FSTC)	金融服务技术联合会（FSTC）
secure communications protocol	安全通信协议
secure payment agreements	安全支付协议
secure sockets layer protocol	保密插口层协议
secure electronic transaction (SET)	安全电子交易（SET）协议
asymmetric encryption	非对称加密
double signature	双联签章
hot money	热门货币
digital cash	数字现金
all in all	总而言之
payment card	支付卡
non-material form	非物质形态
to be stored in	储存
shopping cart icon	购物车图标
checkout button	结账按钮
electronic funds transfer (EFT)	电子资金转账（EFT）
fitness centers	健身中心
online bill pay	在线账单支付
processing fee	处理费
digital certificate	数字证书
electronic checks	电子支票
security schemes	安全机制
public key	公钥
private key	私钥
digital signature	数字签名

| third-party certification authority (CA) | 第三方认证机构（CA） |
| hard disk | 硬盘；硬磁盘 |

Sentences

1. "It made more sense to establish a journal that was trying to be totally objective in Britain than in the United States." Lord Wilson said.

   威尔逊勋爵说："在英国创办一个力图完全客观的刊物，比在美国更合适一些。"

2. The second objective of regulation is to insulate financial markets against the sort of panic seen in recent weeks.

   第二个监管目标是保护金融市场免受最近几周这种恐慌的冲击。

3. In the event of a liquidation, creditors now trying to increase their incremental recoveries would get nothing.

   如果进行清算，那么现在希望尽可能多地收回资金的债权人将一无所获。

4. And if all that isn't enough, the physical casing of the appliance is tamper resistant.

   如果这些还不够，那么设备的物理外壳还能够防篡改。

5. This kind of detail can be invaluable when trying to debug any network protocol that you are using.

   这些详细信息在调试你使用的任何网络协议时都是非常有用的。

6. WHO also understands that there is ongoing dialogue among the parties concerned to resolve the matter.

   世卫组织还了解到，有关各方正为解决这一问题进行对话。

7. The system could not be unlocked. The smartcard certificate used for authentication was not trusted.

   系统无法解锁。用于授权的智能卡证书不被信任。

8. In an age of sophisticated genetic testing, the concept of anonymity is rapidly fading.

   在精密的基因检测时代，匿名的概念迅速消失。

9. China's foreign-exchange regulator then allocates the qualified investor with a limit on how much currency he can exchange into yuan.

   中国外汇监管机构对合格投资者可以将多少货币兑换成人民币设有限制。

10. Created so far, the company received a rapid growth, "focus on integrity, the pursuit of quality" is the motto of the company.

    创立至今，公司获得了快速成长，"注重诚信、追求质量"是公司的座右铭。

11. Users trying to encrypt or decrypt with the specified key must have the required permissions to access the key container.

    尝试用指定密钥进行加密或解密的用户必须具有访问密钥容器的所需权限。

12. The supply of money in circulation was drastically reduced overnight.

    一夜之间流通货币的供应急剧减少了。

13. He was watching a game of tennis on a television monitor.

　　他那时正在电视监控器上观看一场网球赛。

14. Not surprisingly, the system is symmetric and comprehensive.

　　系统是对称和全面的，这不足为奇。

Conversations

1. Agent Commission

Blair: I have to bring up the commission. After all, we are commission agents.

Compton: The bigger the quantity is, the higher the commission rate is.

Blair: How much commission will you grant?

Compton: Usually, we'll give a commission of 4%.

Blair: I'm afraid it's too low. Is it possible to increase it to 5%?

Compton: If your order is a sizeable one, we could reconsider our prices.

Blair: I feel 4% is really out of the question.

Compton: To be frank, you are not the only one applying to be the agent of our company.

Blair: 1 know, however, we expect a high commission, of course. Can't you give an inch?

Compton: Sorry.

1. 代理佣金

布莱尔：我不得不提出佣金。毕竟我们是代理商。

康普顿：订货量越大，佣金率就会越高。

布莱尔：你方愿给多少佣金？

康普顿：通常我们给 4%的佣金。

布莱尔：恐怕太低了。能不能增加到 5%？

康普顿：如果您的订单量够大，我们会重新定价。

布莱尔：我想 4%我们真的做不了。

康普顿：坦率地讲，你方不是唯一向我公司提出申请的代理方。

布莱尔：我知道，可是，我们当然希望能得到较高的佣金。难道你们就不能做一点
　　　　让步？

康普顿：对不起。

2. Negotiation on Price

William: Have you seen our price list?

Kevin: Yes, but I must say the unit price for $35 per kilogram is too high for us to accept.

William: We can't talk about price separately from quality.

Kevin: The quotation we received from others is much lower. Your price is prohibitive.

William: Are their products in the same class with ours?

Kevin: Your products may have certain advantages over others, but the price is almost twice of others.

　　William: What do you have in mind?

Kevin: $25 per kilogram.

William: $25 per kilogram is out of the question. We have never gone as far as that. Our rule is the larger the order, the lower the price. At that time, you will find our prices are very favorable.

2. 价格谈判

威廉：您看过我们的价目表了吗？

凯文：看过了，但我必须指出每千克 35 美元的单价太高了，我们无法接受。

威廉：我们不能离开质量谈价格。

凯文：我们从别处收到的报价要低得多。你们的报价令人望而却步。

威廉：他们的产品和我们的是同一档次吗？

凯文：你们的产品可能存在某些优越之处，但价格却近乎其他产品的两倍。

威廉：您想要多少？

凯文：每千克 25 美元。

威廉：每千克 25 美元是不可能的。我们从来没降过这么多。我们的规定是卖得越多越便宜。到那时您会发现，我们的价格非常优惠。

Text

4.1.1　Electronic Payment System 电子支付系统

The electronic payment system is a network banking system to achieve electronic money data exchange and settlement using digital and electronic form. In general, there are three main types of electronic payment systems: electronic check, payment based on different protocols and payment cards, and electronic money.

电子支付系统是采用数字化、电子化形式进行电子货币数据交换和结算的网络银行业务系统。一般来说，共有 3 种主要的电子支付系统：电子支票、基于不同协议和支付卡的支付、电子货币。

1. Electronic Check 电子支票

The electronic check is a concept combining the traditional checks with electronic payment systems. Electronic signature can be achieved technically. In the legality country, there are no objective obstacles to the development of this system, and only payment habits can lead to the difficulties of development. The use of electronic checks is the same as the paper checks, and the liquidation between the payer and the payee is based on the bank clearing system.

电子支票是一种将传统支票和电子支付系统联系起来的概念。电子签名能够在技术上实现，而且在法制化国家中，对这个系统的发展并不存在客观的障碍，只有人们的支付习惯会导致其发展的困难。电子支票的使用与纸质支票一样，即在付款人和收款人之间的清算是以银行结算系统为基础的。

As an example of electronic check, E-check will be mentioned, which is proposed by the Financial Services Technology Consortium (FSTC). E-check is an electronic replica of paper checks, and it has its own characteristics:

(1) Electronic checks can be transmitted between any two parties with the necessary equipment.

(2) It can be used for all transactions that use traditional checks.

(3) All banks customers with checking accounts can use the electronic check.

作为电子支票的一个范例，人们会提到 E-check，它是金融服务技术联合会（FSTC）提议发起的。E-check 是纸质支票的电子翻版，并具有自身的特点：

（1）只要拥有必要的设备，电子支票就能够在任何两方之间进行传输。

（2）可以用于使用传统支票的所有交易。

（3）所有拥有支票账户的银行客户都可以使用电子支票。

2. Payment Card System 支付卡系统

The following problems may occur in the process of sending the card number in the open Internet network.

(1) Monitoring: Because of its unique structure, and because it goes through different computers before they reach the final recipient, the card number may be intercepted.

(2) Tampering: The raw data is intercepted and changed in the case of ignorance of the sender.

(3) Faking: If you know the details of the payment card, it is easy to pretend to be the owner shopping in the electronic store.

在互联网这样的开放式网络中传送卡片号码的时候可能会出现以下问题。

（1）监听：由于卡片号码具有十分独特的结构，而且在数据到达最终接收者之前要经过不同的计算机，卡片号码可能会被截获。

（2）篡改：在发送者不知情的情况下，截获原始数据并进行改变。

（3）假冒别人：如果知道了支付卡的详细情况，就很容易假装成其他人在电子商店进行购物。

In order to prevent such fraud, several agreements are designed, and these agreements are still in developing. Generally speaking, there are two protocols to protect the payment data in the transmission process of the open network: a secure communications protocol and secure payment agreements.

为了防止这些欺诈行为，人们设计了几种协议，这些协议仍在发展。一般来说，在开放网络的传输过程中，保护支付数据的协议有两种：安全通信协议和安全支付协议。

Secure communication protocol has established a set of system rules to manage the entire communication process and it has provided rules of grammar and dialogue in order to create the necessary exchange of information. An example of such protocol is the "Secure Sockets Layer Protocol" that supports with symmetric encryption developed by Netscape. With this protocol, the card number can be passed to the merchant safely and thus preventing information eavesdropping or tampering during transmission. However, this agreement can neither ensure non-repudiation, nor prevent the fraudulent using credit card numbers, because there is all confidential information concerning the credit card of customer on the server. In the process of SSL transactions, the purchaser cannot ensure that businesses are able to protect the payment card information.

Moreover, the customer cannot determine whether the merchant is certified or can receive credit card payments. In addition to the merchant cannot exactly identify if the customer can use the payment card. This issue is particularly important during the sales of intangible goods.

安全通信协议建立了一套系统规则，用以管理整个通信过程。最为首要的是协议为创建必要的信息交换提供语法和对话规则。这种协议的一个范例是"保密插口层协议"，此协议通过对称加密来支持，这种对称加密是由网景公司开发的。借助这个协议，卡片号码可以被安全地传递到商户，这样就防止了在传输过程中对信息的窃听或篡改。但是这种协议既不能确保不可否认性，也不能防止假冒使用信用卡号码，这是由于商户在其服务器中存有顾客信用卡的所有机密信息。在 SSL 交易的过程中，买主不能确保商户能够保护好支付卡的信息。而且，顾客不能确定商户是否经过认证，是否能够接受信用卡支付。除此之外，商户也不能确切辨认此客户是否可以使用支付卡。在无形商品的销售中，这个问题显得尤为重要。

SSL provides data encryption and server authentication, which ensure the integrity of the information and client authentication for the TCP/IP connection.

安全套接层提供数据加密、服务器认证，保证了信息的完整性，并且可以对 TCP/IP 连接进行客户端认证。

In addition, there are other secure payment protocols developed. The most famous is Secure Electronic Transaction (SET) jointly developed by Visa Company and Master Card Company, and this protocol is based on the RSA algorithm, achieving asymmetric encryption. By means of double signature, the privacy and confidentiality can be protected better. The merchant cannot get financial information because of different keys, and the bank is unable to get commercial information preferred by customers. Part of the information related to the bank is decrypted with the bank's public key encryption (merchant cannot decrypt), the other part with the merchant's public key encryption (bank cannot decrypt). SET widely make up for the service not provided in the SSL protocol.

除此之外，还有其他安全支付协议也被开发出来。最著名的是由维萨卡公司和万事达卡公司联合开发的安全电子交易（SET）协议，这种协议基于 RSA 算法，实现了非对称加密。借助双联签章可以更好地保护隐私和机密。不同的密钥使商户无法得到金融信息，而且银行无法得到有关客户偏好的商业信息。与银行有关的部分信息用银行的公钥进行加密（商户无法解密），另一部分用商户的公钥进行加密（银行无法解密）。安全电子交易协议广泛地弥补了安全套接层协议所无法提供的服务。

3. Electronic Money 电子货币

According to national statistics, the percentage of cash transactions is estimated to reach 75% to 90% in all transactions. Visa Company estimates that $1.8 trillion spent on trading below $10 each year around the world. "Hot money" is so popular due to the following types of problems:

(1) Characteristics of a legal tender;

(2) Anonymity;

(3) Needn't the process of certification, authentication and authorization;

(4) Do not have to spend transaction costs (supply, collection, transportation, and defend it costs excluded);

(5) Widely acceptance for cash is from the legal system and citizens' trust.

根据国家的统计，在所有交易中，现金交易的百分比估计达到 75%~90%。据维萨卡公司估计，每年在全世界有 1.8 万亿美元花在低于 10 美元的交易之上。"热门货币"如此受欢迎可能是由于下列几种问题：

（1）法定货币的特性；

（2）匿名性；

（3）不需要经过认证、鉴别和授权的过程；

（4）不必花费交易成本（在供给、收集、运输和保卫等方面要花费成本的除外）；

（5）对现金的广泛接受源于法制体系和公民的信任。

The advantages of cash using give birth to the concept of digital currency, which plays the same role in the real world. Digital cash has become possible through using state-of-the-art encryption technology. Many projects are in developing for the early use.

使用现金的许多优点催生了数字货币，数字现金与现实世界中的现金起着同样的作用。通过使用先进的加密技术，数字现金已经成为可能。为了客户能早日使用，许多项目正在努力开发中。

All in all, the electronic money is different from checks, bank transfers and payment card. It's not the product requiring network access, which forming a new subclass of currency. Electronic money constitutes a means of payment, monetary value and account unit — which makes electronic money get the same utility as cash.

总而言之，电子货币不同于支票、银行转账和支付卡，它不是需要网络接入的产品，电子货币形成了货币的一个新的子类。同时，电子货币也构成了支付手段、货币价值和账户单元——这使电子货币具有与现金一样的效用。

Based on these definitions and the properties of the real money, the characteristics of the electronic money can be described as follows:

(1) Non-material form of electronic money;

(2) Payment without intermediary;

(3) Electronic money is a versatile tool (phone units stored in the phone card are not electronic money);

(4) Electronic money is stored in the smart card or in the computer's hard disk;

(5) The truly virtual money offers complete anonymity;

(6) The electronic money may be in circulation outside the banking sector;

(7) Electronic money has the exact face amount;

(8) In most circumstances, the electronic money is prepaid, but it's not a regulation way;

(9) Electronic money is used for micro-payment (in the EC, most systems allow customers to pay for less than 100 Euros).

基于这些定义和真实货币的属性，电子货币的特点可以描述如下：

（1）电子货币是非物质形态的；

（2）支付不需要中间媒介；

（3）电子货币是一种多用途的工具（存储在电话卡中的电话单位不是电子货币）；

（4）电子货币存储在智能卡中或存储在计算机的硬盘中；

（5）真正的虚拟货币提供完全的匿名性；

（6）电子货币可以在银行部门之外流通；

（7）电子货币具有确切的票面金额；

（8）在多数情况下，电子货币是预付费的，但这不是一个定规；

（9）电子货币是用来进行小额支付的（在欧共体，多数系统能够让顾客进行低于 100 欧元的支付）。

4.1.2 Security of Electronic Payment System 电子支付系统安全机制

Before we discuss each electronic payment method, it is helpful to look back the security schemes for universal use. Four essential security requirements are commonly used in electronic payment methods:

(1) Certification: Used to verify the identity of the purchaser prior to payment authorization.

(2) Encryption: This process is used to avoid being deciphered, unless they have been granted the decryption key.

(3) Integrity: To ensure that the information have no accidental or malicious tampering or destruction in the process of transmission.

(4) Non-repudiation: Prevent consumers' denying for ordering or businesses, denying that they have accepted the money.

在探讨各种电子支付方式之前，回顾一下在电子支付方式中普遍使用的安全机制是有益的。安全的电子支付有以下 4 个基本的要求：

（1）认证：用来在支付授权之前核实买主的身份。

（2）加密：这个过程用来避免信息被破译，除非拥有被授予的解密密钥。

（3）完整性：保证信息在传输的过程中不会被意外或恶意地篡改或破坏。

（4）不可否认性：防止消费者否认已经进行过订货或者商家否认已经收过钱。

1. Key Encryption 密钥加密

Over the years, people use the security system based on a single key. The secret key encryption method is known as symmetric encryption or private key, and uses the same key as the sender (for encryption) and a receiver (for decrypting). The most widely accepted secret key encryption algorithm is the Data Encryption Standard (DES). Some cryptographer deems that DES algorithm is penetrating.

多年来，人们使用的安全系统基于一个单一的密钥。密钥加密方式也被称为对称加密，或私人密钥加密，是发送方（用于加密）和接收器（用于解密）使用相同的密钥。最广为接受的密钥编码算法是数据加密标准（DES）。有的密码破译者认为，DES 算法也可被破译。

However, DES is considered to be safe enough, as the penetration takes several years and millions of dollars cost. The SET protocol used DES 64-bit key algorithm.

然而，DES 被认为是足够安全的，因为破译需要花费数年、数百万美元成本。SET 协议采用了 DES 的 64 位密钥的算法。

2. Public Key Cryptography 公钥加密

Public key cryptography, also known as asymmetric encryption, uses two different keys: a public key and a private key. Public key is open to all approved users, while the private key is only open to one person — the owner of the private key. The private key is generated by the master computer, and not sent to anyone. In order to use public key cryptography to send information securely to the sender, the sender must use the recipients public key to encrypt the information. This requires passing the recipient's public key in advance. The information encrypted in this manner can only be decrypted by the recipient's private key. The most popular algorithm in public key encryption is the RSA algorithm, which can have a variety of different length of the key, for example, the key with 1024 bits. This algorithm has never been cracked by hackers, which is considered to be the most secure encryption method currently known.

公钥加密也称非对称加密，使用两个不同的密钥：公钥和私钥。公钥针对所有经认可的用户公开，而私钥只有一个人知道——私钥的主人。私钥由主人的计算机产生，不向任何人发送。要想使用公钥加密安全地发送信息，发送者要使用接收者的公钥对信息进行加密。这就需要事先传递接收者的公钥。按照这种方式加密的信息只能通过接收者的私钥来解密。公钥加密中最为流行的算法是 RSA 算法，这种算法可以有各种不同的密钥长度，例如 1024 位的密钥。这种算法从未被黑客破解过，所以被认为是目前已知的最为安全的加密方法。

RSA public key encryption algorithm is usually used to send the DES algorithm, because during encryption and decryption, DES algorithm is more effective and more efficient.

RSA 公钥加密算法通常用于传送 DES 算法，因为在进行加密和解密的时候，DES 算法更有效、更快捷。

3. Digital Signature 数字签名

Digital signature is another way to authenticate the information sender. In order to achieve digital signature, the sender encrypts the information with the private encryption key. In this case, anyone who has her public key can read this message, and the receiver can also confirm that this information is from the master. The digital signature is usually attached to the transmitted information, and is the same as the handwritten signature.

数字签名是对信息发送者进行认证的又一种方法。为了进行数字签名，发送者用自己的密钥对信息进行了加密。在这种情况下，任何一个拥有公钥的人都能读懂这条信息，而且接收者还能确认信息的发送者就是这条信息的主人。数字签名通常附加到被发送的信息之后，就像手写的签名一样。

4. Information Summary 信息摘要

In order to carry out the information summary, the information should be standardized and converted into a predetermined length with 160 bits, regardless of the length of the original information. This standardization transform process can be performed by hash transformation of the original data, and the hash information is called information summary.

要想进行信息摘要，就需要对信息进行标准化的变换，使其成为预定的 160 位的长度，而不管最初的信息长度有多长。这种标准化变换的过程可以通过对最初的数据进行散列变换来进行，这个散列信息就叫作信息摘要。

5. Certificate 证书

Certificate usually refers to authentication certificate issued by a trusted third-party certification authority (CA). Certificate contains serial number, the name of the owner, the owner's public key, algorithms of the key, authentication type (cardholder, merchant or payment gateway), the name of the authentication center, and the signature of the certification center.

证书通常是指由受信任的第三方认证机构（CA）颁发的身份认证证书。证书中包含序列号、主人的名称、主人的公钥、使用这些密钥的算法、认证的类型（持卡人、商户或支付网关）、认证中心的名称和认证中心的数字签名。

Section 4.2　Main Payment Platform of Cross-border E-commerce 跨境电子商务支付主要平台

New Words

initial	*adj.*	最初的；开始的；第一的
	n.	（名字的）首字母；（全名的）首字母
	v.	用姓名的首字母作标记（或签名）于
wholly	*adv.*	完全；全面；整体地
subsidiary	*n.*	子公司；附属公司
	adj.	辅助的；附带的；次要的；附属的
processor	*n.*	处理器；加工机（或工人）；处理机
auction	*n.*	拍卖
	v.	拍卖
procurement	*n.*	（尤指为政府或机构）采购
consumption	*n.*	消费；消耗量
deposit	*n.*	存款；寄存
	v.	沉淀；寄存；储蓄；放置
multichannel	*adj.*	多频道的；多通道的
robust	*adj.*	结实的；耐用的
remittance	*n.*	汇款；汇款金额；汇付

Phrases

online payment platform	在线支付平台
transfer fee	转账费用

Sentences

1. My initial opinion of him has changed since getting to know him better.
   随着对他了解的加深，我对他最初的印象也发生了变化。

2. British people do not use their middle names, but Americans often give the initial: John F.
   英国人通常不用他们的中名，但美国人却常常使用自己中名的首字母缩写，如：John F。

3. It was an affluent life, though the source of Joseph's fortune has never been wholly clear.
   约瑟夫一生富足，尽管其财富来得并非全部清白。

4. WM Financial Services is a subsidiary of Washington Mutual.
   华盛顿互惠银行金融服务公司是华盛顿互惠银行的子公司。

5. The marketing department has always played a subsidiary role to the sales department.
   营销部一直都扮演着销售部的辅助角色。

6. The frozen-food industry could be supplied entirely by growers and processors outside the country.
   冷冻食品行业可以完全由国外的种植者们和加工者们供应。

7. The food processor has thin, medium, and thick slicing discs.
   这个食品加工机有薄、中、厚的切片盘。

8. The painting is expected to fetch up to $400,000 at auction.
   这幅画预计在拍卖会上能卖到 40 万美元。

9. Eight drawings by French artist Jean Cocteau will be auctioned next week.
   法国艺术家让·科克托的 8 幅画作将在下周拍卖。

10. These are some of the problems that can be addressed through more efficient procurement policies.
    这些问题都是可以通过更为有效的采购政策加以解决的。

11. We have now worked with 41 countries around the world on improving the transparency, competitiveness, and efficiency of government procurement.
    我们已经与世界上的 41 个国家开展了合作，以改善政府采购的透明度、竞争性和效率。

12. The laws have led to a reduction in fuel consumption in the U.S.
    这些法律已导致美国燃料消耗的降低。

13. Most of the wine was unfit for human consumption.
    大多数酒都是不适合人类饮用的。

14. They were prepared to put people out of work and reduce consumption by strangling the whole economy.
    他们准备通过遏制整个经济让人们失业、降低消费。

15. Consumption rather than saving has become the central feature of contemporary societies.
现代社会的主要特征是消费而不是储蓄。

16. The initial deposit required to open an account is a minimum 100 dollars.
开户需要的首笔存入额是至少 100 美元。

17. A 10% deposit is payable in advance.
须预付 10%的押金。

18. Please enclose your remittance, making checks payable to Valley Technology Services.
请随信附上您的汇款，支票收款方为瓦利科技服务公司。

Conversations

1. Talking about Discount

Bob: Mr. Johnson, I've considered the offer you made yesterday. I must point out that your price is much higher than other offers we've received.

Johnson: Well, it may appear a little higher, but the quality of our products is much better than that of other suppliers. You must take this into consideration.

Bob: I agree with you on this point. That's why we like doing business with you. This time I intend to place a large order but business is almost impossible unless you give me a discount.

Johnson: If so, we'll certainly give you a discount. But how large is the order you intend to place with us?

Bob: 80,000 sets with a discount rate of 20%.

Johnson: I am afraid I cannot agree to such a big discount. Such a discount won't leave us anything. Our maximum is 10%.

1. 谈谈折扣

鲍勃：约翰逊先生，我已考虑过你昨天的报价了。我得指出你们的价格比我们收到的其他报价高很多。

约翰逊：可能显得高一点，但我们的产品质量比其他供应商的好。你应该考虑到这一点。

鲍勃：这点我同意。那也是我们喜欢和你们做生意的原因。此次我想下一个大订单，但你们要给我一个折扣，否则很难成交。

约翰逊：既然如此，我们当然会给你们一个折扣。但你们要订购多少呢？

鲍勃：80 000 套，折扣 20%。

约翰逊：我恐怕不能同意给这么高的折扣。给这样一个折扣，我们就无利可图了。我们最高给 10%。

2. Meeting Half Way

Martin: That still leaves a gap of $35 to be covered. Let's meet each other half way once more, then the gap will be closed and our business completed.

John: You certainly have a way of talking me into it. All right, let's meet half way again.

Martin: I'm glad we've come to an agreement on price/ We'll go on to the other terms and conditions at our next meeting.

John: Yes, there's one other point I wish to clear up.

Martin: What is it?

John: My friends in business circles all seem to be of the opinion that the U.S. import and export corporations have become more flexible in doing business recently.

Martin: Yes, they're right. In fact, we have either restored or adopted international practices in our foreign trade.

2. 双方让步

马丁：这样还剩下 35 美元的差额。我们再一次各让一半吧。这样差额就可以消除，生意也就做成了。

约翰：你真有办法，把我说服了。好吧，我们再各让一半。

马丁：很高兴我们在价格上达成一致。在下一次谈判中，我们再研究其他条款。

约翰：好。不过我还想澄清另一个问题。

马丁：什么事？

约翰：商界的许多朋友好像觉得美国的进出口公司在贸易中的做法更加灵活了。

马丁：正是这样。事实上，最近我们在国际贸易中恢复或采用了国际惯例和习惯做法。

Text

4.2.1　PayPal 贝宝支付

Established in 1998, PayPal had its initial public offering in 2002 and became a wholly owned subsidiary of eBay later that year. PayPal Holdings, Inc. is an American company operating a worldwide online payments system that supports online money transfers and serves as an electronic alternative to traditional paper methods like checks and money orders.

成立于 1998 年 PayPal 的（贝宝）在 2002 年进行首次公开发行，并于同年晚些时候成为 eBay 的全资子公司。PayPal 是一家主要经营全球性在线支付系统的美国公司。PayPal 支持在线汇款，被作为支票和汇票等传统纸币方式的电子替代品。

PayPal is one of the world's largest Internet payment companies. The company operates as a payment processor for online vendors auction sites and other commercial users to charge fees. PayPal is an account type that is designed for users with international payment requirements. It is currently the world's most widely used online trading tool. It can help us to carry out the convenient foreign trade collection, to track withdrawing and transaction, and to engage in safe international procurement and consumption.

PayPal 是全球最大的互联网支付公司之一，该公司作为在线供应商、拍卖网站和其他商业用户的付款处理器来收取费用。PayPal 是针对具有国际收付款需求用户设计的账户类型。它是目前全球使用最为广泛的网上交易工具。它能帮助我们进行便捷的外贸收款、提现、跟踪交易，进行安全的国际采购与消费。

4.2.2　Alipay 阿里支付

Alipay, or Zhifubao is a third-party mobile and online payment platform in China. It was established in Hangzhou in February 2004 and was founded by Jack Ma of China's Alibaba Group. Alipay mainly provides payment and financial services, including online purchase secured transactions, online payments, transfer, credit card repayment, mobile phone recharge, water and electricity coal payment, personal wealth management and other fields.

阿里支付，即支付宝，在中国是一个第三方移动和在线支付平台，2004 年 2 月在杭州成立，创始人为中国阿里巴巴集团的马云。支付宝主要提供支付及理财服务，涉及网购担保交易、网络支付、转账、信用卡还款、手机充值、水电煤缴费、个人理财等多个领域。

4.2.3　Western Union 西联汇款

1. How Western Union Works

Quick cross-border money transfers are made using an extensive computer network, the center of which is located in the United States. It operates in 200 countries of the world having around 500,000 agent locations worldwide. The digital service network is much smaller, covering only about 60 countries. The most recent online expansion took place in the Middle East and Asia.

快速跨境转账是利用一个广泛的计算机网络进行的，该网络的中心位于美国。它在世界 200 个国家和地区开展业务，在世界各地拥有约 50 万个代理地点。数字服务网络要小得多，只覆盖大约 60 个国家。最近的在线扩张发生在中东和亚洲。

The majority of WU transactions come through the partner network of various organizations such as banks, retailers, and foreign exchange bureaus. In the last couple of years, Western Union has also made partnerships with multiple mobile network operators and mobile wallet companies to make mobile money transfer hassle-free.

西联汇款的大部分交易都是通过银行、零售商和外汇局等各种组织的合作伙伴网络进行的。在过去的几年里，西联汇款还与多家移动网络运营商和移动钱包公司建立了合作伙伴关系，使移动资金转移变得畅通无阻。

2. Western Union Fees 西联汇款费用

The remittance amount plus the fee incurred is charged from your debit/credit card or your bank account. This money is transferred to a Western Union account. The latter is usually located in the sender's country. At this point, your money transfer is deposited. The Western Union branch in the receiver's country is informed and the money transfer is ready for delivery. If requested, money transfer is further redirected to a sender's bank account. The whole process may take from a few minutes to 4-5 business days.

汇款金额加上所产生的手续费将从您的借记卡/信用卡或您的银行账户中收取。这笔钱会转到西联汇款的账户上，后者通常位于寄件人所在的国家。此时，您的转账被存入银行，通知收款人所在国家的西联汇款分公司，转账就准备好了。如果请求，转账会进一步重定向到汇款人的银行账户，整个过程可能需要几分钟到 4~5 个工作日。

The transfer fee is the full responsibility of the sender. There's no single binding receipt address — the recipient may contact any point of the Western Union system in the receiving country.

转账费用由寄件人承担全部责任。没有单一的有约束力的收据地址——收件人可以联系接收国的西联汇款系统的任何地点。

As with many similar services, fees vary greatly depending on the transfer type. Typically, the fixed transaction fees are cheaper when you send money online. Furthermore, paying with your debit or credit card is much more expensive than from a bank account.

与许多类似的服务一样，根据转账类型的不同，费用也会有很大的差异。通常，当你在网上汇款时，固定交易费会更便宜。此外，用你的借记卡或信用卡支付比从银行账户支付贵得多。

While transfers from a bank to a bank account can be as cheap as 0.99 USD or even free of charge, sending money with a debit or credit card for a cash pick-up may bring an additional $70. In general, the fees depend on the location. The more fierce competition on the remittance market, the lower the transfer fees. Moreover, costs have been falling not only as a result of healthier competition but also due to the pressure from the G20 and the UN, who are targeting an average remittance cost to the consumer of 3%-5%.

虽然从银行转账到银行账户的费用可以低至 0.99 美元，甚至是免费的，但用借记卡或信用卡转账提现可能会带来额外的 70 美元的费用。一般来说，费用取决于地点。汇款市场竞争越激烈，转账手续费越低。此外，成本一直在下降，这不仅因为更健康的竞争，也来自 20 国集团和联合国的压力——它们的目标是将消费者的平均汇款成本控制在 3%~5%。

3. Pros and Cons of Western Union 西联汇款的利弊

1) Pros of Western Union 西联电汇的优点

(1) Over 100 years of business experience.

(2) Robust multichannel system.

(3) Good opportunities for unbanked citizens.

(4) Operates in 200 countries and deals with 130 different national currencies.

（1）超过 100 年的商业经验。

（2）健全的多渠道系统。

（3）为无银行账户的公民提供良好的机会。

（4）在 200 个国家开展业务，处理 130 种不同的国家货币。

2) Cons of Western Union 西联电汇的缺点

(1) The digital experiences are still not as convenient as cash options, accounting for only 6% of all transactions.

(2) Some fees are higher than among their competitors.

(3) Mobile money transfers are available in limited regions.

（1）数字体验仍不如现金支付方便，仅占总交易量的 6%。

（2）部分费用高于竞争对手。

（3）移动转账地域有限。

Section 4.3　Overview of International Settlement
国际结算概述

New Words

settlement	n.	解决；结算；处理
transaction	n.	处理；业务；办理
supervise	v.	监督；管理；指导；主管
tangible	adj.	有形的；实际的；真实的；可触摸的
inspect	v.	检查；视察；检阅；审查
appreciation	n.	升值；欣赏；感谢；增值；了解
depreciation	n.	折旧；贬值
timeliness	n.	时间表；大事年表
ownership	n.	所有权；产权；物主身份

Phrases

in simple words	简而言之
international settlement	国际结算
cooperative partners	合作伙伴
visible trade	有形贸易
invisible trade	无形贸易
syndicated loans	银团贷款
credit risks	信用风险
financing costs	融资成本
hard currency	硬通货

Sentences

1. Our objective must be to secure a peace settlement.
   我们的目标必须是确保达成一个和平协议。

2. She accepted an out-of-court settlement of $40,000.
   她接受了 4 万美元庭外和解。

3. The transaction is completed by payment of the fee.
   交易在支付费用之后就完成了。

4. Neither side would disclose details of the transaction.
   双方都不会透露交易的细节。

5. There should be some tangible evidence that the economy is starting to recover.

应该有一些足够清晰的证据表明经济正开始复苏。

6. The tension between them was almost tangible.
   他们之间的紧张关系几乎让人感觉得出来。

7. The Public Utilities Commission inspects us once a year.
   公用设施委员会每年到我们这里视察一次。

8. Please accept this gift in appreciation of all you've done for us.
   承蒙鼎力相助，不胜感激，谨备薄礼，敬请笑纳。

9. Foreign currency depreciation is a result of economic depression in the country concerned.
   外汇贬值是有关国家经济不景气的结果。

10. Many states allow different amounts for depreciation deductions.
    许多州允许不同数额的折旧扣除。

11. The timeline shows important events from the Earth's creation to the present day.
    该年表列出了从地球诞生迄今的重要事件。

12. The restaurant is under new ownership.
    这个餐厅已换了新的东家。

13. We sincerely look forward to being your best strategic cooperative partners and purchasing alliance.
    我们真诚地期待着能够成为你最佳的战略合作伙伴和采购联盟。

14. You need hard currency to get anything halfway decent.
    你得有硬通货才能买到像样点儿的东西。

Conversations

1. Modify the Payment Page

A: I'm interested in your sweaters, but it cost $20 for each one. I think it's difficult for me to try trial sales at such a price.

B: How much do you think is suitable?

A: Think to get the business done, you should at least reduce the price by 10%.

B: We could take a cut on the price if your order is a large one, but 10% reduction is really impossible. What quantity are you going to order from us then?

A: As a trial order, I'll take 50 pieces this time.

B: 50 pieces is by no means a large order, and the most we can offer you is $18 per piece.

A: That sounds reasonable, but how do I pay for it?

B: Just wait a minute for me to adjust the price to $18, and then I'll send you the link.

A: Okay.

B: This is the new payment link. You can click in and click the "Start Order" button.

A: I got it!

1. 修改支付页面

A：我对你们店的运动衫很感兴趣，不过每件运动衫就要 20 美元。我觉得很难以这一价格试销你们的产品。

B：您觉得多少合适呢？

A：我认为要成交的话，你至少应降价 10%。

B：如果您订购数量大的话，我们可以降价，但降价 10%是不可能的。您准备向我们订购多少呢？

A：我打算订购 50 件试销。

B：50 件并不是什么大订单，我们最多只能以每件 18 美元的价格出售。

A：听起来也挺合理的，不过我该怎么支付呢？

B：请您先等我把价格调到 18 美元，再将链接发送给您。

A：好的。

B：这是新的支付链接，您点进去，单击"立即下单"按钮就行了。

A：我知道了。

2. Help Customers Understand the Payment Steps

A: Hello, there?

B: Yes, what can I do for you?

A: Well, it's my first time purchasing goods on Amazon. I like a watch in your store. Can you tell me how to pay for it?

B: Of course, I'd love to. First, you should complete the order information for the item, such as quantity, style, and color. Then click the "Buy Now" button to enter the new page. Select the shipping address on the new page. You can enter a new shipping address, or choose the default address.

A: Please wait a moment. Have entered my shipping address when registering.

B: Then you can click on the "Ship to this address" button and go to the next page to select the payment method. There are many payment options. You may choose a credit card or debit card, and then click the "Continue" button to proceed step by step.

A: Well, it doesn't sound complicated.

B: Yes, you will be very skilled if you do it a few more times.

A: Thank you for your help.

2. 帮客户了解支付步骤

A：你好，在吗？

B：是的，请问有什么吩咐？

A：是这样的，我第一次在亚马逊上买东西，我在你们店内看好了一款手表，能告诉我付款步骤是怎样的吗？

B：当然，我很乐意。首先您要选择商品的基本属性，比如数量、款式和颜色。然后单击"现在购买"按钮，进入新的页面。在新的页面选择送货地址，可以选择默认地址，也可重新添加地址。

A：请稍等，在注册时我已经输入我的收货地址了。

B：那您可以直接单击"送货到该地址"按钮，进入下一个页面选择付款方式。您可以选择信用卡或借记卡，然后单击"继续"按钮，按步骤操作。

A：听起来也不是很复杂。

B：没错，您多操作几次就会很熟练了。

A：谢谢你的帮助。

Text

4.3.1　Concept of International Settlement 国际结算的概念

International settlement refers to financial activities in which payments are made to settle accounts, debts and claims, and etc. occurring among different countries. In simple words, international settlement means money transfer across national borders.

国际结算是指为结算发生在不同国家之间的账目、债务和债权等而进行支付的金融活动。简而言之，国际结算就是跨国界的资金转移。

4.3.2　Three Key Elements Necessarily for International Settlement 国际结算必须具备的三个关键要素

1. Persons in Different Countries 不同国家的人

Buyers and sellers in the international transaction are not competitors, but cooperative partners for seeking long-term and common interests.

国际交易中的买卖双方不是竞争者，而是谋求长远共同利益的合作伙伴。

2. Bank's Participation 银行的参与

Facilitating world-wide funds transfer efficiently, promoting transactions because they can easily supervise both buyer and seller.

促进资金在全球范围内的高效转移，促进交易，因为银行可以方便地监管买家和卖家。

3. Funds Transfer 资金调拨

Funds transfer always happens in the following activities: visible trade such as importing and exporting tangible and visible goods; invisible trade such as service trade, technology transfer，etc.; financial transaction such as foreign exchange market export credits, syndicated loans, etc.; payment between governments such as giving aids and grants, providing disaster relief, etc.

资金转移通常发生在以下活动中：有形贸易，如进出口有形货物；无形贸易，如服务贸易、技术转让等；金融交易，如外汇市场出口信贷、银团贷款等；政府之间的支付，如给予援助和赠款，提供救灾，等等。

4.3.3　Key Issues in International Settlements 国际结算中的几个关键问题

1. Credit Risks 信用风险

Credit risks are caused by giving easy, extended or inexpensive credit terms in international payments. For example, the seller gives the buyer the opportunity to resell the goods before payment, and the buyer pays to the seller before receiving the goods.

Conflicts: Both the seller and buyer want the other, not himself to bear the credit risk. The buyer wants to receive the goods once or even before he pays, while the seller wants to receive payment once or even before he ships the goods.

信用风险是在国际付款中提供宽松、延长或廉价的信用条件所造成的，例如，卖方在买方付款前给买方转售货物的机会，或者买方在收到货物之前向卖方付款。

冲突：买卖双方都希望对方承担信用风险，而不是自己承担信用风险。买方希望一次或甚至在他付款之前收到货物，而卖方希望一次或甚至在他装运货物之前收到付款。

2. Financing Costs and Risks 融资成本和风险

Financing costs and risks for the seller: The costs and risks he bears during the period before receiving payment，including manufacturing, packaging, transporting, inspecting, customs clearing, etc.

Financing costs and risks for the buyer: Those he bears during the period before resale of the goods, including waiting, warehousing, reselling, getting paid, etc.

Conflicts: both parties want the other party to finance the transaction and to bear the costs and risks.

卖方的融资成本和风险：卖方在收到付款前的一段时间内承担的成本和风险，包括制造、包装、运输、检验、通关等。

买方的融资成本和风险：买方在货物转售前的一段时间内承担的成本和风险，包括等待、仓储、转售、收款等。

冲突：双方都希望对方为交易提供资金，并承担成本和风险。

3. Foreign Exchange Risks 外汇风险

Foreign exchange risks are caused by the appreciation or depreciation of the specified currency for the payment between the contract date and the payment date.

Conflicts: The seller wants to get paid in own currency, a hard currency, or a currency expected to increase in value; the buyer wants to pay in own currency, or a currency expected to decrease in value.

外汇风险即在合同日期和付款日期之间，指定货币的升值或贬值所造成的风险。

冲突：卖方希望以自己的货币、硬通货或预期升值的货币付款；买方希望以自己的货币或预期贬值的货币支付。

4. Political and Legal Risk 政治和法律风险

Political and legal risks are caused by political instability, changes in trade policy, restrictions on trade, changes in monetary policy, riots, etc. which are usually beyond control, but predictable and avoidable to some extent.

Conflicts: The seller usually considers these risks more important than the buyer.

政治和法律风险是由政治不稳定、贸易政策变化、贸易限制、货币政策变化、骚乱等带来的风险，这些风险通常是无法控制的，但在一定程度上是可以预测和避免的。

冲突：卖方通常认为这些风险比买方更重要。

5. Transportation Costs and Risks 运输成本和风险

Transportation costs and risks are caused by the shipping of the goods to remote locations, insurance coverage and timeliness.

Conflicts: The buyer wants the seller to bear all these costs and risks, thinking in terms of landed cost in his own market; the seller wants the buyer to bear these costs and risks and to deliver the goods and transfer ownership at a local port or warehouse.

运输成本和风险是货物运往偏远地区所造成的成本和风险、保险范围和及时性。

冲突：买方考虑到自己市场的到岸成本，希望卖方承担所有这些成本和风险；卖方希望买方承担这些成本和风险，并在当地港口或仓库交货并转让所有权。

6. Payment Method Costs and Risks 付款方式成本和风险

Payment method costs and risks are caused by using different methods of international payment, e.g. late payment costs the seller money, while payment in advance means high costs and risks for the buyer. Different methods of international settlement may mean different bank fee charges and different degrees of risks and security for the buyer and the seller.

Conflicts: both parties want the other to bear more of these costs and risks.

付款方式成本和风险是使用不同的国际付款方式所产生的成本和风险，例如逾期付款会让卖方付出代价，而预付款对买方来说意味着很高的成本和风险。不同的国际结算方式可能意味着不同的银行手续费，以及对买卖双方不同程度的风险和保障。

冲突：双方都希望对方承担更多的这些成本和风险。

Section 4.4　Methods of International Settlement 国际电子结算法

New Words

institution	*n.*	制度；建立；（社会或宗教等）公共机构；习俗
stipulate	*v.*	规定；约定；坚持要求以……为协议条件；保证
remitter	*n.*	出票人；【法】（诉讼案件的）移转；复位
obligation	*n.*	义务；责任；职责；（已承诺的或法律等规定的）义务
invoice	*n.*	【商业】发票；发货单
	v.	开（……）发票
beneficiary	*n.*	受益者；受惠人；遗产继承人
persuade	*v.*	说服；劝说；使信服；使相信
amend	*v.*	改良；订正；改变（行为等）；改过
reimbursement	*n.*	补偿；付还
issuance	*n.*	发行；配给
indication	*n.*	显示；表明；标示；象征

Phrases

remitting bank	汇出行

paying bank	汇入行
mail transfer, M/T	信汇
telegraphic transfer, T/T	电汇
remittance by banker's demand draft, D/D	票汇
cash on delivery, COD	货到付款
payment in advance	预付货款
open account transaction	赊销
international chamber of commerce (ICC)	国际商会
commercial credit	商业信用
involved parties	当事人
principal	委托人
remitting bank	托收银行
collecting bank	代收行
presenting bank	提示行
clean collection	光票托收
documentary collection	跟单托收
documents against payment (D/P)	付款交单
documents against acceptance(D/A)	承兑交单
letter of credit	信用证
bill of exchange	汇票
clean bill	光票
documentary bill	跟单汇票
sight draft	即期汇票
time bill or usance bill	远期汇票
endorsement	背书
cash check	现金支票
transfer check	转账支票
bank guarantee	银行保函
standby letter of credit	备用信用证

Sentences

1. I believe in the institution of marriage.
   我相信婚姻制度。

2. Clifford's only stipulation is that his clients obey his advice.
   克里弗德唯一的规定是他的客户必须听从自己的建议。

3. The remitter is responsible for the remittance charge.
   汇款手续费由汇款人承担。

4. Don't forget to write down the telephone number of the remitter.

请不要忘记写上汇款人的电话号码。

5. If you are selling your property, why not call us for a free valuation without obligation.
如果你打算出售房产，为什么不打电话让我们做个免费的评估呢。

6. We will then send you an invoice for the total course fees.
然后我们将寄给你一张全部课程费用的发票。

7. Prompt payment of the invoice would be appreciated.
见发票即付款，将不胜感激。

8. Who will be the main beneficiary of the cuts in income tax?
削减所得税的主要受益者将是谁？

9. The protagonist Emily is endowed with the images of protector of the tradition, and its convict, beneficiary and revolter.
主人公爱米丽同时具有传统的维护者、囚徒、受益人和反抗者多个身份。

10. To forestall is better than to amend; Prevention is better than cure.
与其补救于已然，不如防患于未然。

11. She is demanding reimbursement for medical and other expenses.
她在要求医疗和其他费用的报销。

12. Further confusion arises because the firm's consolidated invoices are titled reimbursement for the month of ×.
由于公司的合并发票的标题为×月份的偿还额，因此进一步引起了混乱。

13. Overseas listing and bond issuance are no longer the only way for property developers to raise money.
海外上市和债券发行不再是房地产开发商筹措资金的唯一途径。

14. He gave no indication that he was ready to compromise.
他没有流露出打算妥协的迹象。

15. He searched Hill's impassive face for some indication that he understood.
他在希尔没有表情的脸上搜寻着一些他理解的迹象。

16. Cash check is a check that can be redeemed for cash at a bank. The bank generally has to be the account holder's bank.
现金支票是可以在银行兑换现金的支票。银行通常为账户持有人银行。

17. People who ordered were given an option of paying cash on delivery or by credit card.
事先订货的客户可以选择货到付现或者信用卡支付。

Conversations

1. Changing or Refunding

A: Hi, are you there?

B: Hello, at your service.

A: I'd like a refund on this CD.

B: Anything wrong with it?

A: It's scratched, and doesn't play properly.

B: I'm sorry about that. But I'm afraid you can't.

A: Why is that? Don't all the goods in your store be returned and exchanged within one month?

B: That's true, but not albums and magazines. These items are not refundable once they are unsealed.

A: Is that so?

B: Yes, sorry again.

1. 退换货

A：你好，在线吗？

B：您好，有何吩咐？

A：这张 CD 我想退换。

B：有什么问题吗？

A：唱片上有很多刮痕，不能正常播放。

B：对此我很抱歉，但您恐怕不能退换。

A：为什么？你们店内的商品不都是一个月内无条件退换吗？

B：是这样的没错，不过不包括唱片和杂志，这些商品一旦拆封概不退换。

A：是这样吗？

B：是的，再次抱歉。

2. Procedure for Refund

A: Hi.

B: Hello, may I help you?

A: Can I have my money back on this skirt?

B: What's wrong?

A: Yes, it is defective. There's a hole in it.

B: Can you take a photo of the item's detail and send it to me?

A: OK, hold on.

B: Oh, I see. I'm very sorry about that. You can change it for another one if you prefer.

A: No, I'd like a refund.

B: OK. May I have your order number, please?

A: The order number is 4165876148.

B: OK, you can do the return application in the backstage.

A: I never return the goods on Amazon. I don't know how to apply for it.

B: First of all, select the order that needs to be returned in "Your Orders" and click the "Exchange or return items" button. Select the quantity and return reason, and confirm the return method delivery address, then follow the steps.

A: Okay, thank you. That's very kind of you.

2. 退款程序

A：你好。

B：您好，有什么可以帮您的吗?

A：这条裙子我能退款吗?

B：怎么了?

A：当然，这条裙子有瑕疵，有个地方破洞了。

B：您能拍一张商品的局部照发给我吗?

A：好的，请稍等。

B：噢，我看到了。实在很抱歉，如果您愿意的话，可以换另外一件。

A：不用了，我想退款。

B：好的，请告诉我您的订单号?

A：订单号是 4165876148。

B：好的，您在后台进行退货申请就可以了。

A：我没有在亚马逊上退过货，我不知道怎么申请。

B：首先，您要在"我的订单"中选择需要退货的订单，单击"需要退换货"按钮。选择退货商品的数量以及退货原因，确认退货方式及上门取货地址，然后按步骤操作即可。

A：好的，谢谢，你真是太好了。

Text

4.4.1　Remittance 汇付结算

1. Definition of Remittance 汇付的定义

Remittance refers to that the payer makes payment to the payee through a bank or other institutions.

For the remittance in the international trade, the buyer makes payment to the seller by bank according to the conditions and the payment time stipulated in the contract.

汇付是指付款人主动通过银行或其他途径将款项汇交收款人。

国际贸易货款采用汇付，一般是由买方按合同约定条件（如收到单据或货物）和时间，将货款通过银行汇交给卖方。

2. The Involved Parties in the Remittance 汇付当事人

Remitter is the party who makes payment by remittance. Usually the importer or the buyer is the remitter.

Payee or beneficiary is the party who receives payment. Usually the seller is the payee or beneficiary.

Remitting bank is the bank which issues a remittance instruction at the request of the buyer. Usually, the remitting bank is the bank in the importer's country.

Paying bank is the bank that transfers the money to the account of the seller following the instruction of the remitting bank. The paying bank is usually the bank in the exporter's country.

The application form of remittance is a contract concluded between the buyer and the remitting bank, and the paying bank is the agency bank of the remitting bank, committed to the obligation of making payment.

汇款人，即汇出款项的人，一般为进口人、买方。

收款人，即收取款项的人，在进出口业务中一般为卖方。

汇出行，即接受买方的委托汇出款项的银行，通常是进口地银行。

汇入行，即解付汇款的银行，一般是出口地银行。

汇款申请书是买方与汇出行之间的一项合同，汇出行与汇入行是代理合同，承担解付汇款的义务。

3. The Classification of Remittance 汇付的种类

1) Mail Transfer, M/T 信汇

Mail transfer refers to that the remitting bank sends a remittance instruction letter by mail to the paying bank at the request of the payer, authorizing the paying bank to make payment of a sum of money to the payee.

Advantages: Low cost;

Disadvantages: Long time for receiving the payment.

信汇是指汇出行应汇款人申请，将信汇委托书寄给汇入行，授权解付一定金额给收款人。

优点：费用低廉；

缺点：收取汇款时间长。

2) Telegraphic Transfer, T/T 电汇

Telegraphic transfer refers to that the remitting bank sends the remittance instruction to the paying bank by telex, tele-transmission or SWIFT at the request of the payer.

Advantages: Speedy, beneficial to the seller's capital running as it can receive the payment in a short time.

Disadvantages: High cost.

电汇指汇出行应汇款人的申请，拍发加押电报或电传或 SWIFT 给另一个国家的分行或代理行（汇入行），指示解付一定金额给收款人的付款方式。

优点：其具有速度快，卖方能尽快收到货款，有利于卖方资金周转的特点。

缺点：费用高。

3) Remittance by Banker's Demand Draft, D/D 票汇

The remitting bank draws a banker's sight draft on its branch bank or agency bank on behalf of the payer after the payer pays some charges for the draft, and sends the draft to the payee; the payee gets the payment from the paying bank with draft.

票汇是汇出行应汇款人的申请，在汇款人向汇出行交款并支付一定费用的条件下，代替汇款人开立的以其分行或代理行为解付行，支付一定金额给收款人的银行即期汇票，寄交收款人，由收款人凭以向汇入行取款。

4. The Usage of the Remittance 汇付的应用

The remittance can be divided into the following two kinds:

1) Cash on Delivery

The buyer will make payment on receipt of the documents or goods from the seller.

Actually, it is a kind of credit offered by the seller to the buyer as well as a kind of open account transaction. For the seller, the risk of it is the greatest. It totally depends on the credit of the buyer whether the seller will be paid after the delivery of the goods.

2) Payment in Advance

The buyer will make payment prior to the seller's delivery of the goods. In this way, the buyer offers credit to the seller while the buyer takes some risks. It is sometimes called cash with order. The buyer will make payment to the seller by T/T or M/T in a few days after the conclusion of the contract.

汇付还可分为货到付款和预付货款两种：

1）货到付款

买方在收到卖方的单据或货物后再付款。实际上是卖方向买方提供的一种信用，也是一种赊销，对卖方来说风险最大，卖方交货以后，能否得到偿付，全凭买方个人信用，也称为商业信用。

2）预付货款

在卖方还未生产交货时，买方预付货款，这种方式买方向卖方提供了信用，买方存在一定的风险，这种做法有的叫作随订单付现。或者在合同签订后若干天，买方将货款电汇或信汇给卖方。

4.4.2　Collection 托收结算

1. Definition of Collection 托收的概念

Collection is an arrangement whereby the seller draws a draft on the buyer and authorizes its bank to collect.

The definition of the International Chamber of Commerce (ICC) URC 522: The collection is the handling by banks, on instructions received, of documents (financial documents and/or commercial documents), in order to: (a) obtain acceptance and/or, as the case may be, payment, or (b) deliver commercial documents against acceptance and /or, as the case may be, against payment, or (c) deliver documents on other terms and conditions.

托收是指债权人（卖方）出具汇票，委托银行向债务人（买方）收取货款的一种支付方式。

国际商会《托收统一规则》522 号给托收下的定义：托收是指由接到托收指示的银行根据所收到的指示处理金融单据以便取得付款或承兑，或凭付款或承兑交出商业单据，或凭其他条款或条件交出单据。

2. Nature of Collection 托收的性质

Collection is a kind of commercial credit, offered to each other by firms and merchants. The collection bank acts only as collector of funds on behalf of the seller and is not committed to the obligation whether the buyer makes payment or not. It is dependent on the commercial credit of the buyer if the seller will be paid after the delivery of goods. Therefore, a collection transaction puts the seller under a great risk.

托收是一种商业信用，也就是商人之间互相提供的信用。通过银行办理托收，银行属于代办性质，对买方是否付款不承担责任。卖方交货后能否收回货款，完全要看买方个人的信誉。托收虽然通过银行办理，但银行只是代收代付，并不承担付款责任，所以托收对卖方仍然存在较大的风险。

3. Procedure of Documentary Collection 托收的程序

The payment method agreed in the sales contract is by collection, in which the seller signs a commission contract with the local bank of the seller's country in form of collection authorization letter, authorizing the local bank of the seller's country (collection bank) to collect the payment through the correspondent bank of it in the buyer's country, and then deliver the shipping documents to the buyer.

在买卖合同中规定的支付方式用托收，卖方与所在地银行以托收委托书的形式签订委托代理合同，约定由当地银行（托收行）通过其在进口国的往来银行（代收行）向买方收取货款，然后交单。

4. The Involved Parties in Collection 托收方式的当事人

1) Principal 委托人

Usually, the principal is the seller.

也称本人，通常是卖方。

2) Remitting Bank 托收银行

The bank in the exporter/country is authorized by the principal to effect the collection on behalf of the principal.

出口地银行（委托行）接受委托人委托，办理托收业务的银行。

3) Collecting Bank 代收行

The bank in the importer's country who receives the authorization from the remitting bank to collect the funds from the payer.

进口地银行，买方所在国银行。接受托收行的委托，向付款人收取货款。

4) Payer 付款人

Namely the buyer, the drawee.

即买方，受票人。

5) Presenting Bank 提示行

The bank who presents the shipment documents with draft to the payer.

向付款人做出提示汇票和单据的银行。

5. The Classification of Collection 托收的种类

Basically there are two types of collection: clean collection and documentary collection.

托收一般有两种类型：光票托收和跟单托收。

1) Clean Collection 光票托收

Clean collection: Clean collection means collection on financial instruments without being accompanied by commercial documents, such as invoice, bill of lading, insurance policy, etc.

Under clean collection, only the draft, if necessary, an instruction letter is sent out for collection. The documents are sent directly by the seller to the buyer or the seller's foreign agent. The seller is, in fact, shipping on open account terms. Clean collection may be used when the goods are shipped to overseas agent on consignment. A clean collection may represent an underlying trade transaction or a purely financial transaction involving no movement of merchandise and, therefore, no documents.

光票托收是指只使用金融工具，而不随附诸如发票、提单、保险单等商业单据的托收。

在光票托收下，仅寄汇票，如果有必要的话，加一封托收函进行托收。单据由卖方直接寄给买方，或卖方的国外代理。实际上，卖方是在按赊销条件交货。光票托收可能在货物按寄售条件运送给海外代理时使用。光票托收可能代表基础贸易交易或不涉及货物，因此也不涉及单据的纯粹的金融交易。

2) Documentary Collection 跟单托收

Documentary collection: A documentary collection is so-called because the seller requires the remitting bank to forward commercial documents(or both the commercial documents and financial documents)relating to the transaction to the buyer via collecting bank. In terms of release of documents, documentary collection can be subdivided into three categories: Documents against payment (D/P)and documents against acceptance(D/A).

之所以称跟单托收，是因为卖方要求汇出行将商业单据（或者交易相关的商业单据和金融单据）通过代收行寄给买方。根据交单条件不同，跟单托收分为两类：付款交单和承兑交单。

4.4.3   Letter of Credit(L/C) 信用证结算

1. Definition of Letter of Credit 信用证的定义

A letter of credit is a written undertaking by a bank (issuing bank) given to the seller (beneficiary) at the request, and in accordance with the buyer's (applicant) instructions to effect payment — that is by making a payment, or by accepting or negotiating bills of exchange (drafts)— up to a stated amount, against stipulated documents and within a prescribed time limit.

The UCP 600 explicitly defines a credit as "any arrangement, however named or described, that is irrevocable and thereby constitutes a definite undertaking of the issuing bank to honour a complying presentation". In simple terms, a letter of credit is a conditional undertaking of payments by a bank.

信用证是一家银行（开证行）应买方的请求开给卖方（受益人）的。其通过书面承诺按买方（申请人）指示进行支付，即通过付款、承兑或议付汇票方式，凭规定单据，在规定时间支付规定金额。

UCP600 定义信用证为"无论如何命名或描述，是不可撤销的，因此构成了开证行承付相符交单的确定保证"。简言之，信用证是银行有条件的付款承诺。

2. The Involved Parties in the Credit 信用证的当事人

1) Applicant or Opener 申请人或开证人

The applicant or the opener is the party (usually the buyer) who fills out and signs an application form, requesting the bank to issue a letter of credit in favor of a seller abroad. He is in duty bound to ensure that the credit is issued in compliance with the terms and conditions laid down in the sales contract within a proper or reasonable time. After the payment is effected by the issuing bank, the opener must pay the bank against correct shipping documents or refuse to pay if the documents are not in order.

申请人或开证人是填写并签署开证申请书，要求银行开立以国外卖方为受益人的信用证的当事人（通常为买方）。他有责任保证信用证在合适时间或合理时间内，按照销售合同条款开立。开证行付款之后，开证人在货运单据符合要求的情况下必须向银行付款。如果单据有差错，则可以拒付。

2) Beneficiary 受益人

The beneficiary is the party(usually the seller) in whose favor the credit is issued. If there is a discrepancy between the credit opened and the sales contract, the beneficiary may have the option to accept it as it stands or persuade the opener to have it amended so as to be in line with the contract. Once the beneficiary accepts the credit, he must deliver the goods in compliance with the contract. Then he tenders to his bank or any other bank all the relevant documents as stipulated in the credit. He is responsible not only for the correctness and genuineness of the documents but also for the goods which must conform with the contract. If the issuing bank does not pay or is in liquidation, the beneficiary can claim from the opener for the payment.

受益人是指以其为受益人开立信用证的一方（通常为卖方）。如果所开信用证与合同不符，受益人可以接受不符信用证，也可要求开证人修改，使信用证与合同一致。受益人一旦接受信用证，就必须按照信用证规定交货。然后，向其银行或任何其他银行交付信用证规定的所有相关单据。他不仅要承担单据正确与真实的责任，还有承担货物与合同相符的责任。如果开证行不付款或在停业清算中，受益人可要求开证人付款。

3) Issuing Bank or Opening Bank 开证行

The issuing bank is one which issues a letter of credit at the request of an applicant. An issuing bank is irrevocably bound to honour as of the time it issues the credit. If the applicant fails to pay after the issuing bank makes payment, the letter has the right to sell the goods and claim from the applicant if the proceeds are not sufficient. It is primarily liable to the beneficiary, no matter whether the applicant is in default or not.

开证行是应申请人的请求开立信用证的银行。开证行自开立信用证时起就不可撤销地受到承兑的约束。如果开证行付款之后，申请人没有向开证行付款，那么后者有权出售货物，并向申请人追索款额不足部分。不管申请人是否拖欠债款，开证行都对受益人负主债务责任。

4) Advising Bank 通知行

The advising bank is one which advises the credit to the beneficiary in accordance with stipulations on the credit. It is located in the place of the beneficiary and is usually the issuing bank's branch or correspondent acting as an agent of the opening bank in accordance with the instructions given.

通知行是按信用证规定，将信用证通知给受益人的当事人。它位于受益人所在地，且通常是开证行的分支机构或代理，作为开证行的代理，按照指示行事。

5) Negotiating Bank 议付行

A negotiating bank is the nominated bank who purchases drafts (drawn on a bank other than the nominated) and/or documents by advancing or agreeing to advance funds to the beneficiary on or before the banking day on which reimbursement is due to the nominated bank.

议付行是在偿付日当天或之前的银行工作日，垫付或同意垫付资金，购买受益人的（以指定银行之外的银行为付款人的）汇票和/或单据的指定银行。

This definition emphasizes that negotiation relates to the purchase of a draft drawn on a bank other than the nominated bank. If it was drawn on the nominated bank, it would be a payment or acceptance credit. Further, negotiation is either the advancing or agreeing to advance funds to a beneficiary. Use of agreeing to advance allows the bank and beneficiary to determine the terms under which negotiation will occur. These terms would include when, for how much and whether or not the advance is with or without recourse.

该定义强调，议付与购买以指定银行之外的银行为付款人的汇票相关。如果汇票以指定银行为付款人，信用证则为付款或承兑信用证。而且，议付既可以向受益人垫付资金，也可以同意向受益人垫付资金。同意垫付资金，等于允许银行与受益人决定议付条件。这些条件包括何时、怎样以及是否带有追索。

The negotiating bank naturally becomes the holder in due course of the draft after its negotiation. And so it normally has a right of recourse against the drawer, namely the beneficiary in the credit, in the event of dishonour by the issuing bank.

议付行在议付之后，自然就成为汇票的持有人。因此，在开证行拒付时，议付行对出票人，即信用证的受益人有追索的权利。

6) Paying Bank 付款行

The paying bank is always the drawee of a draft stipulated in the credit. Or we may say it is a bank nominated by the issuing bank to make payment under the credit. Sometimes the paying bank is the issuing bank itself.

付款行总是信用证上规定的汇票的付款人。或者我们可以说，它是开证行指定的信用证下进行付款的人。有时，付款行是开证行。

7) Reimbursing Bank 偿付行

Reimbursing bank is the agent of the issuing bank. It honours the reimbursement claims of a paying bank or an accepting bank or a negotiating bank under a particular credit in accordance with the instructions or authorization given by the issuing bank.

偿付行是开证行的代理。偿付行按照开证行的指示或授权，对特定信用证下付款行或承兑行或议付行的索偿进行兑用。

3. Procedure for Letter of Credit Operations 信用证业务程序

The documentary credit procedure involves three basic groupings of steps in the procedure: issuance — amendment — utilization.

跟单信用证程序包括三个基本步骤组：开证——修改——使用。

1) Issuance 开证

Issuance describes the process of the buyer's applying for and opening a documentary credit at the issuing bank and the opening bank's formal notification of the seller through the advising bank.

The procedures of issuance are as follows: Contract to settlement by a letter of credit — contract to settlement by a letter of credit — opening of a letter of credit — advising the beneficiary.

开证描述的是买方向开证行申请开立信用证，以及开证行通过通知行通知信用证的过程。

开证的步骤如下：采用信用证支付的合同——请求开立信用证——开证——通知受益人。

2) Amendment 改证

Amendment describes the process whereby the terms and conditions of a documentary credit may be modified after the credit has been issued.

改证是指信用证开立之后，对其中的条款进行修改的过程。

3) Utilization 用证

Utilization describes the procedure for the seller's shipping of the goods, the transfer of documents from the seller to the buyer through the banks, and the transfer of payment from the buyer to the seller through the banks.

用证是指卖方装运货物，单据通过银行从卖方转移给买方，货款通过银行从卖方转移给买方的程序。

4. Contents of a Letter of Credit（L/C）信用证的内容

At present, most L/C are opened by telecommunication. Although the forms are different, their contents are, in the main, the same. The following details are to be found on all credits.

(1) Name and address of the issuing bank.

(2) Type of the credit. Every credit must indicate whether it is revocable or irrevocable. Whether it is a transferable credit or a confirmed credit must also be indicated in the credit.

(3) Name and address of the beneficiary.

(4) Amount of the credit and its currency.

(5) Expiry date of the credit and its place to be expired.

(6) Name and address of the applicant.

(7) L/C number and date of issue.

(8) Drawer and drawee as well as tenor of the draft. The drawer is always the beneficiary, the drawee may be the issuing bank or any other bank.

(9) Full details of the goods.

(10) Full details of the documents to be presented.

(11) Partial shipment permitted/not permitted.

(12) Transshipment allowed/not allowed.

(13) Port of shipment and port of discharge.

(14) Latest date for shipment, and the latest date for presentation of documents.

(15) Instructions to the advising bank, negotiating bank or paying bank.

(16) Other special terms and conditions.

(17) The undertaking clause of the issuing bank.

(18) The indication "This credit is subject to the Uniform Customs and Practice for Documentary Credit (2007 revision), International Chamber of Commerce Publication No. 600".

目前，大部分信用证使用电信方式开立。虽然信用证开立形式各异，但内容总体相同。所有信用证都有以下几项内容：

（1）开证行的名称与地址。

（2）信用证的种类。每个信用证都必须表明是可撤销的，还是不可撤销的。信用证还需表明是可转让信用证还是保兑信用证。

（3）受益人名称与地址。

（4）信用证金额与货币。

（5）信用证的有效期及到期地。

（6）申请人的名称与地址。

（7）信用证号码与开证日期。

（8）汇票的出票人、受票人及汇票期限。出票人总是受益人，受票人可能是开证行或其他任何银行。

（9）货物详情。

（10）应交单据详情。

（11）是否允许分批装运。

（12）是否允许转运。

（13）装运港和卸货港。

（14）最迟装运和交单时间。

（15）给通知行、议付行或付款行的指示。

（16）其他特殊条款。

（17）开证行责任条款。

（18）"本信用证受《跟单信用证统一惯例》（2007 年版）的约束，国际商会第 600 号出版物开立"字样。

5. Features of Letter of Credit Business 信用证的特征

The characteristics of the letter of credit can be summarized as：

(1) It is a kind of bank credit.

(2) It is a self sufficient document.

(3) It is a document deal.

信用证的特点可以概括为：

（1）是一种银行信用证；

（2）是自给自足的单据；

（3）是单据交易。

6. Classification of Letters of Credit 信用证的分类

Based on different criteria, L/C can be classified into different types.

根据不同的标准，信用证可以分为不同的类型：

(1) According to whether the draft is accompanied with the shipping documents, L/C is divided into two kinds: documentary L/C and clean L/C. A documentary L/C means that the bill of exchange should be accompanied with shipping documents. A clean L/C means that the bill of exchange isn't accompanied with shipping documents.

根据汇票是否附带运输单据，信用证分为跟单信用证和光票信用证。跟单信用证是指汇票必须附带运输单据。光票信用证意味着汇票不附带装运单据。

(2) According to the responsibilities that the issuing bank bears, L/C is classified into revocable L/C and irrevocable L/C. Revocable L/C means that the opening bank may amend or revoke the credit before negotiation, acceptance or payment without agreement of the beneficiary. Once the L/C is opened, without the agreement of the beneficiary, the opening bank can't amend or revoke the L/C within its validity. That is called an irrevocable L/C. As long as the beneficiary provides the documents in accordance with the stipulation in the L/C, the opening bank shall perform its duty of payment.

根据开证行承担的责任，信用证分为可撤销信用证和不可撤销信用证。可撤销信用证是指开证行在议付、承兑或付款前，无须受益人同意即可修改或撤销的信用证。信用证一经开立，未经受益人同意，开证行不能在有效期内修改或撤销的就是不可撤销的信用证，只要受益人按照信用证的规定提供单据，开证行就应履行其付款义务。

(3) According to whether the bank confirms, L/C is classified into Confirmed L/C and Unconfirmed L/C. Confirmed L/C means a second guarantee is added to the document by another bank. While unconfirmed L/C means the issuing bank bears the guarantee alone.

根据银行是否保兑，信用证分为保兑信用证和未保兑信用证，保兑信用证是指由另一家银行在单据上增加第二个保函。而未保兑信用证则由开证行单独担保。

(4) According to the time of payment, L/C is divided into sight L/C and deferred L/C. Sight credit means payment is due upon presentation of all documents request in the L/C within the

required timeframe. Deferred L/C is used to provide assurance that payment will be made after a certain period of time.

按付款时间不同，信用证分为即期信用证和延期信用证。即期信用证是指在规定的期限内出示信用证上要求的所有单据即可付款的信用证。延期信用证是用来保证一定时间后付款的信用证。

(5) According to whether the L/C can be transferred, it is classified into transferable L/C and non-transferable L/C. Transferable L/C means that the beneficiary can assign part or whole of the L/C amount to a third-party called second beneficiary. While the non-transferable L/C can not be transferred.

按信用证能否转让分为可转让信用证和不可转让信用证。可转让信用证是指受益人可以将信用证的部分或全部金额转让给称为第二受益人的第三方。而不可转让信用证则不能转让。

(6) According to the way of payment, L/C is divided into sight payment credit, acceptance L/C, negotiation L/C and deferred payment L/C.

信用证按付款方式分为即期付款信用证、承兑信用证、议付信用证和延期付款信用证。

① Acceptance L/C. This kind of L/C is accepted by the bank. When the beneficiary presents the time draft to the bank, the bank will accept it and pay the price on the due date.

承兑信用证。银行承兑这种信用证。当受益人向银行出示远期汇票时，银行将承兑，并在到期日付款。

② Negotiation L/C. The opening bank invites other banks to buy draft and/or documents. This kind of L/C allows the beneficiary to negotiate the purchase price from an indicated bank or any bank.

议付信用证。开证行邀请其他银行购买汇票和/或单据。这种信用证允许受益人向指定银行或任何银行议付购买价格。

4.4.4　Negotiable Instruments 票据结算

1. Bill of Exchange 汇票

1) Definition of Bill of Exchange 汇票的定义

A bill of exchange, also called draft or postal order, is defined as "an unconditional order in writing, addressed by one person to another, signed by the person giving it, requiring the person to whom it is addressed to pay on demand, or at a fixed or determinable future time, a sum certain in money, to, or to the order of a specified person, or to bearer". The operation process of draft includes drawing, presentation, acceptance, payment, endorsement, dishonor and recourse. Drafts are negotiable instrument and may be sold.

汇票（bill of exchange/draft/postal order），被定义为"一种无条件的书面命令"。汇票是一个人向另一个人签发的、要求见票时或在将来的固定时间或可以确定的时间、对某人或其指定的人或持票人支付一定金额的无条件的支付命令。汇票的操作流程包括出票、提示、承兑、付款、背书、退票和追索权。汇票是可转让的票据，可以出售。

2) Parties Involved in Bill of Exchange 汇票当事人

Generally, a bill of exchange involves three parties:

(1) Drawer. The person who writes the order and gives directions to the person to make a specific payment of money. He is usually the exporter or his banker in import and export trade; usually, he is also a creditor of the drawee.

出票人。出票人是开立票据并将其交付给他人的法人、其他组织或者个人，出票人对收款人及正当持票人承担票据在提示付款或承兑时必须付款或者承兑的保证责任。

(2) Drawee. The person to whom the order is addressed and who is to pay the money. He is usually the importer or the appointed bank under a letter of credit in import and export trade. In addition, when a time bill has been accepted by the drawee, he becomes an acceptor who is the same person as the drawee. The drawer and the acceptor must be different persons.

付款人。付款人，或称受票人，是指出票人或者出票人在汇票上记载的委托其支付票据金额的人。付款人并非因出票人的支付委托即成为当然的票据债务人，而是必须经其承兑，才能成为票据债务人，付款人一经承兑后，即成为承兑人，是汇票的主债务人。

(3) Payee. One who receives a payment, through cash, check, money order and promissory note.

受款人。受款人，又称汇票的抬头，受领汇票所规定金额的人，进出口业务中可以是出口人、卖方、指定的银行或正当持票人。

3) Classification of Bill of Exchange 汇票的种类

(1) According to the different drawers.

按出票人不同来分。

(a) Banker's draft. The draft is drawn by a bank, and the drawer is a bank. A banker's draft is sent to payee by remitter, with which the payee can exchange the money from the payer (the bank).

The characteristics of banker's draft: both the drawer and the drawee are banks.

银行汇票是一种汇款凭证，由银行签发，出票人为银行，通常交由汇款人寄给受款人或亲自交给受款人，凭票向付款人（银行）兑取票款。

银行汇票的特点：出票人和受票人都是银行。

(b) Commercial draft. The draft is made out by the seller of one country (exporter) and presented to the importer or the payment bank. Usually, the draft is presented to the importer or the payment bank (L/C opening bank) through the bank in the exporter/place or the correspondent bank of it in the importer's place.

The characteristics of commercial draft: The drawer is a firm or an individual, the payer (the drawee) is a firm, an individual, or a bank.

商业汇票由一国的卖方（出口人）向另一国的进口人或付款银行开出，通常通过出口地银行或其在进口地的代理行向进口人或其委托银行（L/C 开证行）收取票款。

商业汇票的特点：出票人是商号或个人，付款人（即受票人）可以是商号、个人，也可以是银行。

(2) According to the documents accompanied.

按流通转让时有无随附单据来分。

(a) Clean Bill. Without shipment documents to accompany, the banker's draft is usually a clean bill.

不附带货运单据的汇票，银行汇票多为光票。

(b) Documentary bill. The draft is accompanied with shipment documents, which is guaranteed by exporter's credit as well as the goods. The commercial draft is usually a documentary bill.

随附货运单据的汇票。这种汇票既有人的信用担保，又有物的担保。商业汇票多为跟单汇票。

(3) According to payment time.

按付款时间不同来分。

(a) Sight draft. To make payment at sight of the draft.

即期汇票，见票提示即付。

(b) Time bill or usance bill. To make payment within x x days or on a fixed date.

远期汇票。在一定期限或特定日期付款的汇票。

4) Procedure of Using a Bill of Exchange 使用汇票的程序

(1) Issuance. It is made out in written form. The drawer fills in the contents including the payer's name, payment sum, payment time, place, payee's name etc., and signs its name. The issuance is regarded to be fulfilled only after the bill is sent to the drawee.

出票。做成书面汇票，出票人在汇票上填写付款人、付款金额、付款日期、地点、受款人等项目，最后由出票人签字。将汇票交给受票人，只有经交付才算完成出票行为。

(2) Presentation. The holder of the draft presents the draft to the drawee, asking for the acceptance or payment.

持票人将汇票提交受票人，要求承兑或付款的行为。

(a) Presentation for payment. The draft holder presents the draft to the payer asking for the sight payment.

付款提示。持票人向付款人提交汇票，要求付款（即期付款）。

(b) Presentation for acceptance. The draft holder presents the draft to the payer asking for the acceptance at sight of the draft and payment on the maturity time.

承兑提示。持票人向付款人提交汇票，付款人见票后办理承兑手续，到期时付款。

(3) Acceptance. It is a promise made by the payer that it will make payment against a time draft.

The payer writes the word "acceptance" on the bill remarking the acceptance date and affixes its signature, then returns the bill to the draft holder. The payer is regarded as the acceptor after making acceptance for the draft. The first debtor of the draft is the drawer before making acceptance, and it changes into the payer after making acceptance while the drawer becomes the second debtor. Before the payer's acceptance, all the bearers are allowed to recourse to the drawer as the draft is transferable.

承兑是指远期汇票的付款人对远期汇票表示承担到期付款责任的行为。

付款人在汇票上写明"承兑"字样，注明承兑日期，并签字，交还持票人。付款人对汇票做出承兑，即成为承兑人。汇票在付款人承兑前，主债务人是出票人，在付款人承兑后，主债务人是付款人。出票人成为第二债务人。因为出票人可转让其汇票，在付款人承兑前，所有后手都可以向出票人追索。

(4) Payment. For the sight payment, the payer shall make payment against the presentation of the draft; for the time bill, the payer makes payment on the maturity time after the acceptance and all the debts on the draft come to an end after the payment.

对即期汇票，在持票人提示汇票时，付款人即应付款；对远期汇票，付款人经过承兑后，在汇票到期日付款，付款后，汇票的一切债务即告终止。

(5) Endorsement. The endorsement of the draft includes two points: (a) to make endorsement on the overleaf of the draft; (b) to transfer the bill to the endorsee. These two points are both necessary for the fulfillment of the endorsement.

In international market, the draft is a kind of transfer instrument, which is negotiable and transferable in the bill market. The endorsement is one legal procedure of transferring the bill, that is to say, the holder of draft signs its name on the back of the bill or adding the name of the bearer (endorsee), and then transfers the draft to the bearer. After the endorsement, the claim for the payment is transferred to the bearer, too.

The draft can be transferred again and again after endorsements. For the endorsee, all the endorsers and the drawers are its remote holders; for the endorser, all the bearers after its endorsement and transferring are its subsequent parties. The remote holders are committed to the guaranty responsibility of the payment for the subsequent party.

汇票的背书包括两个方面：①在汇票背面背书；②交付给被背书人，只有通过交付，才算完成背书。

在国际市场上，汇票是一种流通工具，可以在票据市场上流通转让。背书是转让汇票权利的一种法定手续，就是由汇票持有人在汇票背面签上自己的名字，或再加上受让人（被背书人）的名字，并把汇票交给受让人的行为。经背书后，汇票的收款权利便转移给受让人。

汇票可以经过背书不断转让下去。对于受让人来说，所有在他以前的背书人以及原出票人都是他的前手；对于出让人来说，所有在他让与以后的受让人都是他的后手。前手对于后手负有担保汇票必被偿付的责任。

(6) Discounting. Discounting means that the usance bill after the acceptance but undue is sold to a bank or a discounting house for the immediate payment with the discounting interest deducted from the payment sum based on a certain discounting rate.

In the international market, in order to receive the payment immediately, a time bill holder may transfer the draft to the others by making endorsement before the bill is mature.

贴现是指远期汇票承兑后，尚未到期，由银行或贴现公司从票面金额中扣除按一定贴现率计算的贴现息后，将余款付给持票人的行为。

在国际市场上，一张远期汇票的持票人如想在付款人付款前取得票款，可以通过背书转让汇票，即可将汇票进行贴现。

(7) Dishonor. It is called the dishonor by non-acceptance or by non-payment in case that the bill is not accepted or not paid when the bill is presented by the bill holder for the acceptance. Dishonor also happens when the payer returns the bill, keeps away from the bill, dies, or is bankrupted.

The draft holder has the right of recourse in case that the draft is not accepted when it is presented within a reasonable time or it is not paid on the maturity date. The bill holder has the right to claim for the shipment documents or payment against the endorser and drawer.

持票人提示汇票要求承兑时，遭到拒绝承兑，或遭到拒绝付款，均称为拒付。付款人避不见票、死亡、破产，也称拒付。

汇票的持票人有权对合理期限内提示的而遭到拒付的汇票或未在到期日付款的汇票行使追索权，持票人有权对运输单据或付款向背书人和开票人进行索偿。

(8) Right of recourse. Upon the dishonor, the bill holder has the right to claim for the settlement of the payment and the relevant charges against the prior endorser (or the drawer).

To exercise the right of recourse, the bill holder shall present the protest (or certificate of dishonor). The protest is an official document made by the local notary public, bank, chamber of commerce or court testifying that the draft has been dishonored. It is the legal proof with which the bill holder can take the right of the recourse against the prior endorser. If the dishonored bill has been accepted, the bill holder can go to court claiming for the payment against the acceptor.

汇票遭到拒付，持票人对其前手（即背书人，出票人）有请求其偿还汇票金额及费用的权利。

在行使追索权时，持票人必须提供拒绝证书。拒绝证书可以由付款地法定公证人，如银行、商会、法院，做出证明拒付事实的文件，这是持票人凭以向其"前手"进行追索的法律依据。如被拒付的汇票已经承兑，出票人可凭以向法院起诉，要求承兑人付款。

2. Promissory Note 本票

1) Definition of Promissory Note 定义

The promissory note is the note issued by the drawer, promising to make unconditionally a definite sum of money to the payee or the note holder at sight of the note. It is stipulated in Negotiable Instruments Law of the People s Republic of China that the promissory note is named as the bank promissory note, issued and signed by the central bank of China or other financial institutions. There are only bank promissory notes in China but no commercial promissory notes.

The key elements in the promissory note are as follows: The words of "promissory note", unconditional payment promise, a sum certain in money, the name of payee, the issuance date, and the signature of the drawer.

本票的定义：本票是出票人签发的、承诺自己在见票时无条件支付确定的金额给收款人或者持票人的票据。《中华人民共和国票据法》规定，本票称为银行本票，由中国人民银行或其他金融机构签发。我国只有银行本票，没有商业本票。

我国《票据法》规定的本票要项包括：表明"本票"字样，无条件支付承诺，确定金额，收款人名称，出票日期，和出票人签字。

2) Classification of the Promissory Notes 本票的种类

(1) Commercial promissory notes. Commercial promissory notes are also called general promissory notes, drawn by the commercial firms. The general promissory notes are divided into sight promissory note and time promissory note.

商业本票。商业本票也称为一般本票，由工商企业签发。一般本票可分为即期一般本票与远期一般本票。

(2) Bank promissory notes. Bank promissory notes are issued and signed by banks. The bank promissory notes are sight, which are mostly adopted in international trade.

银行本票。银行本票是由银行签发的本票。银行本票都是即期的。国际贸易中使用的本票大都是银行本票。

3) Involved Parties to the Promissory Notes 本票当事人

There are two parties usually: The drawer and the payee. The payer of the promissory note is the drawer himself. The time promissory notes needn't the acceptance. Some banks issue the promissory note which is at sight, without stating the payee or the words of "to the order". The kind of promissory note is equal to the currency circulated in the market.

本票相关方主要有两个：出票人和收款人。本票的付款人即出票人本人。远期本票不需承兑。

有的银行发行见票即付、不记载收款人的本票或来人抬头的本票，这种本票相当于纸币在市场上流通。

4) The Differences of the Promissory Note and the Bill of Exchange 本票与汇票的区别

(1) The promissory note is a promise made by the drawer to make payment to the note holder. The B/E is an order made by one party to the other party requiring it to make payment.

(2) There are only two parties in a promissory note, but three parties in a B/E.

(3) The drawer of a promissory note is the payer, and a time promissory note needn't the acceptance. The drawee of a B/E is the payer.

(4) In whatever situation, for a promissory note, the drawer is the first debtor. For a B/E, drawer is the first debtor before the bill is accepted, and the acceptor becomes the first debtor after the acceptance and the drawer turns into the second debtor.

(5) The promissory note is made out in only one original. The B/E is made out in duplicate.

（1）本票是出票人承诺自己向持票人付款，汇票是一个人向另一个人发出的支付命令。

（2）本票只有两个当事人，汇票有三个当事人。

（3）本票的出票人即付款人，远期本票不需承兑；汇票的受票人是付款人。

（4）本票在任何情况下，出票人都是主债务人；汇票在付款人承兑前，出票人是它的主债务人，在承兑后，承兑人是主债务人，出票人成为次债务人。

（5）本票只能开出一张，汇票可开出两张。

3. Check 支票

1) Definition of Check 支票的定义

In Negotiable Instruments Law of the People s Republic of China, a check means a bill issued and signed by the drawer, appointing the bank or other financial institutes to make payment of a sum certain in money unconditionally to the payee or the check holder.

The key elements in a check according to Negotiable Instruments Law of the People's Republic of China are as follows: the words of "check" or "cheque", unconditional payment promise, a sum certain in money, the name of payer, the issuance date, and the signature of the drawer. The check without any one of stipulated elements is regarded as invalid.

《中华人民共和国票据法》规定：支票是出票人签发的，委托办理支票存款业务的银行或者其他金融机构在见票时无条件支付确定的金额给收款人或者持票人的票据。

我国《票据法》规定的支票要项包括：表明"支票"的字样；无条件支付的委托；确定的金额；付款人名称；出票日期；出票人签章。未记载规定事项之一的支票无效。

2) Classification of Check (cheque) 支票的种类

In other countries, checks are divided into crossed check and uncrossed check. The crossed check is crossed with two parallel lines on the up-left of the check, and the payee cannot cash the check but receive the payment through the bank transfer. The uncrossed check can both cash the money and make transfer.

在其他国家，支票可分为划线支票和未划线支票。划线支票的左上角被划上两道平行线，受款人只能通过银行代为收款转账，不能提取现金。未划线支票既可转账也可提取现金。

4.4.5　Bank Guarantee and Standby Letter of Credit 银行保函及备用信用证

1. Bank Guarantee 银行保函

A Bank guarantee is a guarantee from a lending institution ensuring that the liabilities of a debtor will be met. In other words, if the debtor fails to settle a debt, the bank will cover it. A bank guarantee enables the customer (debtor) to acquire goods, buy equipment, or draw down loans, and thereby expand business activity.

银行保函是贷款机构保证债务人债务得到履行的担保。换句话说，如果债务人未能清偿债务，银行将承担这笔债务。银行保函使客户（债务人）能够购买货物、购买设备或提取贷款，从而扩大业务活动。

A bank guarantee is a pledge on the part of a bank to make someone's debt good in the event that he or she cannot pay it. Bank guarantees are essentially like agreements to stand as a consigner on a transaction. In the event that the original party cannot follow through, the bank can be called upon to provide the payment. Many banks offer bank guarantees as a service to their customers for the purpose of facilitating large business operations and deals, and this particular banking tool is primarily used by big customers such as corporations and governments.

银行保函是银行在某人无力偿还债务的情况下保证债务良好的一种担保。银行保函本质上就像是作为交易中的托运人的协议；如果原始当事人不能履行义务，银行可以被要求提供付款。许多银行将银行担保作为一种服务提供给客户，目的是促进大型企业的运营和交易，而这种特殊的银行工具主要是由大客户（如公司和政府）使用的。

From the perspective of a seller in such transactions, a bank guarantee is a letter of surety. It means that if the buyer takes possession and fails to pay, the seller can still recover the payment, from the buyer's bank. Bank guarantees may be used in situations where large amounts of financing are needed and it is not possible to obtain a loan from one location, for example, when the World Bank provides a bank guarantee for a development project, and for deals on a smaller scale.

从此类交易中卖方的角度来看，银行保函是一种保函。这意味着如果买方占有而没有付款，卖方仍然可以向买方银行追回货款。在需要大量融资而无法从一个地点获得贷款的情况下，例如，当世界银行为发展项目和较小规模的交易提供银行担保时，可以使用银行担保。

In a direct guarantee, a bank directly guarantees someone, usually for a set amount and within a set period of time. The guarantee may also be generated for a specific transaction. Indirect guarantees are issued by one bank on behalf of another's customer, for example, when a foreign bank stands surety for someone by arrangement through that person's domestic and primary bank.

在直接担保中，银行直接担保某人，通常是在规定的金额和期限内。也可以为特定交易生成担保。间接担保是由一家银行代表另一家客户出具的，例如，当一家外国银行通过某人的国内银行和主要银行安排为该人担保时。

2. Standby Letter of Credit 备用信用证

Standby letter of credit, also known as a "non-performing letter of credit", is a guarantee of payment issued by a bank on behalf of a client and is used as "payment of last resort" when the client fails to fulfill a contractual commitment with another party. Standby letters of credit are created as a sign of good faith in business transactions, and are proof of a buyer's credit quality and repayment abilities. The bank issuing this kind of L/C will perform brief underwriting duties to ensure the credit quality of the client seeking the letter of client, and then send a notification to the bank of the client requesting the letter of credit (typically a seller or creditor).

备用信用证，又称"不良信用证"，是银行代客户出具的付款担保，在客户未能履行与另一方的合同承诺时，用作"最后付款"。备用信用证是商业交易中诚信的标志，也是买方信用质量和还款能力的证明。开具这种信用证的银行将履行短暂的承销职责，以确保寻求客户信用证的客户的信用质量，然后向要求信用证的客户的银行（通常是卖方或债权人）发出通知。

A standby letter of credit will typically be in force for about one year, allowing for enough time for payment to be made through standard contractual guidelines.

备用信用证的有效期通常为一年左右，以便有足够的时间通过标准合同准则付款。

Standby letters of credit are often used in international trade transactions, such as the purchase of goods from another country. The seller will ask for a standby letter of credit, which can be cashed on demand if the buyer fails to make payment by the date specified in the contract. The cost to obtain a standby letter of credit is typically 1%-8% of the face amount annually, but the letter can be canceled as soon as the terms of the contract have been met by the purchaser or borrower.

　　备用信用证经常用于国际贸易交易，例如从另一个国家购买商品。卖方将要求一份备用信用证，如果买方未能在合同规定的日期前付款，该信用证可以即期兑现。获得备用信用证的费用通常是每年面值的 1%~8%，但一旦买方或借款人满足了合同条款，信用证就可以被取消。

【 Exercise 】

1. Translate the following phrases into Chinese.

secure socket layer (SSL) _____

the electronic payment system_____

electronic money_____

online payment platform _____

international settlement_____

2. Translate the following phrases into English.

合作伙伴_____

信用风险_____

硬通货_____

货到付款_____

光票托收_____

3. Please explain the following words or items.

　　(1) international settlement

　　(2) remittance

　　(3) collection

　　(4) letter of credit

　　(5) bill of exchange

4. Please answer the following questions.

　　(1) What are the key elements necessarily for international settlement?

　　(2) What are the key issues in international settlement?

　　(3) What is the classification of remittance?

　　(4) What are the involved parties in collection?

Chapter 5　Cross-border E-commerce Logistics

跨境电子商务物流

【Knowledge Objective】

❑　Be able to introduce the E-commerce in English 能够用英语介绍电子商务；

❑　Be able to communicate with customers in English 能够用英语与顾客交流；

❑　Be able to read and comprehend some articles related to cross-border E-commerce 能够阅读和理解与跨境电子商务有关的文章。

【Knowledge Objectives】

❑　Master typical expressions about cross-border E-commerce 掌握跨境电子商务的经典表达；

❑　Memorize new words and phrases in the texts 能够记忆文章中的单词与短语。

【Key Words】

international logistics（国际物流）；the third-party logistics（第三方物流）；the fourth-party logistics（第四方物流）；DHL Express（敦豪快递）；United Parcel Service（联合包裹）；express mail service（特快专递）；special Line logistics（专线物流）

Section 5.1　A Brief Introduction to Cross-border Logistics 跨境物流简介

New Words

capacity	*n.*	容量；生产能力；容积；功率
lifeblood	*n.*	生命线；命根子；（事物的）命脉；（人的）命脉
clearance	*n.*	（人、交通工具进出机场或出入境的）许可，准许，清关
tariffs	*n.*	税则；收费；〈英〉（旅馆、铁路等的）价目表
	v.	征收关税；定税率；定收费标准
threshold	*n.*	阈；门槛；起点；开端
disputes	*n.*	争端；争论；争吵；抗辩
	v.	争论；争吵；对……质疑；反抗

outsource	*v.*	（将……业务、工程等）外包
procurement	*n.*	（尤指为政府或机构）采购
integration	*n.*	一体化；结合；融入群体或社会
eminently	*adv.*	非常；特别；极其
outbound	*adj.*	向外的；出港的；离开某地的
	v.	跳过
subsequent	*adj.*	随后的；后来的；之后的；接后的
demurrage	*n.*	逾期费，滞留期；（英格兰银行的）金银块兑换费
extensive	*adj.*	广阔的；广大的；大量的；广泛的
forklift	*n.*	铲车
consulting	*adj.*	咨询的
deployment	*n.*	部署；展开；使用；运用
integrate	*v.*	使结合起来；使（黑人等）不受歧视；表示（面积、温度等的）总和
	adj.	完整的
utilization	*n.*	利用；效用；使用率；利用率
optimization	*n.*	最佳化；网络优化；最优化；最适化
automatic	*adj.*	自动的；无意识的；不假思索的；必然的
	n.	自动步枪；自动变速汽车；自动换挡汽车
ownership	*n.*	所有权；产权；物主身份
margin	*n.*	边缘；差额；余地；界限
	v.	给……镶边；在……加旁注
minimal	*adj.*	极小的；极少的；最小的
	n.	最简单派艺术作品
fulfillment	*n.*	实现；履行；完成；满足
startups	*n.*	开机；创办中的公司；创业公司
	v.	开办；发动（机器、引擎等）
	adj.	新成立的
assets	*n.*	资产；财产；宝贵的人（物）
coordinate	*n.*	坐标；（颜色协调的）配套服装
	v.	协调；使协调；使相配合；使（身体各部位）动作协调
	adj.	同等的；配合的
transaction	*n.*	事务；交易；学报；处理
internally	*adv.*	内部的；体内的
unparalleled	*adj.*	无可匹敌的
bulk	*n.*	大宗货物

Phrases

competitive advantage	竞争优势
be…reflected in	体现在……
offline services	线下服务
the product delivery and distribution services	产品配送服务
inquiry way	查询方式
postal logistics	邮政物流
query page	查询页面
China Post Air Mail	中国邮政航空邮件
China Post Registered Air Mail	中国邮政挂号空邮
customer experience	客户体验
tariff threshold	关税门槛
import tariff	进口关税
third-party logistics	第三方物流
supply chain	供应链
integrated operation	综合运营
value-added services	增值服务
Council of Supply Chain Management Professionals (CSCMP)	供应链管理专业委员会（CSCMP）
cross-docking	跨平台
inventory management	库存管理
freight forwarding	货运
workforce size	员工规模
logistics fix costs	物流固定成本
variable costs	可变成本
dispatch management software	调度管理软件
electronic data interchange(EDI)	电子数据交换（EDI）
to take over	接管
fourth-party logistics	第四方物流
medium-to-large businesses	大中型企业
small-to-medium businesses	中小企业
overseas warehouse	海外仓
folding beds	折叠床
blue ocean	蓝海
word-of-mouth marketing	口碑营销
storage fee	仓储费

Sentences

1. Do you have a delivery service?
   你们有快递服务吗？

2. Where do you want it delivered?
   你想把它快递到哪里？

3. Could you have the ticket delivered to his office on Monday?
   你能把票在周一的时候送到他的办公室吗？

4. Do you want to get the package delivered or to pick it up yourself?
   你想把这个包裹快递过去还是自己过来拿？

5. Please send this parcel by express delivery.
   请用快递寄送这个包裹。

6. You have to pay a premium for express delivery.
   寄快递你得付额外的费用。

7. I'll have the express delivery service send my ski.
   滑雪板用快递寄过去吧。

8. The package was shipped by the express delivery service.
   包裹由特快专递送出。

9. How much does it cost to express to Hong Kong?
   快递到香港需要多少钱？

10. How much do I have to pay to ship a package to Hong Kong?
    寄一个包裹到香港需要多少钱？

11. Logistics service is a balance of service priority and cost.
    物流服务是服务优先与成本间的平衡。

12. We'll send you by air a full set of non-negotiable documents immediately after the goods are loaded.
    货物装船后，我们将立即空运全套不可议付的单据。

13. Information is a key to the success of logistics.
    信息是物流成功的关键。

14. When the goods have been loaded, you can get the B/L signed by the master of the vessel.
    货装上船后，你可以得到由船长签字的提单。

15. Inventory control can effectively reduce logistics cost.
    库存控制能有效地降低物流成本。

16. We'll send you two sets of the shipped, clean bill of lading.
    我们将寄送两套已装运清洁提单。

17. Packing and sorting are two activities in logistics.
    包装和分拣是物流中的两项活动。

18. We arrange shipments to any part of the world.
    我们承揽去世界各地的货物运输。

19. From what I've heard you're ready well up in shipping work.

据我所知，您对运输工作很在行。

20. The two sides finally reached an agreement on the mode of transportation.

双方就运输方式达成了协议。

Conversations

1. Applying for a Patent

A: I'm going to apply for a patent but I'm not sure how to prepare the application. Would you please help me?

B: Sure. Glad to help. First you need to submit a request, a description and a claim. The description is particularly important. If necessary, it should be supported by drawings.

A: How long shall I have to wait for the approval?

B: Well. Examination takes time. The Patent Office will announce the result and notify the application within 18 months. Even then you still don't get the patent certificate.

A: Why?

B: The Patent Office needs 90 days to wait for any possible opposition. Only when everything is OK will the patent be registered.

A: I see. But I have another question. I don't know why the duration of protection is only 15 years?

B: This is only for one of the patent rights. For invention, the duration of protection is 15 years. For utility models and designs, the duration of protection is even shorter, only for 5 years protection.

A: Does every country specify the same duration of protection?

B: No. l5-year protection is the minimum protection any country will grant its patentees. In some countries, the patent right duration for invention is 20 years.

A: What are the criteria for granting patent rights?

B: They are similar in all countries: novelty, inventiveness and practicability.

1. 申请专利

A：我想申请专利，但不知道如何准备，你能帮我吗？

B：当然，很高兴能帮忙，首先，你需要提交一份申请书、一份说明书和一份要求书。说明书尤其重要，必要的话，说明书应配有插图。

A：获得专利要等多长时间？

B：哦，专利审查需要时间。专利局会在 18 个月内公布结果，公告专利。即使到那时，您也拿不到专利证书。

A：为什么？

B：专利局还需要 90 天时间看看是否有异议，只有一切都没问题时，专利方可以注册。

A：我明白了，我还有一个问题。我不知道专利的保护期限为什么只有 15 年？

B：只有一种专利权保护期限是 15 年——发明专利。至于实用新型和外观设计专利，保护期更短，只有 5 年。

A：每个国家规定的保护期限是否都一致？

B：不是，各国都对专利人给予了最低 15 年的专利保护。在一些国家，发明专利的保护期是 20 年。

A：授予专利的标准是什么？

B：标准和别国相似，都要求具备新颖性、创造性和实用性。

2. Complaint

Operator: Hello! This is the Customer Service Center. Can I help you?

Customer: I want to make a complaint about the delay of your delivery.

Operator: Can you tell me the details?

Customer: My business partner sent me a draft by EMS on March 25th from ×××, but I didn't receive it until a week later, which made our manager very angry.

Operator: Have you made an inquiry?

Customer: Yes. I was told that the mail had arrived in ××× the day after it was sent, but there was no further information from your system. I want to know why.

Operator: I will pass on your complaint to the related department right away. Please leave your telephone number and we will call you back.

Customer: When can I expect a reply?

Operator: We will investigate it immediately and give you a reply as soon as possible.

Customer: I'll be waiting for your call.

Operator: Thank you for calling. Good-bye.

2. 客户投诉

客服：您好！这里是客服中心，您有什么需要帮助的吗？

顾客：你们投递太慢了。

客服：您能说得详细些吗？

顾客：我的合作伙伴 3 月 25 日从 ××× 通过 EMS 寄给我一张汇票。但是我一星期后才收到，我们经理为此非常生气。

客服：您查询过吗？

顾客：查过。他们告诉我交寄后的第二天汇票就已经到了 ×××，但是系统查不到进一步的信息了。我想知道是什么原因。

客服：我会将您反映的情况转给相关部门，请您留下联系电话，我们会给您打过去。

顾客：什么时候能得到答复？

客服：我们立即进行调查，尽快给您答复。

顾客：等待你的回复。

客服：感谢来电，再见。

Text

5.1.1　The Introduction of Logistics 物流简介

For cross-border E-commerce business, the competitive advantage of company depends primarily on user-centered customer value. User experience is reflected not only in the quality of products provided by cross-border E-commerce companies, but also in the offline services especially the product delivery and distribution services throughout the process. It shows that cross-border E-commerce must rely on the combination of logistics, business flow and information flow to get better development.

对于跨境电商业务而言，企业的竞争优势主要取决于以用户为中心的客户价值。用户体验不仅体现在跨境电商公司提供的产品质量上，更体现在线下服务尤其是产品配送服务的全程。这表明跨境电子商务必须依靠物流、商流和信息流的结合才能得到更好的发展。

The key to the quality of logistics service is reflected in the capacity of logistics operation, and has the driving effect to the customer value. The logistics information is the lifeblood of E-commerce logistics operation, affecting the entire logistics system, providing favorable conditions to the customer value. The logistics service of cross-border E-commerce requires faster distribution, shorter delivery time, broader coverage, more accurate and efficient logistics information.

物流服务质量的关键体现在物流运营能力上，并对客户价值有带动作用。物流信息是电子商务物流运作的命脉，影响着整个物流系统，为客户价值的实现提供了有利条件。跨境电商的物流服务要求配送更快，配送时间更短，覆盖范围更广，物流信息更准确、更高效。

How to achieve low shipping price, faster distribution, and quick customs clearance is the key for sellers to gain an advantage in the logistics competition. If the seller can communicate with the customer about the delivery method, delivery time, inquiry way for logistics information, receipt time, orders overweight, tariffs and other matters before the sale, he will win more trust and orders.

如何实现低运价、快配送、快通关，是卖家在物流竞争中取得优势的关键。如果卖方能在售前与客户沟通发货方式、发货时间、物流信息查询方式、收货时间、订单超重、关税等事项，则会赢得更多的信任和订单。

There are many logistics methods for cross-border E-commerce, including postal logistics, commercial express, logistics for special line and overseas warehouses. There are great differences in prices and services among different modes of logistics. Shipping fee of EMS is relatively cheaper, with forwarding agent offering up to 50% discount.

跨境电子商务的物流方式很多，包括邮政物流、商业快递、专线物流和海外仓物流。在不同的物流方式下，价格和服务差别很大。特快专递的运费相对便宜，货运代理提供高达五折的优惠。

UPS is known for its high speed and its good service. It usually takes two to four days to ship from China to USA. UPS also provides a quick updating of query information and a quick solution to any problems you may have. UPS provides online delivery and on-site pick-up service, shipping to over 200 countries and regions around the world.

UPS 以其高速和优质的服务闻名。从中国装船到美国通常需要两到四天的时间。UPS 还提供查询信息的快速更新以及您可能遇到的任何问题的快速解决方案。UPS 运往全球 200 多个国家和地区，提供在线送货和现场提货服务。

DHL offers a quick delivery, usually three workdays from China to Europe and two workdays to South and East Asia. It has a quick updating of query page and a quick solution to problems. Goods over 21 kg is charged in bulk. Shipping fee for bulk to most areas is cheaper than that of EMS. Shipping agents usually offer 50% discount for bulk and charges for smaller parcels are more expensive.

DHL 提供快速送货服务，通常从中国到欧洲三个工作日，到南亚和东亚两个工作日。查询页面更新速度快，问题解决速度快。超过 21 千克的货物是散装收费的。散货到大部分地区的运费比特快专递便宜。船运代理通常对大宗货物提供 50% 的折扣，而较小包裹的费用更高。

FedEx has a competitive price for the shipping from China to South and Central America and Europe with a 15% higher discount than that of other shipping companies, while the price for shipping to other areas is relatively higher.

联邦快递从中国运往中南美洲和欧洲的价格具有竞争力，折扣比其他航运公司高出 15%，而运往其他地区的价格相对较高。

TNT is quick in shipping and it takes 3 workdays or so from China to west Europe countries. It can ship to more countries than others.

TNT 运输速度快，从中国到西欧国家需要 3 个工作日左右。它可以运往比其他国家更多的国家。

The charge of China Post Air Mail is relatively cheaper, and it reaches destination countries all over the world, but it takes relatively longer time.

中国邮政航空邮件的费用相对便宜，而且到达世界各地的目的地国家和地区，但需要的时间相对较长。

Sellers can set a reasonable shipping template according to the characteristics of the product and the location of customer. Sellers can describe logistics methods and related matters in details for sellers to choose. As the charge of China Post Air Mail is relatively cheaper, covering almost all countries, most of the current cross-border retail sellers will choose China Post Registered Air Mail.

销售商可以根据产品的特点和客户的位置设置合理的发货模板。卖家可以详细描述物流方式和相关事项，供卖家选择。由于中国邮政空邮的收费相对便宜，而且几乎覆盖所有国家，所以目前的大多数跨境零售卖家都会选择中国邮政挂号空邮。

After the products are shipped, the seller should send a notice of shipment to the buyer to inform him/her of the product logistics, delivery time, tracking number and logistics status link. The shipment notice allows buyers to clearly understand the logistics status of the product, enjoy the seller's quality service, and greatly enhances the customer experience.

产品装运后，卖方应向买方发送装运通知，告知买方产品物流，交货时间，跟踪号和物流状态、环节。发货通知让买家清楚了解产品的物流状况，感受卖家的优质服务，大大提升了客户体验。

As the transaction amount for most of cross-border retail sales are small and the value for parcels are generally low, they will not meet the tariff threshold set by the customs authorities in most cases and buyers do not need to worry about the import tariff. But the threshold of some countries is low, which requires the seller to communicate with the buyer, patiently guide the buyer to understand the customs policy, and make it clear that if there are any additional customs taxes and fees, the buyer need to pay by himself/herself, so as not to cause unnecessary disputes.

由于大多数跨境零售的交易金额不大，包裹价值普遍较低，在大多数情况下没有达到海关设定的关税门槛，买家无须担心进口关税。但有些国家的门槛较低，这就要求卖方与买方沟通，耐心引导买方了解海关政策，并明确如果有任何额外的关税税费，买方需要自行支付，以免造成不必要的纠纷。

The development of cross-border logistics in China is relatively slow. The development of logistics and cross-border E-commerce are complementary to each other. Logistics occupies an important part in whether cross-border E-commerce is satisfactory. Companies should compare a variety of cross-border logistics modes for comprehensive consideration and choose the best logistics method of cross-border E-commerce based on their own situation. They can also create new logistics methods according to the needs of business and customer, and create more customer value through upgrading logistics services for cross-border E-commerce.

我国跨境物流发展相对缓慢。物流和跨境电商的发展是相辅相成的。物流对于跨境电商是否令人满意非常重要。企业应比较多种跨境物流模式进行综合考虑，根据自身情况选择最佳的跨境电商物流方式。企业还可以根据企业和客户的需求创造新的物流方式，通过提升跨境电商的物流服务来创造更多的客户价值。

5.1.2 Third-party Logistics 第三方物流

A third-party logistics (abbreviated 3PL or sometimes TPL) provider is a firm that provides service to its customers of outsourced (or "Third-Party") logistics services for part, or all of their supply chain management functions. Third-party logistics providers typically specialize in integrated operation, warehousing and transportation services that can be scaled and customized to customers' needs based on market conditions, such as the demands and delivery service requirements for their products and materials. Often, these services go beyond logistics and include value-added services related to the production or procurement of goods, i.e., services that integrate parts of the supply chain. When this integration occurs, the provider is then called third-party supply chain management provider(3PSCMP) or supply chain management service provider(SCMSP). 3PL targets a particular function in supply management, such as warehousing, transportation, or raw material provision.

第三方物流（缩写为 3PL，有时缩写为 TPL）提供商是为其客户提供外包（或"第三方"）物流服务的公司，承担部分或全部供应链管理功能。第三方物流提供商通常专注于综合运营、仓储和运输服务，可根据市场条件（如产品和材料的需求和交付服务要求）按照客户需求进行扩展和定制。通常，这些服务超越了物流，包括与货物生产或采购相关的增值服务，即整合供应链部分的服务。当这种整合发生时，提供商随之被称为第三方供应链管理提供商（3PSCMP3）或供应链管理服务提供商（SCMSP）。3PL 针对的是供应管理中的特定功能，例如仓储、运输或原材料供应。

1. Definition of 3PL 第三方物流的定义

According to the Council of Supply Chain Management Professionals (CSCMP), 3PL is defined as a firm that provides multiple logistics services for use by customers preferably. These services are integrated, or bundled together by the provider. Among the services 3PLs provide are transportation, warehousing, cross-docking, inventory management, packaging and freight forwarding.

根据供应链管理专业委员会（CSCMP）的说法，3PL 被定义为"为客户提供多种物流服务的公司"。而且，这些服务最好由提供者整合或捆绑在一起。第三方物流提供的服务包括运输、仓储、跨平台、库存管理、包装和货运。

2. Advantages of 3PL 第三方物流的优点

1) Cost and Time Saving 节省成本和时间

Logistics is the core competence of third-party logistics providers. They have the ability to possess better knowledge and greater expertise than any producing or selling company. This knowledge combined with the global networks of the often large company size enables higher time and cost efficiency. The equipment and the IT systems of 3PL providers are constantly updated and adapted to new requirements of their customers and their customer's suppliers. Producing or selling companies often do not have the time, resources, or expertise to adapt their equipment and systems as quickly.

物流是第三方物流提供商的核心竞争力。第三方物流提供商有能力拥有比任何生产或销售公司更好的物流知识和更多的专业知识。这种知识与规模较大的公司的全球网络相结合，可以实现更高的时间和成本效率。第三方物流提供商的设备和 IT 系统不断更新，并适应客户及其客户提供商的新要求。生产或销售公司通常没有时间、资源或专业知识来快速调整其设备和系统。

2) Low Capital Commitment 低资本投入

The fact that most or all operative functions are outsourced to a 3PL provider means there is no need for the client to own its own warehouse or transport facilities, lowering the amount of capital required for the client's business. This is particularly beneficial if a company has high variations in warehouse capacity utilization, because a bad capacity utilization ratio at equal fixed cost(for warehouse)will reduce a company's profitability.

大多数或所有操作功能外包给第三方物流提供商，意味着客户无须拥有自己的仓库或运输设施，从而降低了客户业务所需的资金数量。如果公司的仓库容量利用率变化很大，这是特别有利的，因为在固定成本（仓库）相等的情况下，容量利用率不足会降低公司的盈利能力。

3) Focus on Core Business 专注核心业务

The outsourcing of logistics departments permits the company to focus even more on their core business. If logistics is one of the firms' core businesses then outsourcing doesn't make sense. But if logistics is no core competency but rather a needed or annoying attachment it should be outsourced to a logistics provider because the continuous increasing of business complexity makes it impossible to be an expert in every division or sector. And if you are no expert in a division, there is always the opportunity to improve. Often only the core competency is really adding value to your product. It is immensely important to be the best in class or one of the market leaders to generate profits, because normally the quality of the core product is the main (not the only, but the main!) reason for the consumer to buy it.

物流部门的外包使公司能够更加专注于核心业务。如果物流是公司的核心业务之一，那么外包就没有意义了。但是，如果物流不是核心竞争力，而只是一种需要甚至还会带来烦恼，那么应该把物流外包给物流提供商，因为不断增加的业务复杂性使工作人员不可能都成为每个部门的专家。如果你不是一个部门的专家，总会有机会改进。通常，只有核心竞争力才能真正为产品增加价值。非常重要的一点是要成为一流企业或市场领导者之一以获取利润，因为通常核心产品的质量是消费者购买它的主要原因（不是唯一的，但是主要的）。

4) Flexibility 灵活性

Third-party logistics provider can provide a much higher flexibility in geographic aspects and can offer a much larger variety of services than the clients could provide for themselves. In addition to that, the client gets flexibility in resources and workforce size and logistics fix costs turn into variable costs.

第三方物流提供商可以在地理方面提供更高的灵活性，并且可以提供比客户自己提供的更多种类的服务。除此之外，客户还可以在资源和员工规模方面具有更大的灵活性，并且物流固定成本会转化为可变成本。

3. Disadvantages of 3PL 第三方物流的缺点

One particular disadvantage is the loss of control a client has by working with third-party logistics, eminently in outbound logistics when the 3PL provider completely assumes the communication and interacting with a firm's customer or supplier. By having a good and continuous communication with their clients, most 3PL's try to charm away such doubts. Some 3PL's even paint the clients logos on their assets and vest their employees like the clients'.

一个特别的缺点是与第三方物流合作会让客户失去控制。在出站物流方面这一缺点尤其突出，因为第三方物流提供商完全承担了与公司客户或提供商的沟通和互动。通过与客户进行良好和持续的沟通，大多数 3PL 试图消除这些疑虑。有些 3PL 甚至会在客户的资产上绘制客户徽标，并让员工穿上与客户员工一样的服装。

The other is that the IT systems of the provider and the client must operate together.

Technology helps increase visibility for the client by way of continuous status updates via dispatch management software and electronic data interchange(EDI), which does involve a cost, but it can help avoid penalty for delays and subsequent financial losses by way of demurrage.

另一个缺点是，提供商和客户的 IT 系统必须协同运作。在技术上，调度管理软件和电子数据交换（EDI）通过持续的状态更新来提高客户的可见性，这确实涉及成本，但它可以通过滞期费来帮助避免因延误和后续财务损失所带来的处罚。

4. Types of 3PL 第三方物流的类型

Third-party logistics providers include freight forwarders courier companies, as well as other companies integrating & offering subcontract logistics and transportation services.

第三方物流提供商包括货运代理、快递公司以及其他整合和提供分包物流和运输服务的公司。

1) Standard 3PL Provider 标准 3PL 提供商

This is the most basic form of 3PL providers. They would perform activities such as pick and pack, warehousing and distribution (business), which are the most basic functions of logistics. For a majority of these firms, the 3PL function is not their main activity.

这是第三方物流提供商的基本形式。它们将开展诸如拣货和包装、仓储和配送（业务）等活动，这些都是物流的基本功能。对于这些公司中的大多数而言，3PL 功能不是其主要活动。

2) Service Developer 服务开发人员

This type of 3PL provider will offer their customers advanced value-added services such as tracking and tracing, cross-docking, specific packaging, or providing a unique security system. A solid IT foundation and a focus on economies of scale and scope will enable this type of 3PL providers to perform these types of tasks.

此类第三方物流提供商将为其客户提供高级增值服务，例如跟踪和追踪、直接换装、特定包装或提供独特的安全系统。坚实的 IT 基础以及对规模经济和范围经济的关注将使这类第三方物流提供商能够执行此类任务。

3) The Customer Adapter 客户适配者

This type of 3PL provider comes in at the request of the customer and essentially takes over complete control of the company's logistics activities. The 3PL provider improves the logistics dramatically, but does not develop a new service. The customer base for this type of 3PL provider is typically quite small.

客户适配者：此类第三方物流提供商应客户的要求，并且基本上完全控制公司的物流活动。第三方物流提供商大大改善了物流，但没有开发新服务。此类 3PL 提供商的客户群通常非常小。

4) The Customer Developer 客户开发者

This is the highest level that a 3PL provider can attain with respect to its processes and activities. This occurs when the 3PL provider integrates itself with the customer and takes over their entire logistics function. These providers will have few customers, but will perform extensive and detailed tasks for them.

这是第三方物流提供商在其流程和活动方面可以达到的最高级别。当第三方物流提供商与客户整合并接管其整个物流功能时，就会发生这种情况。这些提供商的客户很少，但会为其执行广泛而详细的任务。

5. Layers of 3PL 第三方物流的层级

First-party logistics (1PL) providers are single service providers in a specific geographic area that specialize in certain goods or shipping methods. Examples are carrying companies, port operators, and depot companies. The logistics department of a producing firm can also be a first-party logistics provider if they have their own transport assets and warehouses.

第一方物流（1PL）提供商是特定地理区域中的单一服务提供商，专门从事某些商品或运输方式。例如，承运公司、港口运营商、仓库公司都属于此类。生产公司的物流部门如果拥有自己的运输资产和仓库，也可以成为第一方物流提供商。

Second-party logistics (2PL) providers are service providers which provide their specialized logistics services in a larger(national) geographical area than the 1PL does. Often there are frame contracts between the 2PL and the customer, which regulate the conditions for the transport duties that are mostly placed short term. 2PLs provide their own and external logistics resources like trucks, forklifts, warehouses, and etc. for transport, handling of cargo or warehouse management activities. Second-party logistics arouses in the course of the globalization and the uprising trend of lean management, when the companies begin to outsource their logistics activities to focus on their own core companies. Examples are courier, express and parcel services, ocean carriers, freight forwarders and transshipment providers.

第二方物流（2PL）提供商是服务提供商，在比第一方物流更大的（国家）地理区域提供其专业的物流服务。通常在第二方物流和客户之间存在框架合同，这些合同规定了大部分短期运输职责需满足的条件。2PL 提供自有和外部物流资源，如卡车、叉车、仓库等，用于运输、货物处理或仓库管理活动。众多公司纷纷将其物流活动外包，以专注于自己的核心公司，第二方物流随着全球化和精益管理而兴起，如速递、快递和包裹服务、海运承运人、货运代理和转运提供商。

The most significant difference between a second-party logistics provider and a third-party logistics provider is the fact that a 3PL is always integrated in the customs system. The 2PL is not integrated, and in contrast to the 3PL, he is only an outsourced logistics provider with no system integration. A 2PLworks often on call (e.g. express parcel services) whereas a 3PL is almost every time informed about the workload of the near future. Another point that differs 2PL and 3PL is the specification and customizing of services. A 2PL normally only provides standardized services. 3PLs often provide services that are customized and specialized on the needs of their customer. This is possible by the long term contracts that are usual in the third-party logistics market. So if there are customized logistics services needed, the contracts in the 3PL segment have to be long term, because customizing always costs money. A cost effectiveness for the third-party logistics provider is only given over longer periods of time with a stable contract and stable profits.

However, second-party logistic services can't be customized, concerning to the fluctuating market with hard competition and a price battle on a low level. And there we have another distinguishing point between 2PL and 3PL: Durability of contracts. 3PL contracts are long term contracts, whereas 2PL contracts are of a low durability, so that the customer is flexible in responding to market and price changes.

第二方物流提供商和第三方物流提供商之间最重要的区别在于 3PL 始终整合在海关系统中。2PL 没有整合，与第三方物流相比，它只是一个没有系统整合的外包物流提供商。2PL 经常随叫随到（例如快递包裹服务），而 3PL 几乎每次都被告知近期的工作量。另外一点不同在于服务的规范和定制。2PL 通常仅提供标准化服务。3PL 通常提供定制的服务，并专门满足其客户的需求。这可以通过第三方物流市场中常见的长期合同来实现。因此，如果需要定制物流服务，那么第三方物流部门的合同必须是长期的，因为定制总是花费金钱的。第三方物流提供商只有较长时间内合同稳定且利润稳定才能获得成本效益。相比之下，第二方物流服务无法定制，涉及竞争激烈、价格战的波动市场。2PL 和 3PL 的另一个区别点是：合同的持久性。第三方物流合同是长期合同，而第二方物流合同的持久性较低，因此客户可灵活应对市场和价格变化。

With companies operating globally, the need to increase supply chain visibility and reduce risk, improve velocity and reduce costs — all at the same time — requires a common technological solution. Non-asset based providers perform functions such as consultation on packaging and transportation, freight quoting, financial settlement, auditing, tracking, customer service and issue resolution. However, they do not employ any truck drivers or warehouse personnel, and they don't own any physical freight distribution assets of their own-no trucks, no storage trailers, no pallets, and no warehousing. A non-assets based provider consists of a team of domain experts with accumulated freight industry expertise and information technology assets. They fill a role similar to that of freight agents or brokers, but maintain a significantly greater degree of "hands on involvement" in the transportation of products. These providers are 4PL and SPL services.

随着公司在全球运营，它需要提高供应链可见性，降低风险，加快速度和降低成本，这需要一个共同的技术解决方案。非资产提供商执行诸如包装和运输咨询、货运报价、财务结算、审计、跟踪、客户服务和问题解决等功能。但是，它们不雇用任何卡车司机或仓库人员，它们没有自己的任何实际货运配送资产——没有卡车，没有存储拖车，没有托盘，也没有仓库。非资产提供商由领域专家团队组成，拥有累积的货运行业专业知识和信息技术资产。它们扮演类似于货运代理或经纪人的角色，但在产品运输中保持更大程度的"实际操作"。这些提供商提供 4PL 和 5PL 服务。

Fifth-party logistics (5PL) providers provide supply chain management and offer system oriented consulting and supply chain management services to their customers. Advancements in technology and the associated increases in supply chain visibility and inter-company communication have given rise to a relatively new model for third-party logistics operations — the "non-asset based logistics provider".

第五方物流（5PL）提供商提供供应链管理，并为其客户提供面向系统的咨询和供应链管理服务。技术的进步以及供应链可见性和公司间通信的相关增长为第三方物流业务提供了一种相对较新的模式——"非资产型物流提供商"。

5.1.3 Fourth-party Logistics（4PL）第四方物流

1. Definition of Fourth-party Logistics(4PL) 第四方物流的含义

The fourth-party logistics refers to the designed for both parties, the third-party logistics planning, consulting, logistics information system, supply chain management, and other services, through the deployment and management and complementary resources, capabilities, and technology service providers, to provide comprehensive, integrated supply chain solutions.

第四方物流指专为交易双方和第三方提供物流规划、咨询、物流信息系统、供应链管理等服务，通过调配与管理自身及具有互补性的服务提供商的资源、能力和技术，提供综合、全面的供应链解决方案。

The fourth-party logistics, through the influence of the whole supply chain, integrates various social resources to realize the full utilization of logistics information sharing and social logistics resources on the basis of solving the enterprise logistics. Based on the complexity of cross-border e-commerce and cross-border logistics, a number of fourth party logistics enterprises have emerged to inject new factors into cross-border logistics.

第四方物流通过整个供应链的影响力，在解决企业物流的基础上，整合各类社会资源，实现物流信息共享与社会物流资源充分利用。基于跨境电子商务与跨境物流的复杂性，涌现出一批第四方物流模式企业，为跨境物流注入新鲜因素。

2. Advantages and Disadvantages of 4PL 第四方物流的优缺点

1) Advantages of 4PL 第四方物流的优点

(1) Unique and professional operational support,

(2) Effective outsourcing of all logistics needs of a given business,

(3) Offers a single point of contact for all the parties involved in the supply chain,

(4) Gives more sense of ownership and control over your business,

(5) Creates a lean and cost-effective supply chain for improved profit margin,

(6) Outsources all logistics to third-party professionals, letting manufacturers focus on their product.

（1）独特和专业的业务支助。

（2）有效外包给定业务的所有物流需求。

（3）为所有参与供应链的各方提供一个单一的接触点。

（4）赋予你对企业更多的所有权和控制权。

（5）建立一个精益和成本效益高的供应链，以提高利润率。

（6）将所有物流外包给第三方专业人员，让制造商专注于它们的产品。

2) Disadvantages of 4PL 第四方物流的缺点

(1) Minimal control over fulfillment and logistics processes,

(2) Possibly cost-prohibitive for some small businesses and startups.

（1）对履行和物流过程的控制最小化；

（2）对一些小企业和初创企业来说，这可能会造成成本上的限制。

3. The Differences between 3PL and 4PL 第三方物流与第四方物流之间的区别

The main difference between a 4PL and a 3PL is that a 4PL handles the entirety of a supply chain while a 3PL is mainly concerned with handling just the logistical process.

第四方物流和第三方物流的主要区别在于，第四方物流处理整个供应链，而第三方物流主要处理物流过程。

3PL vs. 4PL is hotly debated between companies as to which model is superior. Ultimately, each one works better for different situations and understanding how they differ is crucial for every company.

3PL 和 4PL 公司之间关于哪种模式更好的争论很激烈。归根结底，每一种方法都能更好地适应不同的情况，了解它们的不同之处对每家公司都至关重要。

Some of their key differences include:

(1) Fourth-party logistics are generally better suited for medium-to-large businesses, while third-party logistics are more suitable for small-to-medium businesses.

(2) Fourth-party logistics functions at the optimization and integration level while third-party logistics focuses more on daily operations.

(3) Fourth-party logistics providers may own assets like trucks and warehouses while third-party logistics providers generally don't own such assets.

(4) Fourth-party logistics companies can effectively coordinate the activities of third-party logistics providers.

(5) Fourth-party logistics provides the highest level of logistics services for a great value while third-party logistics is more focused on one-off transactions.

(6) Fourth-party logistics provider maintains a single point of contact for every business' supply chain while with third-party logistics, businesses often must take care of certain aspects of the supply process internally.

它们的一些主要区别包括：

（1）第四方物流通常更适合大中型企业，而第三方物流更适合中小企业。

（2）第四方物流功能处于优化集成层面，而第三方物流更侧重于日常运营。

（3）第四方物流提供商可能拥有卡车、仓库等资产，而第三方物流提供商一般不拥有这些资产。

（4）第四方物流公司可以有效地协调第三方物流提供商的活动。

（5）第四方物流提供最高水平的物流服务。

（6）第四方物流供应商为每个企业的供应链提供一个单一的联系点，而使用第三方物流，企业通常必须在内部处理供应过程的某些方面。

5.1.4　Overseas Warehouse 海外仓

1. Introduction of Overseas Warehouses 海外仓的简介

Overseas warehouses is a new cross-border E-commerce international logistics model that has emerged in recent years. It refers to enterprises that operate cross-border E-commerce to establish or lease warehouses at overseas destinations, and transport goods to overseas destinations by means of sea, land and air transportation. Once the consumer successfully places an order on the platform of cross-border E-commerce, the enterprise can transport the goods from the overseas destination warehouse or cooperate with the overseas third-party logistics organization to start the goods distribution transportation and provide localization service.

海外仓是近年来出现的一种新型跨境电商国际物流模式，是指经营跨境电商的企业在境外目的地设立或租赁仓库，通过海陆空运输方式向境外目的地运输货物。消费者一旦在跨境电商平台成功下单，企业就可以将货物从境外目的仓库运输或与境外第三方物流机构合作，启动货物配送运输，并提供本地化服务。

Compared with the traditional logistics model, the overseas logistics can shorten time and reduce the delivery costs. At the same time, it can effectively solve many problems such as commodity inspection and return. Although it has the unparalleled advantages compared with traditional logistics, due to the huge investment in the construction of "overseas warehouses", many cross-border E-commerce companies are daunting.

与传统物流模式相比，海外物流可以缩短时间，降低配送成本。同时，可以有效解决商检退货等诸多问题。虽然与传统物流相比具有无可比拟的优势，但由于在建设"海外仓"方面投入巨大，令很多跨境电商望而生畏。

Thanks to the rapid growth of cross-border E-commerce export transactions, overseas general warehouses have big demand for market in recent years. In addition, due to the encouragement of local governments at all levels to develop overseas warehouses, the supply and demand in the overseas warehouse market have been booming in the past two years. According to the data released in the *Overseas Warehouse Research Report*, the area of overseas warehouse nearly doubled in 2017, among which the United States is currently a country with overseas warehouses centralized, followed by the United Kingdom and Germany in Western Europe.

得益于跨境电商出口交易的快速增长，近年来海外总仓的市场需求很大。此外，由于地方各级政府鼓励发展海外仓，近两年海外仓市场供需旺盛。根据《海外仓研究报告》中公布的数据，2017 年海外仓面积几乎翻了一番，其中美国是海外仓集中的国家，其次是西欧的英国和德国。

Currently, there are three main types of overseas warehouses. The first one is the self-built warehouse of the platform, such as Amazon FBA. The second is the third-party overseas warehouses, with two ways of cooperation: renting and cooperative construction. The costs are from operation, logistics and warehousing for the rental method, and only the logistics costs will be needed for the cooperation construction. The third one is big sales of self-built overseas warehouses, such as Globalegrow.

目前，海外仓库主要有三种类型。第一种是平台的自建仓库，比如 Amazon FBA。第二种是第三方海外仓，合作方式有两种：租赁和合作建设。租赁的成本来自运营、物流和仓储，合作建设只需要物流成本。第三种是自建海外仓库的大销售，比如 Globalegrow。

"Overseas warehouse" is a key link in the overseas layout of Chinese companies. With this model, the export products of enterprises have the advantage in price and time. It is the only solution to solve the problem of timely response and localization of overseas customer service, including after-sale service.

"海外仓"是中国企业海外布局的关键一环。在这种模式下，企业的出口产品在价格和时间上都具有优势。这是解决海外客户服务包括售后服务的及时响应和本地化问题的唯一方案。

2. Benefits of Overseas Warehouse 海外仓的优点

According to market research, among the big sellers with a monthly sales of more than 500,000 US dollars, 55% of the sellers want to build their own warehouses. Among the sellers who sell more than one million dollars a month, this proportion even reaches 69%. So, what is the advantage of overseas warehouses in the cross-border E-commerce export industry?

据市场调查，在每月销售额超过 50 万美元的大卖家中，55%的卖家想自己建仓库，而在每月销售一百多万美元的卖家中，这一比例甚至达到 69%。那么，境外仓库在跨境电子商务出口行业中的优势是什么？

1) Improve the Shopping Experience 增加购物经验

Through overseas, warehouses products are directly delivered locally, which greatly shortens the delivery time. With local logistics, it is generally possible to check the status of goods online, achieving the whole process of tracking. And from the logistics tracking information, it is shipped from local areas, not China. The head transportation of the overseas warehouse is a traditional foreign trade logistics method, which is imported according to the normal customs clearance process, which greatly reduces the barriers to customs clearance. Local delivery and distribution reduces the transshipment process, thus greatly reducing the damage and packet loss rate. There are various types of commodity stocks in overseas warehouses, so it is easy to return and exchange. These factors will bring a good shopping experience to buyers.

通过海外仓库，产品直接在当地交付，大大缩短了交货时间。有了本地物流，一般可以在线检查货物的状态，实现全程的跟踪。从物流跟踪信息来看，它是从当地而不是中国运来的。国外仓库首运是一种传统的外贸物流方式，是按照正常的通关流程进口的，大大降低了海关通关的壁垒。本地投递和配送减少了转运环节，从而大大降低了损坏和丢包率。国外仓库的商品库存种类繁多，便于退换货。这些因素将给买家带来良好的购物体验。

2) Reduce Logistics Costs 减少物流费用

Postal packages and international logistics have certain restrictions on the weight, volume and value of transported items, resulting in many large items and valuables that can only be shipped by international courier. The emergence of overseas warehouses not only breaks through the restrictions on the weight, volume and value of the goods, but also reduce the overall logistics price, which is equivalent to the price of the small package, which is 20%-50% cheaper than international express.

邮包和国际物流对运输物品的重量、数量和价值都有一定的限制，导致许多大型物品和贵重物品只能由国际信使运送。国外仓库的出现，不仅突破了对货物重量、数量和价值的限制，而且降低了物流的整体价格，相当于小包装的价格，比国际快递便宜 20%~50%。

3) Get Traffic Support from Platforms 从平台获得交通支持

The third-party trading platform will give more exposure and traffic support to the goods that are stored in their overseas warehouses.

第三方交易平台将为存放在海外仓库的货物提供更多的曝光和交通支持。

4) Expand Product Categories 扩大产品类别

Some products have long service period and are not fast-moving consumer products, but the market is large and they will get more benefit if stored in overseas warehouses. There are no special restrictions on products in overseas warehouses. For some large-sized furniture, folding beds and other products, the market competition of them will not be very intense, and it is still a blue ocean overseas.

有些产品服务周期长，不是快速消费品，但市场很大，如果存放在国外仓库里，将会获得更多的收益。对海外仓库的产品没有特别的限制。对于一些大型家具、折叠床等产品，它们的市场竞争不会很激烈，在海外仍然是一个蓝海。

5) Conducive to Opening up the Market 促进市场开放

Overseas warehouses can be easily recognized by foreign buyers. If sellers pay attention to word-of-mouth marketing, their products can not only be recognized by buyers, but also help sellers to accumulate more resources to open up new market and improve the product sales.

Although overseas warehouses have many advantages in cross-border logistics, they also have a lot of requirements for sellers. For example, the seller first needs to pay the storage fee of the overseas warehouse, and the storage costs in different countries are different. Second, the overseas warehouse requires the seller to have a certain amount of stock and the occupied funds are relatively large. Third, the localized operations and management issues are also obstructions that hinder small and medium-sized sellers build their own overseas warehouses.

海外仓库很容易被外国买家识别。如果卖家注重口碑营销，那么他们的产品不仅可以得到买家的认可，还可以帮助卖家积累更多的资源，开拓新的市场，提高产品的销售水平。

国外仓库虽然在跨境物流方面有许多优势，但对卖方也有很多要求。例如，卖方首先需要支付海外仓库的仓储费，而不同国家的仓储成本也不同。其次，海外仓库要求卖方有一定数量的库存，占用的资金相对较大。第三，本地化的经营和管理问题也是阻碍中小型卖家建立自己的海外仓库的障碍。

Section 5.2　Main International Express 主要的国际快递

New Words

courier	*n.*	（递送包裹或重要文件的）信使，快递员
unrivalled	*adj.*	无与伦比的；无双的
portfolio	*n.*	文件夹；职务；有价证券组合；公事包
decisively	*adv.*	果断地；决定性地；肯定；明显
offshore	*adv.*	离岸；向海面；近海岸
	adj.	海上的；近海的；向海的；离岸的
shares	*n.*	〈英〉股票；股份；份额
	v.	共享；分（同）享；共有；均分
territories	*n.*	领土；地区；（科学知识、行动等的）领域
surcharge	*n.*	额外费用；附加费；增收费
	v.	向（某人）收取额外费用

Phrases

Honolulu	檀香山
United Parcel Service	联合包裹服务公司

Sentences

1. Judging from our past sales, I'd say you have little need to call on our guarantee.
   从我们所售出的商品来看，您不需要担心修理问题。

2. We have a one-year warranty on this refrigerator.
   我们这种电冰箱提供一年担保。

3. Regardless of the cause of the trouble, all repairs are guaranteed with in three days.
   不管是什么原因的故障，所有的修理保证在三天内解决。

4. Goods purchased in our factory can be changed within a month, but we don't exchange any item that is improperly used or damaged by the customer himself.
   凡在我厂购买的商品，一个月内可以调换，但对由于顾客自身使用不当造成的损坏，我厂不承担责任。

5. We guarantee the quality of the product we sold in our store for one year.
   我们店卖出的商品在 1 年内保证质量。

6. We will get it fixed soon.
   我们很快就派人去修理。

7. If you are free, our repairman will come to you.
   如果你有时间，我们的修理人员去上门维修。

8. We will send someone to repair it.

我们会派人去修的。

9. I will be ready in a week. We'll call you when it's ready.
   大概需要一个星期，修好时我们会打电话通知您。

10. I can have it ready for you in just a few minutes.
    我几分钟可以为你把它修理好。

11. I think there will be a charge since the warranty has expired.
    我想我还是要收费的，因为保修单已过期。

12. Well, you can leave it here for repairing, but there will be a charge.
    好的，您可以把它放在这儿修理，但要收费。

13. What happens if I am not satisfied with my purchase?
    假如买了以后不满意怎么办？

14. If you are not satisfied, you may return it.
    如果你不满意，你可以退货。

15. We only accept returns for thirty days after the purchase.
    我们这里的货物在卖出后 30 天内可以退货。

16. Bring your receipt to the customer service, and they will refund you.
    把你的收据拿给顾客服务部，他们就会退钱给你。

17. Our bookstore would accept returns provided that books are in good condition.
    我们书店不接受退换的书，除非书完好无损。

18. You can get a full refund if you have the receipt.
    如果你出示发票就可以拿到全额退款。

19. We can't allow returns on sale items.
    特价商品是不能退货的。

20. If it had any quality question, you can have your money back.
    若有质量问题，您可以退款。

21. I'm very sorry. No refunding after it is opened.
    很抱歉，开箱不退。

Conversations

1. Shipping Goods

A: Well, how would you like to ship my order?

B: Usually, we ship goods via EMS.

A: I want to receive the goods as soon as possible. Can it be delivered via DHL?

B: Dear customer, in fact, DHL takes about the same time as EMS. And for the same distance, DHL costs more.

A: However, sometimes it takes longer time via EMS.

B: Yes, there may be problem with EMS, but DHL is often stuck on the way. And you can choose priority, express or standard mail. Well, standard mail can take up to 10 working days. Priority is a bit faster and will arrive in about 5 to 7 working days. Express is the fastest, but it's also the most expensive. It only takes three days.

A: Oh, I see.

B: But if you insist on shipping via DHL, I will accept your advice.

A: No, I don't think that's necessary. EMS is just fine.

1. 寄送商品

A：那么，我订购的商品你们打算怎么寄送呢？

B：通常情况下，我们用邮寄的方式装运货物。

A：我想尽快收到东西，可以通过 DHL 运送吗？

B：亲，其实 EMS 和 DHL 花费的时间差不多，而且同样的距离，DHL 的收费更高。

A：不过 EMS 给人感觉很不稳定。

B：是的，EMS 可能会产生这个问题，不过 DHL 也经常卡在途中。而且邮政还可以选择优先邮递、特快邮递和普通邮递。普通邮递需要至少 10 个工作日。优先邮递快一些，在 5～7 个工作日内能送到。特快邮递是最快的，但也是最贵的，只需 3 天就能送到。

B：不过您如果坚持要通过 DHL 运送，我会接受您的建议。

A：我想不用了，用 EMS 就可以了。

2. Differences between Express Companies

A: Dear customer, generally speaking, if you do not have a special request, we will ship your goods via UPS.

B: What's the difference between UPS and other express companies? It seems that DHL has been chosen more.

A: Indeed, but it is relatively cost effective to send goods over 20kg via UPS.

B: Beyond that, is there any other international express?

A: Well, sometimes goods are shipped via TNT, which is not so far different from UPS and DHL. However, if your item's weight is light, we usually choose small parcel, and the EUB is the cheapest to the United States.

B: What is the weight of my package?

A: I have to check the weight of this parcel first.

2. 不同快递公司的区别

A：亲，一般来说，如果您没有特殊要求，我们通过 UPS 运送您的商品。

B：UPS 跟别的快递公司有什么区别吗？好像 DHL 用得更多些。

A：没错，不过用 UPS 寄送商品，商品重量在 20kg 以上的，费用相对划算些。

B：除此之外，还有哪些国际快递呢？

A：当然，有时候也会用 TNT 运送货物，其与 UPS 和 DHL 差别不大。不过如果您的商品重量轻，我们一般会选择国际小包，到美国的话 EUB 是最便宜的。

B：我的包裹有多重？

A：那我要先称一下。

3. Special Line Logistics

A: Hello, what is international special line logistics?

B: Dear customer, special line refers to the line to designated countries. Generally, there are British line, American line, Japanese line. And there are air transport, sea transport, rail transport and other methods of transport.

A: Can you ship goods via special line logistics?

B: Dear customer, although the special line is more efficient, but the price is not cheap, the thing you bought is a small item, so the small parcel is more suitable.

A: But the thing that I bought also was quite costly. It's more reassuringly shipped via special line logistics.

B: OK, all right, I see.

3. 国际专线物流

A：你好，什么是国际专线物流呢？

B：亲，国际专线是指到特定国家的线路渠道，一般有英国专线、美国专线、日本专线，有空运、海运、铁运和其他运输方式。

A：那你们可以用专线物流发货吗？

B：亲，虽然国际专线时效更高，但是价格也不便宜，您买的东西很小件，所以用国际小包更加适合。

A：但是我买的东西也挺贵重的，用专线物流更放心一点。

B：好的，我知道了。

Text

5.2.1　DHL Express 敦豪快递

DHL is a company owned by Deutsche Post DHL, a famous postal and logistics group in the world, which provides international courier, parcel and express mail services. Deutsche Post DHL is the world's largest logistics company operating around the world, particularly in sea and air mail. It provides an unrivalled portfolio of logistics services ranging from national and international parcel delivery, E-commerce shipping and fulfillment solutions, international express, road, air and ocean transport to industrial supply chain management. DHL is decisively positioned as "the logistics company for the world".

DHL 是全球著名的邮递和物流集团 Deutsche Post DHL 旗下公司，提供国际快递、包裹和快递服务。德国 DHL 是世界上最大的物流公司，在世界各地运营，特别是在海运和空运方面，它提供无与伦比的物流服务组合，从国内和国际包裹递送、电子商务航运和履行解决方案、国际快递、公路、空运和海洋运输到工业供应链管理。DHL 被明确定位为"面向世界的物流公司"。

Founded in the United States in 1969 to deliver documents between San Francisco and Honolulu, the company had expanded its service throughout the world by the late 1970s. The company was primarily interested in offshore and inter-continental deliveries, but the success of FedEx prompted their own intra-US expansion starting in 1983.

该公司于 1969 年在美国成立，在旧金山和檀香山之间递送文件，到 20 世纪 70 年代末，该公司将服务扩展到世界各地。该公司主要对离岸和洲际递送感兴趣，但联邦快递的成功促使其从 1983 年开始在美国国内扩张。

In 1998, Deutsche Post began to acquire shares in DHL. It reached majority ownership in 2001, and 100% ownership by December 2002. The company then absorbed DHL into its Express division, while expanding the use of the DHL brand to other Deutsche Post divisions, business units and subsidiaries. Today, DHL Express shares its DHL brand with business units such as DHL Global Forwarding and DHL Supply Chain.

1998 年，德国邮政开始收购 DHL 的股份。它在 2001 年获得了多数股权，到 2002 年 12 月达到了 100%的所有权。该公司随后将 DHL 并入其快递部门，同时将 DHL 品牌的使用扩大到德国邮政的其他部门、业务部单位和附属公司。如今，DHL 快递与 DHL 全球货运和 DHL 供应链等业务部门共享其 DHL 品牌。

5.2.2　United Parcel Service 联合包裹

United Parcel Service was founded in 1907. It has locations in the United States as well as around the world. Its corporate headquarter is located in Atlanta, Georgia. UPS is the world's largest package distribution company delivering more than 13 million documents and parcels every day and generating revenues of more than $27 billion a year. UPS is also the world's largest express package and document delivery company, delivering more packages in two days or less that are tracked and guaranteed than any other company in the industry. It serves more than 200 countries and territories. The company operates in five international regions: Europe/Middle East Africa, Asia Pacific, Latin America/Caribbean, Canada and the United States. The company is broken down into several divisions because of this. These divisions include UPS Air Cargo, UPS Aviation Technologies, UPS Capital Corporation, UPS Consulting, UPS Mail Innovations, Mail Boxes Etc., Inc., UPS Professional Services, UPS Supply Chain Solutions, and UPS Tele Services.

联合包裹服务公司成立于 1907 年。它在美国和世界各地都有分店。它的公司总部设在佐治亚州的亚特兰大。UPS 是世界上最大的包裹分发公司，每天递送超过 1300 万份文件和包裹，每年产生超过 270 亿美元的收入。UPS 也是世界上最大的快递包裹和文件递送公司，在两天或更短的时间内递送的包裹比业内任何其他公司都多，而且受到跟踪和保证。它服务于 200 多个国家和地区。该公司在五个国际地区开展业务：欧洲/中东、非洲、亚太地区、拉丁美洲/加勒比、加拿大和美国。正因为如此，公司被分成了几个部门。这些部门包括 UPS 航空货运公司、UPS 航空技术公司、UPS 资本公司、UPS 咨询公司、UPS 邮件创新公司、邮箱等公司、UPS 专业服务、UPS 供应链解决方案和 UPS 电信服务。

5.2.3　Express Mail Service 特快专递

Express mail is an accelerated mail delivery service for which the customer pays a surcharge and receives faster delivery. Express mail is a service for domestic and international mail and is in most countries governed by a country's own postal administration. Since 1998, the international accelerated delivery services have been governed by the EMS Cooperative.

特快专递是一种加速邮件递送服务，客户支付附加费，可收到更快的递送。特快专递是一种国内和国际邮件服务，在大多数国家都由一个国家自己的邮政管理机构管理。自1998年起，国际加速递送服务由特快专递合作社管理。

5.2.4　Special Line Logistics 专线物流

Special line logistics is also a new type of cross-border logistics mode under the background of the development of cross-border E-commerce. Special line logistics specifically refers to the cross-border logistics mode formed in two or more countries or regions, the transport route, transport time, logistics starting point and destination, and means of transport are all fixed, especially for fixed cross-border logistics routes.

专线物流也是在跨境电子商务发展背景下出现的一种新型跨境物流模式。专线物流具体指在两个及两个以上国家或地区形成的跨境物流模式，运输线路、运输时间、物流起点与终点、运输工具都是固定的，尤其是针对固定跨境物流线路而言。

As far as cross-border E-commerce is concerned, special line logistics can play the function of long-distance cross-border transportation and has high scale attributes through the special line logistics model. It can give full play to economies of scale, which is of great significance to reduce cross-border logistics costs, especially for cross-border E-commerce in a fixed market. It is an effective cross-border logistics solution.

专线物流对跨境电子商务而言，可以起到长途跨境运输的功能，具有很高的规模化属性，通过专线物流模式，能够发挥规模经济效应，对于降低跨境物流成本意义重大，尤其对固定市场的跨境电子商务而言，更是一种行之有效的跨境物流解决方案。

Section 5.3　The Selection of Cross-border Logistics Mode 跨境物流模式的选择

New Words

statistic	*n.*	统计学；统计数字（资料）
vendor	*n.*	〈正式〉供应商；小贩
calculated	*adj.*	精心策划的；蓄意的

Phrases

the postal system	邮政体系
international E-mail treasure	国际 e 邮宝
packet loss rate	丢包率
direct mail mod	直邮模式
transport mode	运输模式

Sentences

1. It will cause a lot of problems in our transportation.
   这将给我们的运输带来很多问题。

2. Usually, it is cheaper to have the goods sent by sea than by railway.
   通常，海运较陆运便宜。

3. Sometimes, the way of combined transportation has the complicated formalities.
   有时联运的手续十分烦琐。

4. I'm afraid we can't refund you after it's washed.
   恐怕洗过后我们就不能给您退款了。

5. We do not accept merchandise for return unless items are defective.
   若非商品瑕疵，我们是不收退货的。

6. You can exchange it, provided that you haven't taken off the tag.
   只要你没有把吊牌拿掉便可以换货。

7. I'm sorry, I can't exchange your shirt without the receipt.
   很抱歉，没有发票，我不能给您换这件衬衫。

8. We may either pay you an allowance or have the goods replaced.
   我们或者给你折价，或者给你换货。

9. Since the establishment of our company, it has received universal praise by virtue of good reputation, high quality and perfect after-service.
   我公司自成立以来，凭借良好的商业信誉和绝对的质量保证以及完善的售后服务得到了全国各地众多客户的高度评价和赞赏。

10. Buyer would has 24 hours for checking after he get goods, please confirm and give your suggestion in time. Base on spiteful evaluate, we will cancel the after service!
    买家有 24 小时来对收到的货物进行检测，并确认和给出自己的评价，基于不合理的评价，我方不负责售后！

11. The automotive reliability analysis method based on failure information from after-service webs of automobile manufacture is discussed in this paper.
    文中介绍了利用汽车制造企业售后服务网络反馈的故障信息对汽车进行可靠性评价的方法。

12. Improve the service not only includes the hardware, but also covers technology consulting, the company also hopes membership with the perfect service to build customer good

evaluation.

完善的售后服务不只包含了硬件，也涵盖了技术咨询，本公司更寄望借着完善的售后服务建立客户的良好评价。

13. The good quality of the products and the wide-ranging after-sale service have been highly appraised by our customers.

依靠优质的产品、全方位的售后服务赢得了用户的高度评价。

14. We have some questions about after-sale services.

我们对售后服务有几点疑问。

15. Make sure they know how much you appreciate them, and make sure that your after-sales support reflects this.

确保他们知道你很感谢他们，并确保你给予他们的售后服务反映了这一点。

16. Because not only do we custom build the equipment to your requirements but our computers and after-sales service is first class.

我们不仅可以按照你们的要求生产设备，而且我们的电脑和售后服务都是一流的。

17. This will ensure you'll enjoy decent after-service care.

这将确保你能够享受到充分的售后服务。

18. The company persists in the principle of "quality first" and "clients supreme" all along and trusts its clients with quality products, considerate post-sales services and truehearted management ideas.

公司始终以"质量第一、用户至上"为宗旨，承诺以诚信的经营理念提供优质的产品、优质的售后服务。

19. And what about your after-sale service?

你们的售后服务怎样？

20. After the grand opening of our joint venture in China last year, we established as of the beginning of this year our own sales, marketing, after-sales services and distribution organization in China.

去年我们举行中国合资企业的盛大开幕典礼，今年初，我们在中国建立了自己的销售、市场推广、售后服务与分销团队。

21. Please give us detailed accounts concerning functions of these new products and after-sale service.

请给我们提供关于产品性能和售后服务的详细记录。

Conversations

1. The Third-party Logistics Company

Wayne: I have some suggestions to talk with you, Bonnie.

Bonnie: Just go ahead. I'm all ears.

Wayne: I think our company logistics business should be outsourced to the third-party logistics company.

Bonnie: Why do we use third-party logistics?

Wayne: Because third-party logistics companies can do it better, and outsourcing the logistics function can free up resources to focus on core competencies. In addition, 3PL companies can share responsibility with us.

Bonnie: That sounds good. I will call a meeting to discuss whether the logistics outsourcing out. Thanks for your suggestion.

Wayne: You're welcome.

1. 第三方物流公司

韦恩：邦妮，我有些建议想和你说。

邦妮：说吧，我洗耳恭听。

韦恩：我认为我们公司的物流业务应该外包给第三方物流公司。

邦妮：我们为什么要使用第三方物流？

韦恩：因为第三方物流公司可以把它做得更好。外包物流功能可以释放资源，使自己专注于核心竞争力，还可以分摊责任。

邦妮：听上去很不错。我会召开会议商量是否该把物流业务外包出去。谢谢你的建议。

韦恩：不客气。

2. Not Allow Refund

Clerk: May I help you?

Sarah: Yes, I would like to return these slacks.

Clerk: All right. How long do you have it?

Sarah: I bought them last week.

Clerk: And why are you returning them?

Sarah: 1 bought them to go with a blouse of mine. But they don't really match.

Clerk: I see. Oh, wait. Ma'am, I'm sorry. These slacks were on sale.

Sarah: Yes, they were thirty percent off.

Clerk: I'm sorry, but we don't allow returns on sale items.

Sarah: I know many stores have that policy. But I have returned sale items here before.

Clerk: I'm sorry, but we usually don't do it. It is our policy.

Sarah: I just bought these slacks a week ago. And I am a regular customer here. Can you make an exception this time?

Clerk: Well. Let me talk to the manager for a moment.

(A moment later)

Clerk: Customer, the manager says I can do it this time.

Sarah: Good. I'm a regular customer here. I am glad you can make an exception for me.

Clerk: Please show me your trading record again.

Sarah: Here it is.

Clerk: I will have to give you store credit, customer. If you find something else you like in the store, you can use the credit.

Sarah: Store credit is okay with me. I'm sure I will find something I like. I shop here a lot.

Clerk: We appreciate your business, customer.

2. 不接受退款

店员：亲，有什么需要帮助的吗？

莎拉：是的，我想退回这些长裤。

店员：好的。你什么时候拍的？

莎拉：我上星期才拍的。

店员：为什么要退呢？

莎拉：我本想买来配一件衬衫，但是它们配起来不好看。

店员：我明白了。等一等，女士，对不起，这是打折商品。

莎拉：没错，它们是七折品。

店员：对不起，打折商品不能退货的。

莎拉：我知道很多店都是这样，但是我曾经在你们的店退过商品。

店员：对不起，我们通常不接受的，这是规定。

莎拉：我上个星期才买的，而且我是你们的常客。这次可以例外吗？

店员：那么，让我和经理说说看。

（一会儿后）

店员：女士，经理说这次可以。

莎拉：太好了，我是你们的常客，我很高兴你们可以为我破例。

店员：再让我看一看你与我们店铺的交易记录好吗？

莎拉：这里。

店员：我会给你一些点数，女士。你可以用这些点数来挑你喜欢的东西。

莎拉：给我点数也可以。我会找到我喜欢的东西，我常常来你家店铺购物。

店员：谢谢惠顾，女士。

Text

5.3.1 Cross-border E-commerce Export Logistics Mode
跨境电商出口物流模式

According to incomplete statistics, China's current cross-border E-commerce has more than 60 percent of the goods shipped through the postal system. China post actively carries out cross-border logistics and express delivery service, and has customized the new international postal and delivery products for eBay China sellers. International E-post is a new economical international mail delivery product tailored for Chinese E-commerce vendors to meet the needs of the international E-commerce delivery market. International E-mail treasure and the Hong Kong international as for light small items of airmail parcel service products. At present, the business is limited to provide Chinese electricity sellers sender sent to the United States, Canada, Britain, France and Australia package Posting and delivering services. The international E-mail treasure economy is economical, support to be charged according to the total weight, 50 grams first weight, continue to be calculated according to each gram, free registration fee. In 2013, the international E-mail service has covered more than 40 cities in China, with an average daily processing of 100,000 parcels. Although China post has a global postal network, it still has a long transportation time and high packet loss rate in terms of logistics service.

据不完全统计，中国目前跨境电子商务有超过 60%的商品通过邮政体系运输。中国邮政积极开展跨境物流快递业务，为 eBay 中国大陆卖家量身定制了全新国际邮递产品国际 e 邮宝。国际 e 邮宝是中国邮政为适应国际电子商务寄递市场的需要，为中国电商卖家量身定制的一款全新经济型国际邮递产品。国际 e 邮宝和香港国际小包服务一样是针对轻小件物品的空邮产品，目前，该业务限于为中国电商卖家寄件人提供发向美国、加拿大、英国、法国和澳大利亚的包裹寄递服务。国际 e 邮宝经济实惠，支持按总重计费，50 克首重，续重按照每克计算，免收挂号费。2013 年，国际 e 邮宝服务已覆盖中国 40 多个城市，日均处理包裹达 10 万件。中国邮政虽然拥有覆盖全球的邮政网络，但物流服务仍存在运输时间长、丢包率高等问题。

5.3.2　Cross-border E-commerce Import Logistics Mode 跨境电商 进口物流模式

The import logistics mode under the cross-border e-commerce environment mainly includes direct mail mode and transport mode. Among them, direct mail mode is divided into commercial express direct mail and two countries express cooperation direct mail. The transport mode has sunshine overseas online shopping and grey overseas online shopping.

跨境电子商务环境下的进口物流模式主要包括直邮模式和运输模式。其中，直邮模式分为商业快递直邮和两国快递合作直邮；运输模式有阳光海外网购和灰色海外网购。

【 Exercise 】

1. Translate the following phrases into Chinese.

economic globalization_____

tariff barrier _____

global supply chain _____

upstream and downstream companies _____

green logistics _____

2. Translate the following phrases into English.

邮政物流_____

中国邮政航空邮件_____

进口关税_____

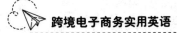
增值服务_____

物流固定成本_____

电子数据交换（EDI）_____

3. Please explain the following words or items.

    (1) 3PL

    (2) 4PL

4. Please answer the following questions.

    (1) What are the benefits of overseas warehouse?

    (2) What are the advantages of 4PL?

    (3) What are the advantages of 3PL?

Chapter 6 Cross-border E-commerce Market Theory
跨境电子商务市场理论

【Ability Objectives】

- ❑ Be able to introduce the E-commerce in English 能够用英语介绍电子商务；
- ❑ Be able to communicate with customers in English 能够用英语与顾客交流；
- ❑ Be able to read and comprehend some articles related to cross-border E-commerce 能够阅读和理解与跨境电子商务有关的文章。

【Knowledge Objectives】

- ❑ Master typical expressions about cross-border E-commerce 掌握跨境电子商务的经典表达；
- ❑ Memorize new words and phrases in the texts 能够记忆文章中的单词与短语。

【Key Words】

platform marketing（平台营销）；SNS marketing（SNS 营销）；SEO & SEM marketing（搜索引擎优化与搜索引擎营销）；mobile marketing（移动营销）；store description（店铺描述）；product description（产品描述）；title description（标题描述）；product selecting of cross-border E-commerce（跨境电商选品）；product pricing of cross-border E-commerce（跨境电子商务产品定价）

Section 6.1 Overview of Cross-border E-commerce Marketing 跨境电子商务市场营销概述

New Words

institution	*n.*	制度；制定；建立；设立
interconnect	*v.*	互相连接；（使）互相联系
interdependent	*adj.*	（各部分）相互依存的
approaches	*n.*	手段；接近；探讨；进路
	v.	探讨；临近；处理；走近
premier	*n.*	总理；地区总理
	adj.	首要的；最著名的；最成功的；第一的

component	*n.*	成分；部件；组成部分
	adj.	构成的
innovation	*n.*	创新；改革；（新事物、思想或方法的）创造；新思想
extension	*n.*	延伸；延长；延期；扩大
target	*n.*	目标；指标；靶子
	v.	面向；把……作为攻击目标；把……作为批评的对象
recipient	*n.*	接受者；受方
	adj.	容纳的；感受性强的
typical	*adj.*	典型的；有代表性的；一贯的；平常的
spam	*n.*	（非正式）滥发的电邮，垃圾电邮
	v.	在互联网上向（大量的新闻组或用户）发送垃圾信息，群发
segmentation	*n.*	分割；割断；细胞分裂
technique	*n.*	技巧，技术；手法
personalization	*n.*	个性化
bombardment	*n.*	轰炸；炮击
permission	*n.*	允许，许可
unsolicited	*adj.*	未经请求的；主动提供的
profile	*n.*	侧面；轮廓；外形；剖面；简况
	vt.	描……的轮廓；扼要描述
	vi.	给出轮廓
category	*n.*	种类，分类；【数】范畴
selection	*n.*	选择，挑选；选集；精选品
potential	*adj.*	潜在的，可能的；强势的
	n.	潜能，可能性
consistent	*adj.*	始终如一的，一致的；坚持的
coupon	*n.*	优惠券；息票
conceivable	*adj.*	可想象的；可相信的
astute	*adj.*	机敏的；狡猾的，诡计多端的
overwhelm	*vt.*	淹没；压倒；受打击；覆盖；压垮
sweeping	*n.*	扫；打扫；清扫；掠
profitable	*adj.*	有利可图的；赚钱的；有益的
fundamentally	*adv.*	根本地，从根本上；基础地
participatory	*adj.*	供人分享的；吸引参与的
collaborative	*adj.*	合作的，协作的
channel	*n.*	电视台；频道；波段；途径
	v.	为……引资；引导；贯注；提供帮助
homepage	*n.*	主页
stickiness	*n.*	黏性；胶黏

concise	*adj.*	简明的，简洁的
occupation	*n.*	职业；占有；消遣；占有期
budget	*n.*	预算；政府的年度预算
	adj.	价格低廉的；花钱少的
	v.	谨慎花钱；把……编入预算
originator	*n.*	创始人；发明者；提出者
surpassed	*vt.*	超越；胜过，优于；非……所能办到或理解
filter	*v.*	过滤；（消息）走漏
	n.	滤器；【无线】滤波器；【物】滤光镜
upload	*v.*	【计】上传
millennial	*adj.*	一千年的；千禧年的
bio	*n.*	个人简历，小传
exquisite	*adj.*	精致的；细腻的；优美的，高雅的；异常的；剧烈的
	n.	服饰过于讲究的男子
recognition	*n.*	识别；承认，认出；重视；赞誉；公认
tag	*n.*	标记；标签；标志；标牌，给……起诨名
distract	*vt.*	转移；分心
raffle	*n.*	废物；抽彩售货
	vt.	抽彩售货
	vi.	抽彩
launched	*v.*	发射；发起；开展；开始
	n.	发射；汽艇
uniform	*adj.*	统一的；一致的；相同的；均衡的；始终如一的
	vt.	使成一样
referral	*n.*	参照；提及；被推举的人；引荐来源（指给某个网站带来了流量的其他网站）
inventory	*n.*	存货，存货清单；详细目录；财产清册
trustworthy	*adj.*	可靠的；可信赖的
convey	*vt.*	传达；运输；让与
inseparable	*adj.*	（与某事物）不可分离的；形影不离的
	n.	不可分的事物；好友
constantly	*adv.*	不断地；时常地
appropriately	*adv.*	适当地
insightful	*adj.*	有深刻了解的；富有洞察力的
optimization	*n.*	最佳化，最优化
indicate	*vt.*	表明；指出；预示；象征
login	*n.*	【计】进入系统
	vt.	【计】登录；注册
	vi.	【计】登录；注册

navigation	*n.*	航行；航海
tablet	*n.*	平板电脑
	vt.	用碑牌纪念；将（备忘录等）写在板上；将……制成小片或小块
initially	*adv.*	最初，首先；开头
unsolicited	*adj.*	未经请求的；主动提供的
maximize	*v.*	（使）增加到最大限度；充分利用；找到……的最高值；（使计算机视窗）最大化
essentially	*adv.*	本质上；本来
sponsor	*v.*	发起；担保；做广告节目的资助人
	n.	（船只的）命名人；保证人；发起者
aggressive	*adj.*	侵略性的；好斗的；有进取心的；有闯劲的
integrate	*v.*	成为一体；（使）加入
	adj.	完全的
organically	*adv.*	有机地；有组织地；器官上地
substantial	*adj.*	大量的；实质的；内容充实的
	n.	本质；重要材料
revenue	*n.*	税收收入；财政收入；收益
acquaintance	*n.*	熟人；相识；了解；知道

Phrases

QR code	二维码
American Marketing Association	美国营销协会
platform marketing	平台营销
in contrast to	与……形成对照
to make…sense to	对……合乎情理；有道理；有意义
SNS marketing	SNS 营销
social signature	社交签名
monthly active users(MAU)	月度活跃用户
social media	社交媒体
search engine optimization (SEO)	搜索引擎优化
search engine marketing (SEM)	搜索引擎营销
search engines	搜索引擎
on the basis of	根据；基于……
to pay per click(PPC)	点击付费

Sentences

1. Let us imagine the light earth dreams begin to interconnect into a global web due to each focused upon this anchoring at this time.

让我们想象一下，由于每个人此时都专注于这个锚定，光明地球的梦想开始相互连接到一个全球网络中。

2. We live in an increasingly interdependent world.
　　我们生活在一个日益相互依赖的世界。

3. Trust is a vital component in any relationship.
　　在任何关系中，信任都是一个至关重要的因素。

4. We must promote originality, inspire creativity and encourage innovation.
　　我们必须提倡独创性，激发创造力，鼓励创新。

5. Usually, you will not use all the features for customer segmentation.
　　通常情况下，您将不会使用所有客户细分的功能。

6. Net-language is characterized as visualization, popularization and personalization etc.
　　网络语言具有视觉化、时尚化与个性化等特点。

7. The unsolicited ads appear prominently on the screen and are a pet peeve for many users.
　　不请自来的广告显眼地出现在屏幕上，对于许多使用者来说是件恼人的事。

8. Selection is based solely on merit.
　　选拔唯贤。

9. We must be consistent in applying the rules.
　　我们在实施这些规则时必须保持一致。

10. No difficulty can overwhelm us.
　　困难压不倒我们。

11. Fundamentally, there are two different approaches to the problem.
　　从根本上说，这个问题有两种不同的处理方法。

12. Most wikis are collaborative websites.
　　大多数维基网站是合作网站。

13. We have continued to exercise caution in our budgeting for the current year.
　　在今年的预算方面，我们继续小心谨慎。

14. He hopes one day to surpass the world record.
　　他希望有一天能刷新世界纪录。

15. Legal aid can often provide referral to other types of agencies.
　　法律援助机构通常能提供转介到其他类型的机构。

Conversations

1. Promote Products to Guests

A: Hi, dear customer. Summer is coming. We have a new series of the summer clothes. I wonder if you would like to have a look at them. This is our new product link.

B: Oh, I'm going to buy summer wear.

A: We can supply all kinds of styles and colors of summer clothes. I think you will be interested in some of our new products. We always keep the pace of the fashion, so as to catch the interest of our customers.

B: I know, so I'm always the fan of your clothes. I must be interested in your products if they are the styles I want.

A: If you are not satisfied with the new summer clothes. As you know, we also take orders for clothes made according to specifications.

B: I see. I need to take my time.

A: OK, please feel free to contact me if you need anything.

1. 向客人推广产品

A：亲，您好。夏天就要到了，我们店上架了很多新款夏装，我想您可能愿意看看，这是本店的新品链接。

B：哦，我正要购买夏装呢。

A：我们可以供应各种款式、各种颜色的夏装。我觉得我们的一些新产品您会感兴趣的。我们一直紧跟时尚，并抓住消费者的兴趣。

B：我知道，所以我一直很喜欢你们店的衣服，如果你们的产品是我想要的类型，我一定愿意购买。

A：如果最近上的几款夏装您不满意，你知道，我们也可以根据您的具体要求定制衣服。

B：我知道了，我需要慢慢挑选。

A：好的，如有任何需要，请随时联系我。

2. Shoes Promotion

A: Dear customer, sorry to disturb you. Recently, in order to take advantage of the shopping festival, all the leather shoes in our store are promoting. Buy one get one free. Want to know the details? Click on the link below!

B: Buy one get one free! That's great! But why buy leather shoes get sneakers free?

A: Our sports shoes are newly launched. You can wear a pair of leather shoes when you go to work and wear sports shoes in the gym. Keep a work-life balance.

B: That sounds good.

A: If you order now, we will send you the best shoe polish, which can help you maintain your shoes at home.

B: I do like a pair of shoes, but it's a little expensive. Do you have any discount?

A: Sorry, we offer you promotional price now.

B: Okay, I'll place the order now.

2. 鞋子促销

A：亲，抱歉，打扰了。最近为了配合购物节的到来，我们店内的所有皮鞋都在搞促销，买一双送一双。想知道详情吗？快来点击下面的链接吧！

B：买一送一！这太好了！不过为什么是买一双皮鞋送一双运动鞋呢？

A：我们的运动鞋都是新推出来的，您买一双皮鞋可以上班的时候穿，平日您健身的时候就可以穿运动鞋。工作生活两不误。

B：听起来不错。

A：如果您现在下单，我们还送顶级鞋油，可以让您在家也能保养皮鞋。

B：我倒是看好了一双皮鞋，不过有一点贵，有折扣吗？

A：不好意思，这已经是促销价了。

B：好吧，我现在就去下单。

Text

6.1.1　Introduction of Marketing 市场营销简介

Marketing is defined by the American Marketing Association as "the activity, set of institutions, and processes for creating, communicating, delivering, and exchanging offerings that have value for customers, clients, partners, and society at large". The term developed from the original meaning which referred literally to going to a market to buy or sell goods or services. Sales process engineering views marketing as "a set of processes that are interconnected and interdependent with other functions, whose methods can be improved using a variety of relatively new approaches".

美国营销协会将营销定义为"创造、沟通、交付和交换对客户、顾客、合作伙伴和整个社会有价值的产品的活动、机构和流程"。这个词的本意即字面意思，是指去市场购买或销售商品或服务。销售流程工程将营销视为"一套与其他职能相互联系和相互依赖的流程，其方法可以使用各种相对较新的方法加以改进"。

Marketing is used to create, keep and satisfy the customer. With the customer as the focus of its activities, it can be concluded that marketing is one of the premier components of business management—the other being innovation. Other services and management activities such as operations (or production), human resources, accounting, law and legal aspects can be "bought in" or "contracted out".

营销是用来创造、留住和满足顾客的。以客户为活动的中心，可以得出结论：营销是企业管理的首要组成部分之一——另一个是创新。其他服务和管理活动，如运营（或生产）、人力资源、会计、法律和法律问题，可以"买入"或"外包"。

6.1.2　Platform Marketing 平台营销

Platform marketing is an extension of marketing, which mainly happens on a web platform. So sellers man get many ways to carry out their marketing. Here we introduce three common platform marketing ways.

平台营销是市场营销的延伸，主要发生在网络平台上。所以卖家有很多方法来进行他们的营销。这里我们介绍三种常见的平台营销方式。

1. Direct E-mail Marketing 电子邮件直销

1) Introduction of Direct E-mail Marketing 电子邮件直销简介

Direct E-mail marketing is a new form of advertising that ads are sent to a targeted list of recipients by E-mail. The messages, which may be texts, HTML, or media movies, and etc. Web-based ads are more than typical E-mail messages. A number of elements make direct E-mail marketing different from spams or other regular E-mail ads. For example, the sender may use customer segmentation techniques to ensure that the message is sent to the right customer, and use personalization techniques to ensure the E-mail be sent to recipient himself or herself.

直接电子邮件营销是一种新型的广告形式，通过电子邮件将广告发送给目标受众。消息可以是文本、HTML 或媒体电影等。基于网络的广告比典型的电子邮件消息更多。许多因素使得电子邮件营销不同于垃圾邮件或其他常规电子邮件广告。例如，发送者可以使用客户细分技术确保将消息发送给正确的客户，并使用个性化技术确保将电子邮件发送给接收者自己。

In contrast to the bombardment approach of spams, the concept behind direct E-mail marketing is that it makes more sense to send attractive, professional, and evocative ads to a smaller group of recipients that might actually be interested in receiving such messages. Direct E-mail marketing is generally E-mails based on the permission of users, rather than unsolicited commercial E-mail.

与垃圾邮件的轰炸方法不同，电子邮件直销背后的概念是，向可能真正有兴趣接收此类邮件的一小部分收件人发送吸引人的、专业的和唤起人心的广告。直接电子邮件营销通常是基于用户许可的电子邮件，而不是未经请求的商业电子邮件。

2) Tips for Direct E-mail Marketing 电子邮件直销的技巧

(1) Understand your target customers. Knowing about your best customers is a key factor in targeted direct marketing. Knowing the customers' basic structures and features, such as males aged 18 to 34 or females with children, is a start. However, a more complete understanding of your customers profiles like their shopping and purchasing behaviors in other categories, their attitudes toward trends, products, marketing and media, or their lifestyle habits can help you become even more effective in both your customer selection and the message you will use in communicating with the customers.

了解您的目标客户。了解你最好的客户是有针对性的直销的关键因素。了解客户的基本结构和特征，如 18 岁至 34 岁的男性或有孩子的女性，是一个开始。然而，更全面地了解客户的概况，如他们在其他类别的购物和购买行为；他们对趋势、产品、营销和媒体的态度；或者他们的生活习惯，可以帮助你在客户选择和与客户沟通时使用的信息更加有效。

(2) Target your ideal customer. Once you understand your customers, you can use this information to build a targeted list of potential customers. Targeted direct mailing lists can be expensive, but they are likely to result in the best response rate and generate future loyal customers.

瞄准您的理想客户。一旦您了解了您的客户，您就可以使用此信息构建潜在客户的目标列表。有针对性的直接邮件列表可能很昂贵，但它们可能会产生最好的响应率，并产生未来的忠诚客户。

(3) Create a mailing list. Once you have a mailing list, it is time to create your direct mail

message. The direct mail piece you create delivers your message. Make it consistent with what you are selling. If you are offering a professional high-quality service, your direct mail piece needs to reflect that quality.

创建邮件列表。一旦您有了邮件列表，就可以创建直接邮件消息了。您创建的直邮邮件会传递您的邮件。让它与您销售的东西保持一致。如果您提供的是专业的高质量服务，您的直邮邮件需要反映这种质量。

2. Coupons 优惠券

Coupons are a great way to attract and get existing customers to come to your business. Here are some tips to use coupons to advertise your business.

Coupons have proven themselves to be highly effective sales tools for every conceivable size and type of business.

For coupons that "pull in the business"，they have gained remarkable acceptance and popularity among astute marketing managers. A simple explanation for their acceptance by advertisers is their overwhelming acceptance and use by the consumers.

It is very easy to see why coupon advertising is sweeping the country. Regular use of good couponing stagey will provide a steady stream of new customers and high quality sales leads.

You are also being given the opportunity to sell-up to a more profitable product or service. You would not have had this opportunity had it not been for the coupon getting the customer through the door in the first place.

优惠券是吸引和吸引现有客户来你的企业的一种很好的方式。这里有一些使用优惠券为你的企业做广告的小贴士。

优惠券已经证明，对于任何可以想象到的规模和类型的企业来说，优惠券都是非常有效的销售工具。

对于"吸引生意"的优惠券，它们受到了精明的营销经理的显著的接受和欢迎。它们被广告商接受的一个简单解释是它们被消费者压倒性地接受和使用。

很容易理解为什么优惠券广告席卷全国。定期使用优惠券将提供源源不断的新客户和高质量的销售线索。

你也有机会出售更有利可图的产品或服务。如果不是因为优惠券让客户在第一时间通过了这扇门，你就不会有这样的机会。

3. Promotion 促销

Promotion refers to raising customer awareness of a product or brand, generating sales, and creating brand loyalty. It is one of the four basic elements of the market mix, which includes the four Ps: product, promotion, price and place.

Fundamentally, there are three basic objectives of promotion, including

❑　to present information to consumers and other,

❑　to increase demand,

❑　to differentiate a product.

促销指的是提高消费者对产品或品牌的认识，创造销售额，并创造品牌忠诚度。它是市场组合的四个基本要素之一，它包括产品、促销、价格和地点四个 P。从根本上讲，推广有三个基本目标：向消费者和其他人展示信息；增加需求；区分产品。

The purpose of a promotion and thus its promotional plan can have a wide range, including sales increase, new product acceptance, creation of brand equity, positioning, competitive retaliations, or creation of a corporate image.

促销的目的及促销计划的范围可以很广，包括增加销售、接受新产品、创造品牌资产、定位、竞争报复或创建企业形象。

There have been different ways to promote a product in person or with different media. Both person and media can be either physically real or virtual. Promotion can be done by different media, namely print media which include newspaper and magazines, electronic media which include radio and television, digital media which include Internet, social networking and social media sites and lastly outdoor media which include banner ads out of home.

促销产品可以通过面对面或者不同的媒介来实现。人和媒介都可以是真实的，也可以是虚拟的。推广可以通过不同的媒介进行，包括报纸和杂志的印刷媒体，包括电台和电视的电子媒体，包括互联网、社交网络和社交媒体网站的数码媒体，以及包括横额广告的户外媒体。

Digital medium is a modern way of brands interaction with consumers as it releases news, information and advertising from the technology limits of print and broadcast infrastructures. Mass communication has led to modern marketing strategies to continue focusing on brand awareness, large distributions and heavy promotions. The fast-paced environment of digital media presents new methods for promotion to utilize new tools now available through technology. With the rise of technology across geographic borders to reach a greater number of potential consumers, the goal of a promotion is then to reach the most people in a time-efficient and a cost-efficient manner.

数字媒体是一种品牌与消费者互动的现代方式，它从印刷和广播基础设施的技术限制中发布新闻、信息和广告。大众传播导致现代营销策略继续注重品牌知名度、大规模分销和大力促销。数字媒体的快节奏环境提供了新的推广方法，以利用现在通过技术可获得的新工具。随着跨越地理边界的技术的兴起，为了接触更多的潜在消费者，那么促销的目标就是以节省时间和成本效益的方式接触最多的人。

Social medium, as a modern marketing tool, offers opportunities to reach larger audiences in an interactive way. These interactions allow for conversation rather than simply educating the customer. Facebook, Twitter, LinkedIn, Pinterest, Tumblr and Instagram are rated as some of the most popular social networking sites. As a participatory media culture, social media platforms or social networking sites are forms of mass communication that allow large amounts of product and distribution of content to reach the largest audience possible through media technologies.

社交媒体作为一种现代营销工具，提供了以互动的方式接触更多受众的机会。这些互动允许对话，而不是简单地教育客户。Facebook、Twitter、LinkedIn、Pinterest、Tumblr 和 Instagram 被评为最受欢迎的社交网站。作为一种参与性媒体文化，社交媒体平台或社交网站是大众传播的形式，其通过媒体技术使大量产品和内容的分发能够接触到尽可能多的受众。

6.1.3　SNS Marketing SNS 营销

SNS(social networking sites), also known as social media, refers to the sites and technologies that allow people to write, share, comment, discuss, and communicate with each other. It is a platform for content creation and exchange based on user relationships on the Internet. SNS marketing means to conduct marketing, public relations, and customer service using social networks, online communities, blogs or other online collaborative platforms. Since SNS marketing has the advantages of low cost and high reach, it is becoming a hot and key marketing spot in recent years. The first step in social media marketing is to attract customers to visit our social media pages and become fans. We should make full use of existing channels or pages that we have. For example, we can place icons of social media sites in the eye-catching location of our store and link them to our social media pages, or just put our QR code directly. In our marketing E-mails to our customers, we can also set up "social signature", that is to place links to our social media pages in the E-mail signature. We can also promote our social media pages offline, such as printing the links of our social media pages on the thank you card.

SNS（社交网站），也称为社交媒体，指的是允许人们相互写作、分享、评论、讨论和交流的网站和技术。它是一个基于互联网上的用户关系进行内容创建和交换的平台。SNS 营销是指利用社交网络、在线社区、博客或其他在线协作平台进行营销、公关和客户服务。由于 SNS 营销具有低成本、高覆盖率的优势，近年来正成为营销热点和重点。社交媒体营销的第一步就是吸引客户访问我们的社交媒体页面，使其成为我们的粉丝。我们应该充分利用现有的频道或页面。例如，我们可以将社交媒体网站的图标放在我们商店的醒目位置，并将它们链接到我们的社交媒体页面，或者直接放置我们的二维码。在我们发给客户的营销电子邮件中，我们还可以设置"社交签名"，即在电子邮件签名中放置指向我们社交媒体页面的链接。我们还可以在线下推广我们的社交媒体页面，例如在感谢卡上打印我们的社交媒体页面的链接。

On a global scale, the most popular social media sites include Facebook, Instagram, Pinterest, Twitter, Youtube, VK, LinkedIn and so on.

在全球范围内，最受欢迎的社交媒体网站包括 Facebook、Instagram、Pinterest、Twitter、YouTube、VK、LinkedIn 等。

1. Facebook 脸书

After more than a decade of development since 2004, Facebook has become the No.1 social media site globally with nearly 2 billion monthly active users(MAU) and 20% market share. According to the comprehensive website ranking from Alexa, Facebook's website traffic and the number of visitors are both ranked top three among all global sites.

自 2004 年以来，经过十多年的发展，Facebook 已经成为全球第一大社交网站。社交媒体网站在全球拥有近二十亿月度活跃用户（MAU）和 20%的市场份额。根据 Alexa 的综合网站排名，Facebook 的网站流量和访问量都位居全球所有网站的前三名。

If Chinese sellers want to promote their online stores and products on Facebook, firstly they need to have a Facebook account. Facebook uses the real-name system. So sellers must ensure the authenticity and accuracy of the information provided, so that they can get back the account with a photo ID in case the account is restricted or blocked. Besides, personal accounts sellers can also create a Facebook page for the store, which is similar to a public homepage. Sellers can interact with fans on Facebook page to improve customer stickiness.

如果中国卖家想在 Facebook 上推广他们的网店和产品。首先,他们需要有一个 Facebook 账户。Facebook 使用实名制。因此,卖家必须确保提供的信息的真实性和准确性,以便在账户受到限制或被屏蔽的情况下,他们可以用带照片的身份证取回账户。除了个人账户,卖家还可以为商店创建一个 Facebook 页面,类似于公共主页。卖家可以在 Facebook 页面上与粉丝互动,以提高客户黏性。

The main paid methods of marketing that Facebook offers are Facebook ads and promotion post.

Facebook 提供的主要付费营销方式是 Facebook 广告和促销帖子。

Facebook ads consists of the title, body image and URL. It generally uses very concise but attractive texts and images to deliver our message and attract customers to click the link to visit our store or product. We can set the target audience for every advertisement, using age, gender, location, occupation, hobbies and other conditions to make our advertisements more precise, and to reach our target customers more accurately. Moreover, we can analyze the effect of advertisements with the data provided by Facebook, and timely adjust our marketing strategies.

Facebook 广告由标题、主体图像和 URL 组成。它通常使用非常简洁但有吸引力的文字和图像传递我们的信息,并吸引客户点击链接访问我们的商店或产品。我们可以为每个广告设定目标受众,根据年龄、性别、地点、职业、爱好等条件,使我们的广告更精准、更准确地触达我们的目标客户。此外,我们还可以利用 Facebook 提供的数据分析广告的效果,并及时调整我们的营销策略。

In addition, we can also post on our personal accounts or Facebook page to advertise and promote our products or stores. We can promote any of the posts, and we can also set the target audience we want to reach, as well as our daily promotion budget. This is a very convenient and low-cost way to promote on Facebook, but very effective at the same time.

此外,我们还可以在我们的个人账户或 Facebook 页面上张贴,为我们的产品或商店做广告和促销。我们可以推广任何一个帖子,我们也可以设定我们想要接触到的目标受众,以及我们的日常推广预算。这是在 Facebook 上进行推广的一种非常方便和低成本的方式,但同时也非常有效。

2. Instagram 照片墙

Founded in 2010, Instagram was the originator of the picture social media sites. In December 2014, the active users of Instagram officially surpassed Twitter, making it the world's second largest social media. Currently, Instagram has more than 700 million monthly active users. In October 2012, Facebook acquired Instagram for 735 million. Before that, Instagram had only 13 employees and never promoted their site.

Instagram 成立于 2010 年，是第一家图片社交媒体网站。2014 年 12 月，Instagram 活跃用户正式超过推特，成为全球第二大社交媒体，目前 Instagram 月活跃用户超过 7 亿。2012 年 10 月，Facebook 以 7.35 亿美元收购了 Instagram。在此之前，Instagram 只有 13 名员工，从未推广过自己的网站。

The use of Instagram is very simple. Users post beautiful pictures with short texts, while others are free to give likes, comments and shares.

Instagram 的使用非常简单。用户用短文字发布漂亮的图片，而其他人则可以自由点赞、评论和分享。

Instagram is an interest-based social media. Users can search for contents that interest them, and the platform will recommend the content you may be interested in based on the users' browsing history.

Instagram 是一种基于兴趣的社交媒体。用户可以搜索他们感兴趣的内容，平台将根据用户的浏览历史向您推荐您可能感兴趣的内容。

Instagram has dozens of different and beautiful filters, making the uploaded photos more artistic. Users can also do some simple editing for photos with the editing function. What's more, these beautiful filters can even be used on short videos.

Instagram 有几十种不同的漂亮滤镜，让上传的照片更具艺术性。用户还可以使用编辑功能对照片进行一些简单的编辑。更重要的是，这些漂亮的滤镜甚至可以用在短视频上。

Instagram users are mainly female, and users under 35 years old account for up to 90%. More than 50% of the millennials think that Instagram has the greatest impact on their online shopping options, while Facebook ranked second with just over 30% of the vote, and only 10% for Twitter. It can be said that Instagram is the most influential social media for young people. So, for sellers in the industries of fashion, women, pets, home and children, Instagram is a key marketing platform that sellers should pay great attention to.

Instagram 用户以女性为主，35 岁以下用户占比高达 90%。超过 50% 的千禧一代认为 Instagram 对他们的网购选择影响最大，Facebook 以略高于 30% 的得票率位居第二，推特的得票率仅为 10%。可以说，Instagram 是对年轻人最具影响力的社交媒体。所以，对于时尚、女性、宠物、家居、儿童等行业的卖家来说，Instagram 是卖家应该高度重视的重点营销平台。

Instagram does not allow any links in the posts, so the bio on the personal homepage becomes the only place where we can put the store link. Remember to write "Click the link in my bio" on each post to remind customers to purchase the product by clicking the link on the personal homepage.

Instagram 不允许在帖子中有任何链接，因此个人主页上的简历成为我们可以放置商店链接的唯一位置。记住在每个帖子上写上 "单击我的简历中的链接"，以通过单击个人主页上的链接提醒客户购买产品。

Instagram is a picture social media, so the photos we upload on Instagram must be exquisite, attractive, and let the photos represent our products. The tone of all pictures should suit the style of our brand, maintain consistency, and improve brand recognition.

Instagram 是图片社交媒体，所以我们上传到 Instagram 上的照片一定要精美、有吸引力，让照片能代表我们的产品。所有图片的色调都要与我们的品牌风格相适应，保持一致性，以提高品牌认知度。

Instagram users will search the contents they are interested in by tags, so we must be efficient at using tags to mark our pictures, and attract more people to read our posts. We can use some keywords or phrases associated with the brand, or some of the popular and most searched tags. We can also create our own tags, so that the tags are unique and easy to be found. Furthermore, our fans can put our unique tags with their photos to interact with us. A post should not have too many tags, so that the tags will not be distracting.

Instagram 用户会通过标签搜索他们感兴趣的内容，所以我们必须高效地使用标签来标记我们的图片，并吸引更多的人阅读我们的帖子。我们可以使用一些与品牌相关的关键字或短语，或者使用一些流行的、被搜索次数最多的标签。我们还可以创建自己的标签，这样标签就是唯一的，并且很容易找到。此外，我们的粉丝可以在他们的照片上贴上我们独特的标签，与我们互动。一篇帖子不应该有太多的标签，这样标签就不会分散人们的注意力。

Another common marketing tool is to create some activities, such as a raffle or a competition. Through raffles or competition, we can not only advertise and promote our products, but also interact with our fans and increase customer stickiness. Finally, Instagram also offers paid promotion services. Sellers with enough budget can also choose to use these services based on demand.

另一种常见的营销工具是创建一些活动，如抽奖或比赛。通过抽奖或比赛，我们不仅可以宣传和推广我们的产品，还可以与我们的粉丝互动，增加客户黏性。最后，Instagram 还提供付费促销服务。有足够预算的卖家也可以根据需求选择使用这些服务。

3. Pinterest

Officially launched in 2010, Pinterest is also a picture social media site, and the first to use "infinite scrolling" to display pictures. In 2016, the monthly active users of Pinterest exceeded 150 million, and more than half of the users come from outside the United States.

2010 年正式上线的 Pinterest 也是一个图片社交媒体网站，也是第一个使用"无限滚动"来显示图片的网站。2016 年，Pinterest 的月活跃用户超过 1.5 亿，超过一半的用户来自美国以外的国家。

Pinterest was inspired by Pin and Interest which means users gather the contents of interest and pin them to an online board. The core components of Pinterest are Pin and Board. Pin means to post a picture or video on board, and Board is a picture or video group, similar to an album.

Pinterest 的灵感来自 Pin 和 Interest，这意味着用户收集感兴趣的内容，并将它们固定在一个在线告示牌上。Pinterest 的核心组件是 Pin 和 Board。Pin 是指将图片或视频发布到告示牌上，Board 是图片或视频组，类似于相册。

Like other social media, users can like or comment on the contents of their interest, or repin it to their own board. Users can also add sources of pictures or videos with the link to the website of the product. Other users can click the link to browse and purchase directly.

与其他社交媒体一样，用户可以点赞或评论他们感兴趣的内容，也可以将其转发到自己的告示牌。用户还可以添加带有产品网站链接的图片或视频来源。其他用户可以点击链接直接浏览购买。

和 Instagram 一样，Pinterest 的用户大多是女性，但年龄相对较大。年龄在 36~45 岁的女性用户使用 Pinterest 的时间最长，也是 Pinterest 的主要目标受众。在 Pinterest 上分享最多的内容是生活方式、家庭花园、美容健康、餐饮和购物。

We usually start with uploading a picture and completing the profile, which should fit our product and brand positioning. Take home products as the example. It is best to use a warmer color to create a comfortable home feeling.

我们通常从上传图片和填写个人资料开始，这应该符合我们的产品和品牌定位。以家居产品为例，最好用暖色营造舒适的家居感觉。

It is best to design a highly recognizable style, and apply it to every post we upload. It can make our marketing contents more uniform, as well as increase our credibility and professionalism.

最好是设计一种高度可识别的风格，并将其应用于我们上传的每一篇帖子。它可以使我们的营销内容更加统一，也可以增加我们的公信力和专业性。

We can add the "Pin It" button on the store's homepage to make it easier for our fans to post our products to Pinterest, so that their friends can see our products and visit our store. Relevant data shows that Pinterest can bring a lot of referral traffic for many brands.

我们可以在商店的主页上添加"Pin It"按钮，让我们的粉丝更容易将我们的产品发布到 Pinterest 上，这样他们的朋友就可以看到我们的产品并参观我们的商店。相关数据显示，Pinterest 可以为众多品牌带来大量的引荐流量。

"Rich Pins" is a new feature introduced by Pinterest that will show the source of the product, product details, inventory and price. It makes our post more professional and trustworthy.

"Rich Pins"是 Pinterest 推出的一项新功能，它将显示产品的来源、产品详细信息、库存和价格。它让我们的帖子更专业，更值得信赖。

Creating Pins related to popular topics, or actively repinning other users' interesting posts can both attract more traffic and fans to our Pinterest page. We can also organize raffles or competitions to better interact with fans and increase customer stickiness.

创建与热门话题相关的 Pin，或者主动回复其他用户感兴趣的帖子，都可以吸引更多的流量和粉丝到我们的 Pinterest 页面。我们还可以组织抽奖或比赛，以更好地与粉丝互动，增加客户黏性。

Finally, Pinterest also offers paid promotion services. Sellers with enough budget can also choose to use these services according to demand.

最后，Pinterest 还提供付费促销服务。有足够预算的卖家也可以根据需求选择使用这些服务。

In addition to the above social media platforms, VK is currently the most popular social media site in Russia. Since Russia is one of the largest markets of AliExpress, sellers should pay attention to the marketing on VK.

除上述社交媒体平台外，VK 目前是俄罗斯最受欢迎的社交媒体网站。由于俄罗斯是全球速卖通最大的市场之一，卖家应该注意在 VK 上的营销。

6.1.4　SEO & SEM Marketing 搜索引擎优化与搜索引擎营销

Store promotion and marketing is not just about creating a message for consumers to see, or to spend your budget. In the era of mobile Internet, it is more important to closely follow the trend, so that the marketing budget can fully receive the expected return.

商店促销和营销不仅仅是创造一个信息，让消费者看到，或者花掉你的预算。在移动互联网时代，更重要的是紧跟潮流，让营销预算充分收到预期回报。

Search engine optimization (SEO) means to improve the website's keywords ranking and increase exposure of the company's products through optimizing and repairing the site (web structure adjustment, web content building, web code optimization and coding, etc.) and off-site optimization. Search engine marketing (SEM) is based on the users' habit of using search engines, and tries to convey as much marketing information as possible to the target audience through this process.

搜索引擎优化（SEO）是指通过优化和修复网站（网站结构调整、网站内容建设、网站代码优化和编码等）和站外优化，提高网站的关键词排名，增加公司产品的曝光率。搜索引擎营销以用户使用搜索引擎的习惯为基础，试图通过这个过程向目标受众传达尽可能多的营销信息。

Just like our daily life is inseparable from Baidu, our overseas customers will open Google, Bing or other search engines whenever they need information. It can be said that the most important way for today's Internet users to search for online information and resources is through search engines. Moreover, for cross-border E-commerce websites, more than 35% of visitors are from natural search of Bing, Yahoo and other search engines. Therefore, SOM(SEO+SEM) model is becoming increasingly important in the current Internet marketing.

就像我们的日常生活离不开百度一样，我们的海外客户无论何时需要信息都会打开谷歌、必应或其他搜索引擎。可以说，今天的网民搜索网络信息和资源最重要的方式就是通过搜索引擎。而且，对于跨境电商网站来说，超过 35% 的访问者来自必应、雅虎等搜索引擎的自然搜索。因此，SOM（SEO+SEM）模式在当前的网络营销中变得越来越重要。

It is worth noticing that the search rules of search engines are constantly changing. The change of search rules will directly lead to the change of keywords ranking on the search engine, so SEO is not once and for all. This is in line with the characteristics of the Internet age: the only thing unchangeable is the change itself. This requires our marketing group to continually adjust and optimize on the basis of the original SEO or SEM strategy to adapt to the changing search rules and consumer search habits.

值得注意的是，搜索引擎的搜索规则在不断变化。搜索规则的改变会直接导致关键词在搜索引擎中排名的改变，所以 SEO 不是一劳永逸的。这符合互联网时代的特点：唯一不变的是变化本身。这就要求我们的营销团队在原有 SEO 或 SEM 策略的基础上不断调整和优化，以适应不断变化的搜索规则和消费者搜索习惯。

The advertising mode of SEO or SEM is mainly pay per click(PPC). Compared with the traditional way of paid promotion, the advantage of PPC is that it can bring more accurate customers with lower cost, and achieve better promotion effect. For cross-border E-commerce sellers who want to improve the ranking of their products or stores in Bing and other search engines, they can make efforts in the following aspects.

SEO 或 SEM 的广告模式主要是按点击付费（PPC），与传统的付费推广方式相比，PPC 的优势在于能够以更低的成本带来更精准的客户，达到更好的推广效果。对于想要提升产品或门店在必应等搜索引擎排名的跨境电商卖家，可以在以下几个方面下功夫：

1. Choose a Good Title for the Product 为产品选择好的标题

Besides naming the product according to what we usually refer to as the "three- stage method", we should also add some hot keywords appropriately in the title to attract more consumers with strong purchase intentions by using some keyword analysis tools, such as keyword spy and keyword planner.

除了按照我们通常所说的"三阶段法"来命名产品，我们还应该在标题中适当加入一些热门关键词，通过一些关键词分析工具，如关键词间谍和关键词策划来吸引更多有强烈购买意向的消费者。

2. Put More Efforts in Content Marketing 加大内容营销力度

Many cross-border E-commerce sellers rely solely on product pages to drive SEO. However, sellers can only add some product description on the product page. Although the product description can display the features and advantages of the product in many ways, the brand will lose the opportunity to tell the insightful story that can touch the consumers. Telling some vivid brand stories can make customers to stay on our website for a longer time and drive them to share the stories with their friends and bring more potential buyers to us.

很多跨境电商卖家完全依靠产品页面带动 SEO。但是，卖家只能在产品页面上添加一些产品说明。虽然产品描述可以在很多方面展示产品的特点和优势，但品牌将失去讲述能够触动消费者的真知灼见的故事的机会。讲一些生动的品牌故事可以让客户在我们网站停留的时间更长，并带动他们与朋友分享故事，为我们带来更多的潜在买家。

3. Combine Duplicate Content 合并重复内容

Marketing staff has a common misunderstanding for SEO: the more content the better. The really good marketing content is to maintain the balance between quantity and quality. When multiple pages are showing the same product, the search engine will let them compete with each other, and sometimes it will even lower the ranking. By combining duplicate contents, you can prevent this from happening.

营销人员对 SEO 有一种普遍的误解：内容越多越好。真正好的营销内容是保持数量和质量的平衡。当多个页面显示相同的产品时，搜索引擎会让它们相互竞争，有时甚至会降低排名。通过组合重复内容，可以防止这种情况发生。

4. Create Better Mobile Experience 创造更好的移动体验

It is not that the mobile age is coming but it is already here. There are already more than half of the cross-border E-commerce orders coming from mobile devices, and this figure is still rising. The focus time for mobile users is often very short, and they do not have enough patience to scroll down the page. In order to create better mobile experience we need to design quick login page to make the menu as simple as possible. Moreover, the contact information or contact button should be put on an eye-catching place, and the use of flashing fonts, plug-ins, pop-up pages and interstitial ads should be reduced. We also need to optimize the local search with GPS positioning technology, and track users' different keywords searched on the PC and mobile devices.

这并不是说移动时代即将到来，而是它已经到来了。目前已经有超过一半的跨境电商订单来自移动设备，而且这一数字还在不断上升。手机用户的聚焦时间往往很短，他们没有足够的耐心向下滚动页面。为了创造更好的移动体验，我们需要设计快速登录页面，使菜单尽可能简单。而且，联系方式或联系按钮要放在醒目位置，减少使用闪烁字体、插件、弹出式页面和插页广告。我们还需要利用 GPS 定位技术优化本地搜索，并跟踪用户在 PC 和移动设备上搜索的不同关键字。

5. Get Links through Product Reviews and Public Media 通过产品评论和公共媒体获取链接

It is a new way of marketing to send the product sample to influential public figures, and ask them to publish reviews online. The positive reviews of some opinion leaders or online celebrity often bring us a lot of visitors and high conversion rates. Product reviews are also a simple and effective way of SEO, so we have to encourage customers to leave positive comments in a variety of ways.

把产品样品寄给有影响力的公众人物，并让他们在网上发表评论，这是一种新的营销方式。一些意见领袖或网红的正面评价往往会给我们带来很多访问量，高转化率的产品评论也是一种简单有效的 SEO 方式，所以我们要通过多种方式鼓励客户留下正面评价。

6. Reduce Website Bounce Rate 降低网站跳出率

"Visitor participation and website bounce rate" also have certain proportion in search ranking. If customers stay on the website for a short time but the bounce rate is high, it indicates that this website is not meaningful for most users, and the ranking will be lowered. So we have to find ways to reduce our website bounce rate, such as canceling the pop-up window, using an attractive website design, speeding up the page login time, creating an intuitive navigation bar and so on.

在搜索排名中，"访问者参与度和网站跳出率"也有一定比例。如果客户在网站停留时间短，但跳出率高，则表明该网站对大多数用户没有意义，排名将会降低。所以我们必须想方设法降低我们网站的跳出率，比如取消弹出窗口、采用有吸引力的网站设计、缩短页面登录时间、创建直观的导航栏等。

6.1.5   Mobile Marketing 移动营销

Mobile marketing is a multi-channel online marketing technique focused on specific audience through their smart phone, tablets, or any other related devices through websites, E-mail, SMS and MMS, social media or mobile applications. Mobile marketing can provide time and location sensitive customers with personalized information that promotes goods, services and ideas. In a more theoretical manner, academic Andreas Kaplan defines mobile marketing as "any marketing activity conducted through a ubiquitous network to which consumers are constantly connected using a personal mobile device".

移动营销是通过网站、电子邮件、短信和彩信、社交媒体或移动应用程序，使用智能手机、平板电脑或任何其他相关设备，针对特定的受众进行的一种多渠道的在线营销技术。移动营销可以为对时间和地点敏感的客户提供个性化的信息，以推广商品、服务和想法。学者安德烈亚斯·卡普兰以一种更具理论性的方式将移动营销定义为"通过消费者使用个人移动设备不断连接到的无处不在的网络进行的任何营销活动"。

1. SMS Marketing 短信营销

Marketing through cellphones SMS (short message service) became increasingly popular in the early 2000s in Europe and some parts of Asia when businesses started to collect mobile phone numbers and send off wanted (or unwanted) content.

21 世纪初，当企业开始收集手机号码并发送想要的（或不想要的）内容时，通过手机短信（SMS）进行的营销在欧洲和亚洲的一些地区变得越来越流行。

Mobile marketing approaches through SMS has expanded rapidly in Europe and Asia as a channel to reach the consumer. SMS initially received negative media coverage in many parts of Europe for being a new form of spam as some advertisers purchased lists and sent unsolicited content to consumer's phones. However, as guidelines are put in place by the mobile operators, SMS has become the most popular branch of the mobile marketing industry with several 100 million advertising SMS sent out every month in Europe alone.

作为一种接触消费者的渠道，通过短信进行移动营销的方式在欧洲和亚洲迅速扩展。最初，由于短信是一种新的垃圾邮件形式，欧洲许多地区的媒体都对其进行了负面报道，因为一些广告商购买了名单，并将未经请求的内容发送到消费者的手机上；然而，随着移动运营商制订指导方针，短信已成为移动营销行业最受欢迎的分支，仅在欧洲一个月就有数亿条广告短信发出。

2. APP-based Marketing 基于应用程序的营销

With the strong growth in the use of smart phones, App usage has also greatly increased. Therefore, mobile marketers have increasingly taken advantage of smartphone Apps as a marketing resource. Marketers aim to optimize the visibility of an App in a store, which will maximize the number of downloads. This practice is called App store optimization (ASO).

随着智能手机使用量的强劲增长，App 使用量也大幅提升。因此，移动营销人员越来越多地利用智能手机应用程序作为营销资源。营销人员的目标是优化应用程序在商店中的可见性，这将使下载次数最大化。这种做法称为应用商店优化（ASO）。

There are lots of competitions in this field as well. However, just like other services, it is not easy anymore to rule the mobile Apps market. Most companies have acknowledged the potential of mobile Apps to increase the interaction between a company and its target customers. With the fast growth of the smartphone market, high-quality mobile App development is essential to obtain a strong position in a mobile App store.

这个领域也有很多竞争。然而，就像其他服务一样，要统治移动应用市场已经不是一件容易的事情。大多数公司都承认移动应用程序有助于增加公司与目标客户之间的互动。随着智能手机市场的快速增长，高质量的手机应用开发对于在手机应用商店中获得强势地位至关重要。

3. In-game Mobile Marketing 游戏移动营销

There are essentially three major trends in mobile gaming right now: interactive real-time 3D games, massive multi-player games and social networking games. This means a trend towards more complex and more sophisticated, richer game play. In addition to, there are the so-called casual games, i. e. games that are very simple and very easy to play. Most mobile games today are such casual games and this will probably stay for quite a while.

目前手机游戏基本上有三大趋势：交互式实时 3D 游戏、大型多人游戏和社交网络游戏。这意味着游戏表现出更复杂、更丰富的趋势。除此之外，还有所谓的休闲游戏，也就是非常简单、非常容易玩的游戏。今天的大多数手机游戏都是这样的休闲游戏，这种情况可能会持续很长一段时间。

Brands are now delivering promotional messages within mobile games or sponsoring entire games to drive consumer engagement. This is known as mobile ad-gaming or ad-funded mobile game.

各大品牌现在都在手机游戏中传递促销信息，或者赞助整个游戏，以推动消费者的参与度。这就是众所周知的手机广告游戏或广告资助的手机游戏。

In in-game mobile marketing, advertisers pay to have their name or products featured in the mobile games. For instance, racing games can feature real cars made by Ford or Chevy. Advertisers have been both creative and aggressive in their attempts to integrate ads organically in the mobile games.

在游戏中的移动营销中，广告商付费让他们的名字或产品出现在手机游戏中。例如，赛车游戏可以展示福特或雪佛兰制造的真车。广告商一直在尝试将广告有机地整合到手机游戏中，他们既有创意又有攻击性。

Although investment in mobile marketing strategies like ad-gaming is slightly more expensive than what is intended for a mobile App, a good strategy can make the brand derive substantial revenue. Games that use ad-gaming make the users remember better the brand involved. This memorization increases vitality of the content so that the users tend to recommend them to their friends and acquaintances, and share them via social networks.

虽然广告游戏等移动营销策略的投资略高于移动应用程序的投资，但好的策略可以让品牌获得可观的收入。使用广告游戏的游戏会让用户更好地记住所涉及的品牌。这种记忆增加了内容的活力，因此用户倾向于将它们推荐给他们的朋友和熟人，并通过社交网络分享。

Section 6.2　Store & Product & Title Description
商店、产品以及标题描述

New Words

neglect	v.	忽视；忽略
visual	adj.	视觉的；形象化的
patent	n.	专利权；专利证书
philosophy	n.	人生信条；人生哲学
credible	adj.	可信的；可靠的
rotation	n.	轮换；交替
alternately	adv.	交替地；轮流地
campaign	n.	运动（为社会、商业或政治目的而进行的一系列有计划的活动）
intuitive	adj.	直观的；易懂的
proportion	n.	比例
crucial	adj.	至关重要的；关键性的
keyword	n.	关键词；关键字
maximize	v.	使增加到最大限度
exposure	n.	曝光；曝光量
stimulate	v.	促进；激发；激励
accurate	adj.	准确的；精确地
attribute	n.	属性；性质；特征
conscientious	adj.	认真的；尽责的；小心谨慎的
template	n.	样板；模板；范例
accordingly	adv.	相应地
coherent	adj.	有条理的；清楚易懂的
burst	n.	爆发
promote	v.	促进；推销

profitability	*n.*	盈利能力；收益性
reserve	*v.*	储备；保留；预留
peak	*n.*	最高点；顶点
comprehensive	*adj.*	广泛的；全面的
common	*adj.*	共同的；共有的
dispute	*n.*	纠纷
load	*v.*	加载；载入
logistics	*n.*	物流；后勤；组织工作
custom	*adj.*	定做的；定制的
module	*n.*	模块；组件

Phrases

business scope	业务范围；经营范围
corporate culture	企业文化
supply channel	供货渠道
return policy	退货政策
after-sales-service	售后服务
consistent with	符合；与……一致
brand image	品牌形象
in turns	依次；轮流
customer stickiness	用户黏性
release products	发布产品
consist of	由……组成；由……构成；包括
plus size	大尺码；加大码
a variety of	种种；多种的
a series of	一系列；一连串
up to	一直到；多达
data analysis	数据分析
pile up	堆砌；堆积
added value	附加值
profit margin	利润率；边际利润
page view	访问量；浏览量
inseparable from	不可分的
expected profit	预期利润
decision making	决策；判定
buying experience	购买体验

Sentences

1. A lot of men who have successful careers have given too much to work and neglected their family.

   很多事业成功的男士为了工作付出了太多，而忽略了家庭。

2. We can never neglect minor issues.

   我们决不能忽视细小问题。

3. Buildings designed by Gaudi give us a tremendous visual impact.

   高迪设计的建筑给人以极其深刻的视觉印象。

4. Our products are protected by patent.

   我们的产品受专利保护。

5. You have to apply for a patent on this invention.

   你必须为这一发明申请专利。

6. Our business philosophy of responsibility ensures our product quality.

   负责任的经营理念保证了我们的产品质量。

7. Detailed product description and high quality pictures make a store more credible.

   详细的产品描述和高质量的图片可以让一家店铺更加可信。

8. All the employees in our company take duty in rotation.

   我们公司的所有员工轮流值班。

9. I owe two apartments where I live alternately.

   我拥有两套公寓并交替居住。

10. An effective marketing campaign can raise the page view and bring more customers to the store.

    一次成功的营销活动能够提高页面访问量，并为店铺带来更多顾客。

11. Apple products have intuitive interface and are very easy to use.

    苹果的产品拥有直观界面，易于使用。

12. The proportion of women in the decision-making positions has risen to 20%.

    决策层中女性占比已经提升到 20%。

13. Our business scope is men's and women's clothing.

    我们的业务范围是男女服装。

14. The contents of the sector expression in a company name shall conform to the business scope of the enterprise.

    企业名称中行业用语表述的内容应当与企业经营范围一致。

15. If an enterprise wants to have an invincible position in the market, it must have its own unique corporate culture.

    一家企业如果想要在市场上立于不败之地，就必须拥有自己独特的企业文化。

16. We want our employees to acknowledge our corporate culture and be loyal to the company.

我们希望员工认同我们的企业文化，并且对企业忠诚。

17. Due to the different supply channels, the price of clothing may vary a lot.
    由于供货渠道不同，服装价格可能相差甚远。

18. The reporter wanted to know the supply channel of Japanese cosmetics, but the store owner just jumped to the next question.
    记者想了解日本化妆品的供货渠道，但是店主直接跳入下一个问题。

19. Groupon offers a "no questions asked" return policy.
    Groupon 提供无条件退货政策。

20. We offer a 30-day return policy.
    我们提供 30 天的退货政策。

21. They are trying to keep buyers as long-term customers by offering high quality after-sales service.
    他们正在努力通过提供优质的售后服务使买家成为长期客户。

22. Siemens is known for its quality products and after-sales service.
    西门子以产品品质和售后服务闻名。

23. Our actions must be consistent with the corporate culture.
    我们的行为必须符合企业文化。

24. His action is always consistent with his words.
    他始终言行一致。

25. Apple is known for its innovative brand image.
    苹果以创新的品牌形象闻名。

26. Brand image is how consumers perceive a product or a company.
    品牌形象是指消费者对一个产品或一家公司的印象。

27. The family members go to the hospital in turns to take care of grandmother.
    家庭成员轮流去医院照顾奶奶。

28. The European Union members take it in turns to chair EU.
    欧盟成员国轮流担任欧盟主席。

29. Highly interactive social networking platforms help to enhance customer stickiness of a company or a brand.
    企业或品牌可以通过高互动的社交媒体平台提高用户黏性。

30. We offer a registration coupon to increase customer stickiness.
    我们通过提供新会员注册的代金券增加用户黏性。

Conversations

1. Spring Festival Promotion

A: Dear customer, Spring Festival is coming. Our shop has a special Spring Festival promotion. All the goods in our shop are 50% off. Choosing and ordering are welcome!

B: Yes, it's Spring Festival in a month. I want to buy a toy for my daughter. Why don't you recommend some?

A: How about the toys below? They are all sold well in our shop. Now they are all 50% off. The more you buy, the cheaper it will be, and your daughter will be very happy.

B: I want to buy Peppa Pig's doll, and my daughter likes to watch this cartoon all the time. How much is this set all together?

A: Well, a set of five is $240. And you need to pay $120 after a 50% discount.

B: That's a good deal. I want to place order now.

1. 春节促销

A：亲，春节就要到了。本店特别推出春节促销活动，全店的商品打 5 折，快来选购吧!

B：没错，还有一个月就到春节了，我想给我的女儿买个玩具，你推荐一些吧。

A：您喜欢下面这些东西吗？都是店里卖得很好的，现在全部 5 折。您买得越多就越便宜，您女儿也会很高兴的。

B：我想买小猪佩奇的玩偶，她平时最喜欢看小猪佩奇了。这一套一共多少钱呢？

A：嗯，一套 5 个，一共 240 美元，打 5 折后是 120 美元。

B：这很划算啊，我现在就买一套。

2. Brand Activities

A: Dear customer, we launched SILK brand week in mid-April for brand promotion, with a 40% discount on orders and a further reduction of $50 for two items.

B: Really? What kind of products do you mainly promote in this brand week?

A: In order to cooperate with the brand image, the main product of this brand week is the most classic "Water" series in our store. The style is unique, and you will like it.

B: Oh, I'm very interested.

A: Dear customer, here's the link.

B: OK.

A: The main products of this series are cyan, with hand embroidery. There are only 3 pieces in each style, and they will not be launched in the future. If you like it, you should place order as soon as possible.

B: I really like it, especially the sea-foam green one. The embroidery on it is my favorite lily.

A: Dear customer, if you like it, you must place the order quickly. This one is the last one.

2. 品牌活动

A：亲，为了推广品牌，我们在 4 月中旬推出了 SILK 品牌周活动，买一件打 6 折，买两件可再降 50 美元。

B：是吗？你们这次活动主要推出哪些商品呢？

A：为了配合品牌形象，本次品牌周活动的主打产品是我们店最经典的"水纹"系列，款式独特，您一定会喜欢的。

B：哦，我很感兴趣。

A：亲，这是链接。

B：好的。

A：该系列的产品以青色为主，加上手工刺绣。每一款只有 3 件，以后也不再推出，您如果喜欢，要尽快入手。

B：我的确很喜欢，尤其是这件海绿色的旗袍，上面的刺绣也是我喜欢的百合。

A：亲，喜欢的话一定要赶紧下单啊，这款只剩最后一件了。

Text

6.2.1　Store Description 店铺描述

Store description is where we introduce the basic information of the store and show the advantages and strength of it, and thus cannot be neglected. In general, cross-border E-commerce stores can be divided into business stores and personal stores. These two types of store descriptions have different focuses. The business store description is richer in content, while the personal store description is usually more concise, and pays more attention to visual marketing tools such as store decoration.

店铺描述是介绍店铺的基本信息、展示店铺的优势和实力的地方，是一个不容忽视的环节。一般来说，跨境电商店铺可以分为商务店和个人店。这两种类型的商店描述有不同的侧重点。商务店铺描述内容更丰富，而个人店铺描述通常更简洁，更注重店铺装修等视觉营销工具。

The business store description generally begins with a company profile, such as company history, main business scope, awards or patent certificate, well-known customers and etc. In addition. there may also be brief introduction of the company's business philosophy or corporate culture, leaving a reliable first impression to the buyer. Due to the special nature of cross-border E-commerce, the store description will also introduce the supply channels, logistics, delivery time, return policy, contact information for after-sales service and etc. In the store description, the seller can also add some pictures properly, such as real shots of the factory, real shots of the packaging process, to make the store more credible.

店铺描述一般以公司简介开头，如公司历史、主营业务范围、获奖或专利证书、知名客户等。还可能简要介绍公司的经营理念或企业文化，给买家留下可靠的第一印象。由于跨境电商的特殊性质，店铺描述中还会介绍供货渠道、物流、发货时间、退货政策、售后服务联系方式等，卖家还可以在店铺描述中适当添加一些图片，比如工厂的真实镜头、包装过程的真实镜头，让店铺更具公信力。

The description of personal stores is relatively concise, and focuses more on the store decoration. The design of the home page is significant for all cross-border E-commerce platforms. Taking AliExpress as an example. Store decoration is divided into multiple parts, including shop sign, picture rotation, recommended products, and customized contents and so on.

个人门店的描述相对简洁，更侧重于店铺装修。首页的设计对所有跨境电商平台都具有重要意义。以速卖通为例，店铺装修分为多个部分，包括店铺标识、图片轮换、推荐产品、定制内容等。

The first step of store decoration is to decide the overall style and color of the store. In this process, we should take full consideration if the selected style and color is consistent with our main business scope or brand image. For example, the store decoration of baby products is generally more lovely and warm, and the color is usually pink and white. The store decoration of digital products or men's clothing is generally more concise and business-style, and the color is usually blue or black and white.

店铺装修的第一步是决定店铺的整体风格和颜色。在这个过程中，我们应该充分考虑所选择的款式和颜色是否与我们的主营业务范围或品牌形象相一致。比如，婴儿用品的门店装修一般比较可爱、温馨，颜色通常是粉白相间的；而数码产品或男装的门店装修一般更简洁、更有商务气息，通常是蓝色或黑白搭配的。

Once the style and color of the store has been decided, we need to design a sign for the store. Shop sign appears at the top of home page. It not only is a simple sign of the store, but also shows the features of it. We can put the name of the store or the company, as well as some main product information in the shop sign. It is also allowed to include a link in the shop sign. The link can be the home page, information for a group of products or any single product. We can use links of the home page, activities, or products alternately according to the goals of marketing campaigns to make the full use of the shop sign.

一旦决定了商店的风格和颜色，我们就需要为商店设计一个招牌。商店标志出现在主页的顶部。它不仅是商店的一个简单标志，还展示了商店的特色。我们可以在招牌上写上商店或公司的名称，以及一些主要的产品信息。商店招牌中允许添加链接。链接可以是主页，可以是一组产品的信息，也可以是任何单个产品的链接。我们可以根据营销活动的目标，交替使用主页、活动或产品的链接，以充分利用商店标志。

Picture rotation is generally located below the shop sign, displaying the advertising pictures in turns, showing the characteristics of products in a more intuitive and vivid way. We usually set the featured products hot-selling products or new products as the advertising pictures. It should be noted that the size and proportion of pictures for the use of picture rotation must be uniform.

轮番海报一般位于店牌下方，将广告图片摆放在圆筒中，以更直观、更生动的方式展示产品特点。我们通常把特色产品、热销产品或新产品作为广告图片。需要注意的是，使用轮番海报的图片大小和比例必须统一。

The use of recommended products is very efficient. We can automatically select the products of the highest sales as the hot products recommendation. A store can add more than one module of recommended products. So in addition to hot products recommendation, we can also add recommendation for new products or seasonal products.

推荐产品的使用效率非常高。我们可以自动选择销量最高的产品作为热销产品推荐。一家商店可以添加多个推荐产品模块。所以除了推荐热销产品，我们还可以添加新产品或季节性产品的推荐。

Finally, we can show our products and store more comprehensively by adding customized contents. For example, you can add custom languages for the convenience of non-English speaking buyers. We can also show our social media accounts to buyers in this area to attract more fans, increase customer stickiness and loyalty.

最后，我们可以通过增加定制内容来更全面地展示我们的产品和商店。例如，您可以添加自定义语言，以方便不会说英语的买家。我们还可以将我们的社交媒体账号展示给这一领域的买家，以吸引更多的粉丝，增加客户黏性和忠诚度。

6.2.2　Product Description 产品描述

Products are key to cross-border E-commerce. It can be said that good products can help companies gain the world. In general, products that are suitable for cross-border E-commerce sales have the following characteristics: small, light and high added value. In short, "small and beautiful" products are most suitable for sales on cross-border E-commerce platform.

产品是跨境电商的关键。可以说，好的产品可以帮助企业赢得世界。一般来说，适合跨境电商销售的产品具有以下特点：体积小、重量轻、附加值高。总之，"小而美"的产品最适合在跨境电商平台上销售。

When looking for products for online shops, pay attention to the product structure. There are mainly three types of cross-border E-commerce products: burst sells, flow-increase products and profitable products.

在为网店寻找产品时，要注意产品结构。跨境电商产品主要有三类：爆款、增流型产品和赢利型产品。

Burst sells are hot products, with high flow, high exposure, large orders and other characteristics. However, burst sells are not the source of profits for shops. Usually, the price of burst sells is low, and the direct impact is that the profit margins are small, even no profit margins. Thus, it is recommended that shops only set 1-2 burst sells per store. Create burst sells by reducing price, increasing discount rates, which will bring a lot of page views and orders in the short term for the shop, as well as promote the sale of other products.

爆款属于热销产品，具有高流量、高曝光率、大订单等特点。然而，爆款并不是商店的利润来源。通常情况下，爆款的价格都很低，直接影响就是利润率很小，甚至没有利润率。因此，建议每家商店只设置 1~2 个来促销。通过降价、提高折扣率等方式创造爆发式销售，短期内会为店铺带来大量的页面浏览量和订单，同时也会促进其他产品的销售。

Flow-increase products refer to the products that can increase page views for the shop. Same as burst sells, the price of flow-increase products is also low, and they are not the main source of profits. It is recommended that each shop set about 5 flow- increase products, so that shops do not need to invest a lot to increase the flow. If shops choose flow-increase products and burst sells reasonably, it will help shops grow rapidly in the early stage.

引流的产品是指能够为商店增加页面浏览量的产品。和爆款一样，增流产品的价格也很低，并不是主要的利润来源。建议每家店铺设置 5 个左右的引流产品，这样商铺引流就不需要投入太多。如果商家合理选择引流的产品和爆款，将有助于商铺在早期快速成长。

The operation of a shop is inseparable from profits, and profitable products are the main source of profits for shops. In general, in addition to burst sells and flow-increase products, other products in the shop are all profitable products. Profitability is determined by the seller's valuation on the expected profit of the products. The page view of this kind of products is not large, but the profit of a single product is high. The seller should reserve discount space for this kind of products, so the seller can discount them during the flow peak of platform or promotion period.

商铺的经营离不开利润，有利可图的产品是商铺的主要利润来源。一般情况下，店里除了爆款、引流产品，其他产品都是有利可图的产品。盈利能力是由卖方对产品预期利润的估值决定的。这类产品的页面浏览量不大，但单品利润高。卖家应该为这类产品预留折扣空间，这样卖家可以在平台流量高峰期或促销期进行打折。

Once we have decided the product structure of store, we need to have a more comprehensive understanding of the product category, so that we can better introduce and display the attributes and characteristic of the products in the product description. Although the major platforms have different rules about the product description, there are still some common skills and tricks:

一旦我们确定了商店的产品结构，我们就需要对产品类别有一个更全面的了解，这样才能更好地在产品描述中介绍和展示产品的属性和特点。虽然各大平台对产品描述的规则各不相同，但还是有一些共同的技巧和诀窍：

(1) Follow the "FAB" method, which refers to feature, advantage and benefit.

(2) Truthfully describe the products, otherwise there will be follow-up disputes such as products not as described.

(3) Do not include too many pictures, otherwise the loading time will be too long and that will probably result in negative effect on the buyer's decision making process, best between 10-12 pictures.

(4) Be as simple as possible in the product description, generally between 100-300 words.

(5) Include logistics, payment, after-sales service and other information in the product description.

(6) Paragraph the description to enhance the buyer's buying experience.

(7) Make use of custom modules such as related sales to increase the sales of similar products, new or profitable products.

（1）遵循"FAB"方式，即功能、优势、效益；

（2）如实描述产品，否则会有后续争议，如产品描述不符；

（3）图片不要太多，否则下载时间太长，可能会对买家的决策过程产生负面影响，最好是 10～12 张图片；

（4）产品描述尽量简单，一般是 100～300 字；

（5）产品说明尽量简单，一般是 100～300 字；

（6）对产品描述有所解释，提升买家购买体验；

（7）利用关联销售等自定义模块，增加同类产品、新产品或盈利产品的销售额。

6.2.3　Title Description 标题描述

Title description is usually the first step of releasing products, and is crucial to cross-border E-commerce products. When buyers select products on third-party cross-border E-commerce platforms, they often search through keywords. A good title allows your products to be searched by buyers, maximizes the page views of products, increases product exposure, improves product ranking, as well as stimulates buyers desire to buy.

标题描述通常是发布产品的第一步，对跨境电商产品至关重要。买家在第三方跨境电商平台选购产品时，往往会通过关键词进行搜索。一个好的标题可以让买家搜索你的产品，最大化产品的页面浏览量，增加产品曝光率，提高产品排名，同时刺激买家的购买欲望。

A good title description should stimulate buyers' desire to buy directly after they see the title and without even clicking into the details. The first thing to follow is that you need to make sure the title description is a collection of product keywords. Therefore, we must put the core and most accurate keywords of products in the title description.

一个好的标题描述会激发买家在看到标题后直接购买的欲望，甚至不需要点击细节。标题描述要遵循的第一件事是：您需要确保标题描述是产品关键字的集合。因此，我们必须把产品的核心和最准确的关键字放在标题描述中。

In general, title description consists of core words, attribute words, long tail keywords and so on. In simple terms, the core words are the key words to describe the products. For example, the core word of a women's dress can be "dress" or "women's dress". Attribute words are used to describes products' attributes, such as color, size material, style, use, and so on. Long tail keywords, also known as flow words, refer to the keywords that do not have much relationship with the products, but can bring more page views, such as "plus size", "free shipping", "wholesale" and so on. After a period of shop operation, there will often be hundreds or even thousands of products, and many of them belong to the same category. If we are conscientious about each title description, the workload is too heavy. So for the same category of products, we can use title templates. That is, the core words stay the same, change attribute words accordingly, and replace the long tail keywords.

标题描述一般由核心词、属性词、长尾关键词等组成。简单地说，核心词就是描述产品的关键词。例如，女装的核心词可以是"着装"或"女装"。属性词用来描述产品的属性，如颜色、大小、材质、款式、用途等。长尾关键词，又称流量词，是指与产品关系不大，但能带来更多页面浏览量的关键词，如"加码""免运费""批发"等。店铺运营一段时间后，往往会有上百种甚至上千种产品，很多都属于同一品类。如果我们认真对待每一个标题描述，工作量就太大了。因此，对于同一类别的产品，我们可以使用标题模板。也就是说，核心词保持不变，相应地更改属性词，并替换长尾关键字。

For example, under the category of women's dress, we may upload a variety of products. Every product has different colors, styles, materials and so on. First, we can set core words for this category of products, such as "2020 Fashion Women's Dress". Then it can be used as the beginning of all products' title under this category. Then we can set different attribute words according to the different attributes of products, such as different colors, length, etc., so there is a difference between each product. Finally, we can set the long tail keywords that will bring us more page views. In this way, we can produce a series of high-quality title descriptions quickly and efficiently.

比如女装类目下，我们可能会上传各种各样的产品。每种产品都有不同的颜色、款式、材质等。首先我们可以为这个品类的产品设置核心词，比如"2020时尚女装"，然后可以作为这个类目下所有产品标题的开头；然后我们可以根据产品的不同属性设置不同的属性词，比如不同的颜色、长度等，所以产品之间是有区别的；最后我们可以设置长尾关键字，其可为我们带来更多的页面浏览量，这样我们就可以快速高效地产生一系列高质量的标题描述。

The rules of the major cross-border E-commerce platforms are not the same. For example, the title of products on AliExpress can be set up to 128 characters, but DHgate allows 140 characters. However, some tips of product description are common. Here are some tips:

(1) Use the data analysis tools to set the hot keywords.

(2) Try to put core words as early as possible, best in the first five words.

(3) Capitalize the first letter of each keyword except for "the" "a" and other prepositions.

(4) Maximize the use of characters.

(5) Do not pile up keywords.

(6) Do not use keywords that do not match the products' real information.

(7) Avoid the use of sensitive words, such as cheap, fake and so on.

(8) Make the title as clear and coherent as possible.

各大跨境电商平台的规则不尽相同。例如，速卖通上的产品标题可以设置为最多 128 个字符，但敦煌网上允许 140 个字符。然而，产品描述的一些提示是共同的。以下是一些提示：

（1）使用数据分析工具设置热点关键字；

（2）尽量先放核心字，最好放在前 5 个字中；

（3）除"the""a"等介词外，每个关键字的首字母大写；

（4）尽量使用字符；

（5）不要堆积关键字；

（6）请勿使用与产品真实信息不符的关键字；

（7）避免使用敏感词汇，如廉价、假冒等；

（8）尽可能使标题清晰连贯。

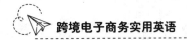

Section 6.3　Product Selecting and Pricing of Cross-border E-commerce 跨境电子商务选品与定价

New Words

specific	*adj.*	特殊的，特定的；明确的；详细的
	n.	特性；细节
fiercely	*adv.*	猛烈地；厉害地
leather	*n.*	皮革；皮革制品
	vt.	用皮革包盖；抽打
	adj.	皮的；皮革制的
preference	*n.*	偏爱；优先选择；【法】优先权；特惠
adequate	*adj.*	充足的；适当的；胜任的
arrange	*vt.*	安排；排列；整理
	vi.	安排；排列；协商
best-selling	*adj.*	最畅销的；畅销作品的
	n.	畅销品
subcategory	*n.*	子范畴；亚类
therefore	*adv.*	因此；所以
stimulate	*vt.*	刺激；鼓舞，激励
	vi.	起刺激作用；起促进作用
flagship	*n.*	旗舰；（作定语）一流；佼佼者
specialized	*adj.*	专门的；专业的
stable	*adj.*	稳定的；稳固的；牢固的；稳重的
	v.	使（马）入厩；把（马）拴在马厩
whereby	*conj.*	凭借；通过……；借以；与……一致
	adv.	凭此；借以
elasticity	*n.*	弹性；弹力；灵活性
campaign	*n.*	运动；活动
prevailing	*adj.*	普遍的；盛行的；流行的；（指风）某地区常刮的
tactical	*adj.*	战术的；策略的；善于策略的
substitute	*n.*	代用品；代替者
	v.	替代
energetic	*adj.*	精力充沛的；积极的；有力的
distributor	*n.*	经销商，配销商，分销商

surplus	*n.*	剩余；【贸易】顺差；盈余；过剩
	adj.	剩余的；过剩的
entrants	*n.*	进入者；新会员；参加竞赛者；新工作者
opponent	*n.*	对手；反对者；敌手
	adj.	对立的；敌对的
firm	*n.*	公司；企业；事务所；商行
	adj.	坚固的；稳固的；坚决的；【商业】固定的（货币）坚挺的
	adv.	稳固地
	v.	使（变）坚实
premium	*n.*	保险费；额外费用；奖金；津贴
	adj.	优质的；昂贵的；价格更高的
palatable	*adj.*	美味的，可口的；愉快的
perceive	*vt.*	察觉，感觉；理解；认知
	vi.	感到，感知；认识到
segment	*n.*	段；部分；片；弓形
	v.	分割；划分
incredibly	*adv.*	非常；极其；难以置信地；不可思议地
patronage	*n.*	赞助；光顾；任免权
innovative	*adj.*	革新的，创新的；新颖的；有创新精神的
admittedly	*adv.*	诚然；公认地

Phrases

to be divided into	被分成
Red Sea	红海
Blue Sea	蓝海
manufacturing cost	制造成本
to be converted into	被转换成
in response to	响应；回答；对……有反应
premium pricing	溢价定价
price skimming	撇脂定价
left-digit effect	左位数效应

Sentences

1. She arranged an appointment for Friday afternoon at four-fifteen.
   她安排了一个星期五下午四点一刻的约会。

2. The company plans to open a flagship shop in New York this month.
   该公司计划本月在纽约开一家旗舰店。

3. Cocaine addicts get specialized support from knowledgeable staff.
   可卡因上瘾者从知识丰富的人员那里得到专业化的帮助。

4. The company operates an arrangement whereby employees may select any 8-hour period between 6 a.m. to 8 p.m. to go to work.

该公司做出了一种安排，据此员工可以在上午 6 点到晚上 8 点任意选择 8 个小时去上班。

5. During his election campaign he promised to put the economy back on its feet.

竞选活动期间，他许诺要致力于恢复经济。

6. Japan's annual trade surplus is in the region of 100 billion dollars.

日本每年的贸易顺差约有一千亿美元。

7. Solicit a continuance of customer's patronage.

敬请顾客继续惠顾。

Conversations

1. Guests Want to Know about the New Products

A: Hello.

B: Hello, what can I do for you?

A: Well, I'd like to know what new products are available in your store recently. However, no relevant pages or links were found.

B: Dear customer, this is actually quite simple. You can find it on our homepage.

A: Homepage?

B: Yes, click the store name on the right side of the product order page to access the store home page.

A: And what?

B: View the homepage, you can see that there are many parts, including "New" part and "Hot" part. Click on the "New" part to see our new product.

A: Right.

B: You can choose the products you need from them.

A: Okay, I see. Thank you.

1. 客人想了解新品

A：你好，在线吗？

B：您好，有什么吩咐吗？

A：嗯，我想了解你们店铺最近新上了哪些产品。不过没有找到相关页面和链接。

B：亲，这很简单，在我们店铺主页就能找到。

A：店铺主页？

B：没错，在商品订单页面的右侧单击店铺名称的链接就可以进入店铺主页。

A：然后呢？

B：在店铺主页往下浏览，您可以看到有很多版块，有"新"版块，也有"火爆"版块，单击"新"版块就可以查看我们的新品。

A：没错。

B：您可以从中选择自己需要的产品。

A：好的，我知道了，谢谢。

2. Products Selecting

A: Hi.

B: Hello, may I help you?

A: I'm going to buy some tableware, but there are many kinds of products in your shop, I can't find it for a while.

B: Dear customer, because of the large number of products in our shop, we categorise the products for the convenience of customers.

A: So what am I supposed to do?

B: First, you enter the store home page. At the top of the home page you can see "Product Categories".

A: Yup, you're right.

B: In the expanded dropdown menu, you can see links to products categories, such as arts and crafts, vase kitchen, etc. Click the relevant link to choose from this category.

A: Oh, I see.

B: If there is anything remaining unclear, you are always mostly welcomes to contact us.

2. 选择商品

A：你好，在线吗？

B：您好，请问有什么能帮您的吗？

A：我打算买一些餐具，但是你们店内的产品种类有点多，我一时找不到。

B：亲，由于我们店内的产品较多，所以我们将产品进行了分类，以方便客人选购。

A：那我要怎么做呢？

B：您首先进入店铺主页，在主页上方可以看到"产品分类"。

A：是的。

B：在展开的菜单中可以看到产品的分类链接，比如艺术手工品、花瓶、餐具等。点击相关链接就可以在该类产品中进行选购了。

A：我明白了。

B：好的，如还有任何不清楚的，请随时联系我们。

Text

6.3.1　Product Selecting of Cross-border E-commerce 跨境电商选品

1. Introduction of Product Selecting 选品简介

Product selecting refers to selecting a business you are going to deal in and specific products under specific categories according to some data analysis and your own competitive power, which can be divided into three steps as follows.

选品是指根据一定的数据分析和自身的竞争力，选择自己要经营的业务和特定类别下的具体产品。产品选择可以分为以下三个步骤：

1) Business Selecting 业务选择

Business selecting means what kind of business you are going to deal in according to the current situation of the platform. There are a variety of businesses in current cross-border E-commerce platforms. Some of them are called "Red Sea", and which means they are fiercely competitive, such as jewelry industry, wedding, wig industry, etc. Others are called "Blue Sea", which means they are less competitive.

业务选择就是根据平台的现状选择要做什么样的业务。目前跨境电商平台商家种类繁多。有些是"红海"，意思是竞争激烈，比如珠宝业、婚庆、假发业等；有些是"蓝海"，意思是竞争力不强。

2) Category Selecting 品类选择

Category selecting refers to the choice of categories under a certain business, such as categories of adult shoes, baby shoes, children's shoes and other shoes under shoes industry.

品类选择是指某一业务下的品类选择，如鞋业下的成人鞋、童鞋、其他鞋等品类。

3) Product Selecting 产品选择

Product selecting refers to the choice of products under a certain category, such as products of leather shoes, sports shoes, casual shoes and many other shoes under the category of adult shoes.

产品选择是指对某一品类下的产品进行选择，如成人鞋品类下的皮鞋、运动鞋、休闲鞋等众多鞋子的产品。

Product selecting should focus on many factors, say, the product competitiveness, foreign buyers' preferences, timely supply, adequate stock, better price for better quality, product's size and weight, and etc.

选择产品要考虑很多因素，比如产品竞争力、国外买家的喜好、供应及时、库存充足、优质优价、产品的大小和重量等。

2. Tips for Product Selecting on DHgate as a New Seller 新手卖家敦煌网选品技巧

1) To Select Suitable Products for the Platform 选择适合平台的产品

(1) The way to check the hot-selling items on the platform. If you are new sellers on DHgate, there are two methods for you to select the suitable products for the platform.

查看平台热销产品的方法。如果你是敦煌网上的新卖家，有两种方法可以让你选择适合平台的产品。

Method 1. Accurate search

Go to DHgate homepage by typing the web address to enter the keywords in the searching bar. For example, if you enter "Sports & Outdoors" in the bar, and click the search button, you will get all relative results. You can arrange the best-selling items of "Sports & Outdoors" in high-to-low order of volume of sales by click the "Items Sold" button on top right.

Method 2. Classification search

You can find the category in the "All Categories" column on left of home page. To take the same example, you can search the subcategory in "All Categories", such as "Athletic & Outdoor

Shoes", click and enter it. You may find the items ranging from high to low sales volume by going on clicking "Items Sold".

方法 1. 精确搜索

进入敦煌网主页，在搜索栏中输入关键字。例如，如果您在栏中输入"运动与户外"，然后点击"搜索"按钮，您将获得所有相关结果。点击右上方的"已售商品"按钮，您可以按销量从高到低的顺序排列"运动与户外"的畅销商品。

方法 2. 分类搜索

您可以在主页左侧的"所有类别"栏中找到该类别。举个例子，您可以在"所有类别"中搜索子类别，如"运动鞋和户外鞋"，点击进入，点击"售出的商品"就可以找到销量从高到低的商品。

(2) Suitable products for the platform. First of all, hot-selling items must be good products, but sometimes it may not suit for your requirements. Many big or medium-sized sellers have already taken account of the product ranking, quality and price, which is too competitive for new sellers. Therefore, we must make good use of the network flow of the best-selling items to stimulate the exposure of other products. Here, we must highlight the keyword "NEW" to take the rare products on platform as our flagship products, say, "Strange and New Products".

适合平台的产品。首先，热销商品必须是好产品，但有时热销品可能不适合你的要求。许多大中型卖家已经考虑到了产品档次、质量和价格的问题，这对新卖家来说太有竞争力了。因此，一定要利用好畅销单品的网络流量，拉动其他产品的曝光。在这里，我们一定要突出"新"这个关键词，把平台上的稀有产品作为我们的旗舰产品，比如说"新奇产品"。

2) Purchase Channels 购买渠道

(1) From the offline specialized market. You can purchase the products for local specialized wholesale market, to get a low cost and stable supply.

来自线下专业市场。你可以为当地的专业批发市场购买产品，以获得低成本和稳定的供应。

(2) From the online wholesale mall. This is a general way to get the products without geographical restrictions, and with more convenience, low cost and stable supply.

来自网上批发商城。这是一种不受地域限制、更方便、成本更低、供应更稳定的一般产品获取方式。

(3) Directly from the factory. It is the best way for you to cooperate with factory. You will get the products directly in a lowest cost and get stable supply.

To summarize, the first choice is to purchase from the local specialized market, and then online wholesale mall. As to the factory channel, it may be the best way for your future development, but small volume product makes factory difficult to cooperate with.

直接从工厂购买。与工厂合作是购买商品的最好方式。您将以最低的成本直接获得产品，并获得稳定的供应。

综上所述，首选是从当地专业市场采购，然后是网上批发商城。至于工厂渠道，这可能是你们未来发展的最好方式，但是小批量的产品使工厂很难合作。

6.3.2　Product Pricing of Cross-border E-commerce
跨境电子商务产品定价

1. Introduction of Product Pricing 产品定价简介

Pricing is the process whereby a business sets the price at which it will sell its products and services, and it may be part of the business' marketing plan. In setting prices, the business will take into account the price at which it could acquire the goods, the manufacturing cost, the market place, competition, market condition, brand, and quality of product.

定价是企业设定销售产品和服务的价格的过程，它可能是企业营销计划的一个部分。在制定价格时，企业会考虑商品的售价、制造成本、市场位置、竞争、市场状况、品牌和产品质量等因素。

Pricing is a fundamental aspect of financial modeling and is one of the four Ps of the marketing mix. The other three Ps of the marketing mix are product, promotion, and place. Price is the only revenue generating element among the four Ps, the rest being cost centers. However, the other Ps of marketing will contribute to decreasing price elasticity and so enable price increases to drive greater revenue and profits.

定价是财务建模的一个基本方面，是营销组合的 4 个 P 之一；营销组合的其他 3 个 P 分别是产品、促销和分销渠道。价格是 4 个 P 中唯一的产生收入的元素，其余均是成本中心。然而，营销组合中的其他 P 将有助于降低价格波动，从而使价格上涨，产生更多收入和利润。

Pricing can be a manual or automatic process of applying prices to purchase and sales orders, based on factors such as a fixed amount quantity break, promotion or sales campaign, specific vendor quote, price prevailing on entry, shipment or invoice date, combination of multiple orders or lines, and many others. Automated systems require more setup and maintenance but may prevent pricing errors. The needs of the consumer can be converted into demand only if the consumer has the willingness and capacity to buy the product. Thus, pricing is the most important concept in the field of marketing. It is used as a tactical decision in response to comparing market situations.

定价可以是将价格应用于购买和销售订单的人工或自动过程，并以诸如固定金额、数量突破、促销或销售活动、特定供应商报价、入市时的普遍价格、发货或发票日期、多个订单或多个产品线组合等因素为基础。自动化系统需要更多的设置和维护，但可以防止定价错误。只有当消费者愿意并有能力购买产品时，消费者的需求才能转化为产品需求。因此，定价是市场营销中最重要的概念。它被用作对比较市场情况做出反应的战术决策。

2. Objectives of Pricing 定价的目标

The objectives of pricing should include：

(1) The financial goals of the company (i.e. profitability).

(2) The fit with marketplace realities (Will customers buy at that price?).

(3) The extent to which the price supports a product's market positioning and be consistent with the other variables in the marketing mix.

(4) The consistency of prices across categories and products.

定价的目标应包含以下内容：

（1）公司的财务目标（即盈利能力）。

（2）符合市场现实（客户会以这个价格购买吗？）。

（3）价格在多大程度上支持产品的市场定位并与营销组合中的其他变量保持一致。

（4）产品类别和产品价格的一致性。

Price is influenced by the type of distribution channel, the type of promotions, and the quality of the product. Price can act as a substitute for product quality, effective promotions, or an energetic selling effort by distributors in certain markets.

价格受分销渠道类型、促销类型和产品质量的影响。在某些市场上，价格可以代替产品质量、有效的促销或分销商积极的销售努力。

From the marketer's point of view, an efficient price is a price that is very close to the maximum that customers are prepared to pay. In economic terms, it is a price that shifts most of the consumer economic surplus to the producer. A good pricing strategy would be the one which could balance between the price floor (the price below which the organization ends up in losses) and the price ceiling (the price by which the organization experiences a no-demand situation).

从市场营销人员的角度来看，有效价格非常接近客户愿意支付的价格上限。从经济学的角度来说，它是将消费者的大部分经济盈余转移到生产者的一个价格。一个好的定价策略应该是能够平衡价格下限（低于这个价格，组织最终会亏损）和价格上限（即使组织的产品处于无市场需求状态的价格）的策略。

3. Pricing Strategy 定价策略

A business can use a variety of pricing strategies when selling a product or service. The price can be set to maximize profitability for each unit sold or from the market overall. It can be used to defend an existing market from new entrants, to increase market share within a market or to enter a new market. The firm's decision on the price of the product and the pricing strategy impact the consumer's decision on whether or not to purchase the product. When firms are deciding to consider applying any type of pricing strategy, they must be aware of the following reasons in order to make an appropriate choice which will benefit their business. The competition within the market today is extremely high, and for this reason, businesses must be attentive to their opponent's actions in order to have the comparative advantage in the market. The technology of Internet usage has increased and developed dramatically, therefore, price comparisons can be done by customers through online access. Consumers are very selective regarding the purchases they make due to their knowledge of the monetary value. Firms must be mindful of these factors and price their products accordingly.

企业在销售产品或服务时可以使用多种定价策略。设定价格旨在使每个销售单元或从整体市场中获取的利润最大化。它可以用来防止新的企业进入现有市场，用来增加市场份额或进入一个新的市场。企业对产品价格和定价策略的决定影响着消费者是否购买产品的决策。当企业决定采用任何类型的定价策略时，它们必须意识到以下原因，以便做出对其业务有利的适当选择。当今市场内部的竞争非常激烈，因此企业必须注意竞争对手的行动方案，才能在市场中获得相对优势。互联网应用技术已经有了极大的提高和发展，因此，客户可以通过在线访问的方式比较价格。由于消费者了解钱的价值，他们在购买时都会精挑细选。企业必须注意这些因素，并相应地对产品进行定价。

Broadly, there are six key pricing strategies mentioned in the marketing.

一般来说，市场营销中的关键性定价策略有以下 6 种。

1) Premium Pricing 溢价定价

Businesses use a premium pricing strategy when they're introducing a new product that has distinct competitive advantages over similar products. Premium-priced product is priced higher than its competitors.

当企业推出一种新产品时，会使用一种溢价定价策略，这种新产品与同类产品相比具有明显的竞争优势。溢价产品的定价高于竞争对手的产品。

Premium pricing is most effective at the beginning of a product's life cycle. Small businesses that sell goods with unique properties are better able to use premium pricing.

溢价定价在产品生命周期的初期最为有效，出售具有独特属性的商品的小企业能够更好地使用溢价定价。

To make premium pricing palatable to consumers, companies try to create an image in which consumers perceive that the products have value and are worth the higher prices. Besides creating the perception of a higher quality product, the company needs to synchronize its marketing efforts, its product packaging and even the decor of the store must support the image that the product is worth its premium price.

为了让高价位更容易为消费者所接受，企业试图创造一种形象，让消费者认为产品有价值，值得更高的价格。除了给人一种高质量产品的印象，企业还需要同步其营销力度、产品包装，甚至店内的装饰都必须支持产品物有所值的形象。

2) Penetration Pricing 渗透定价

Achieving an initial high volume of sales, with a new product, is the primary objective of penetration pricing. Instead of setting a high price to skim off small but profitable segments of the total market, a company can choose to use penetration pricing. Although this strategy calls for a product to be widely promoted, it allows the setting of a low initial price to enable the company to penetrate the market quickly and deeply. Using the penetration pricing strategy, the company can attract a large number of buyers quickly while it also captures a large share of the market. However, there are conditions that must be met.

通过新产品实现最初的高销量，是渗透定价的主要目标。企业可以选用渗透定价法从整个市场中攫取虽小但可盈利的份额，而不是设定一个高价格。虽然这一策略要求产品得到广泛推广，但它可以设定一个较低的初始价格，使企业能够迅速而深入地渗透市场。采用渗透定价策略使公司既能快速吸引大量买家，又能抢占较大的市场份额。但是，必须满足以下条件：

Condition 1: The market for the product must be highly price sensitive, so that a low price produces more market growth.

Condition 2: The market must be large enough to sustain low profit margins and production and distribution costs must fall as sales volume increases.

Condition 3: The low price must help keep out the competition.

Condition 4: The company must be able to maintain its low-price position, otherwise, the price advantage will be just temporary. Once competitors enter the market, they may also lower prices.

条件 1：产品的市场必须对价格高度敏感，这样低价才能带来更大的市场增长；

条件 2：市场规模必须足够大，以维持较低的利润率，生产和分销成本必须随着销量的增长而下降；

条件 3：低价必须有助于阻止竞争；

条件 4：企业必须能够保持其低价地位，否则价格优势将只是暂时的。一旦竞争者进入市场，它们也可能降低价格。

3) Economy Pricing 经济定价

An economy pricing strategy sets prices at the bare minimum to make a small profit. Companies minimize their marketing and promotional costs. The key to a profitable economy pricing program is to sell a high volume of products and services at low prices. Used by a wide range of businesses including generic food suppliers and discount retailers, economy pricing aims to attract the most price-conscious consumers. With this strategy, businesses minimize the costs associated with marketing and production in order to keep product prices down. As a result, customers can purchase the products they need without frills.

经济定价策略将价格设定在最低限度，以获得少量利润。企业会尽量将营销和促销成本降到最低。一个有利可图的经济定价方案的关键是以较低的价格销售大量的产品和服务。包括普通食品供应商和折扣零售商在内的许多企业都在使用经济定价，目的是吸引对价格最敏感的消费者。通过这种策略，企业可以以将与营销和生产相关的成本最小化，从而降低产品价格。因此，顾客可以购买他们需要的产品，而不需要花费太多。

While economy pricing is incredibly effective for large companies like Wal-Mart and Target, the technique can be dangerous for small businesses. Because small businesses lack the sales volume of larger companies, they may struggle to generate a sufficient profit when prices are too low. Still, selectively tailoring discounts to your most loyal customers can be a great way to guarantee their patronage for years to come.

尽管对沃尔玛和塔吉特这样的大企业来说，经济定价非常有效，但对小企业来说，这种方法可能是危险的。由于小企业缺乏大公司的销量，当价格过低时，它们可能难以产生足够的利润。不过，精心地为最忠实的顾客调整折扣，可能是保证他们在未来几年继续光顾你的好办法。

4) Price Skimming 撇脂定价

Price skimming is a strategy of setting prices high by introducing new products when the market has few competitors. This method enables businesses to maximize profits before competitors enter the market, when prices then drop.

撇脂定价是在市场竞争对手很少的情况下，通过推出新产品来制定高价格的一种策略。这种方法使企业能够在竞争对手进入市场之前实现利润最大化，而在竞争对手进入市场之后，价格就会下降。

Price skimming is a strategy that works for a new product that is also a new type of product, one that has no copycat competitors or substitutes yet. Companies that create innovative new products can set high initial prices allowing them to "skim" revenues from the market. However, skimming pricing only works under certain conditions.

撇脂定价是一种适用于新产品的策略。这种新产品也是一种新类型的产品，还没有产品模仿的竞争者或替代品。创造革新产品的公司可以设定较高的初始价格，从而"攫取"市场收入。然而，撇脂定价只在某些情况下有效：

Condition 1: The product's quality and image must be strong enough to support its high price, and enough buyers must want and be willing to buy the product at the high price.

Condition 2: Costs involved in producing a smaller volume of the product cannot be so high that they "eat up" the advantage of charging more.

Condition 3: It cannot be easy for competitors to enter the market and swiftly undercut the high price.

With skimming pricing, the goal is to siphon off maximum revenues possible from the market prior to the introduction of substitutes or copycat offerings. Once the market has been skimmed, the company is free to lower the price drastically to capture low-end buyers while rendering competitors unable to compete on price.

条件 1：产品的质量和形象必须足以支撑其高的价格，并且有足够多的买家想要并愿意以较高的价格购买该产品。

条件 2：生产小批量产品的成本不能高到"吃掉"高价带来的优势。

条件 3：竞争对手进入市场并迅速降低价格是很容易做到的。

采用撇脂定价的目的是在替代品或仿制品进入市场之前，从市场上尽可能多地攫取收入。一旦市场被"撇脂"，该产品就可以大幅降价，以吸引低端买家，同时让竞争对手无法在价格上展开竞争。

5) Psychological Pricing 心理定价

Psychological pricing is a pricing strategy based on the theory that certain prices have a psychological impact. There's evidence that consumers tend to perceive "odd prices" as being nearly lower than they actually are, tending to round to the next lowest monetary unit. Thus, prices such as $1.99 are associated with spending $1 rather than $2. The theory that drives this is that lower pricing such as this institutes greater demand. Marketers use psychological pricing to encourage consumers to buy products based on emotions rather than on common-sense logic.

心理定价是一种定价策略，其理论基础是某些价格能产生心理影响。有证据表明，消费者倾向于认为"奇数价格"几乎低于其实际价格，奇数价格倾向于四舍五入到下一个最低的货币单位。因此，像 1.99 美元这样的价格经常与花费 1 美元而不是 2 美元联系在一起。这一现象的理论基础是，像这样的较低价格会带来更大的需求。营销人员利用心理定价鼓励消费者基于情感而不是常识逻辑购买产品。

For example, setting the price of a watch at $199 is proven to be able to attract more consumers than setting it at $200, even though the true difference here is quite small. This is known as the "left-digit effect". One explanation for this trend is that consumers tend to put more attention on the first number on a price tag than the last. The goal of psychology pricing is to increase demand by creating an illusion of enhanced value for the consumer.

例如，事实证明，将一块手表的价格定在 199 美元比定在 200 美元更能吸引消费者，尽管两者之间的真正差别很小。这就是所谓的"左位数效应"。这种趋势的原因是，消费者往往更关注价格标签上的第一个数字，而不是最后一个数字。心理定价的目的是通过为消费者创造一种价值提升的错觉来增加需求。

6) Bundle Pricing 捆绑定价

Businesses use bundle pricing to sell multiple products together for a lower price. This is an effective strategy to move unsold items that are simply taking up space. Bundling also creates the perception in the mind of the consumer that he's getting a very attractive value for his money.

企业使用捆绑定价，旨在以更低的价格销售多个产品。这是一个有效的策略，以推动那些占着大量空间的难以售出的产品的销售。捆绑销售还会让消费者产生这样一种感觉：他的钱花得值。

Bundle pricing works well for companies that have a line of complimentary products. For example, a restaurant could offer a free dessert with an entree on a certain day of the week. Older video games that are reaching the end of their lives are often sold with a Blu-ray to sweeten the deal. Companies need to study and develop pricing strategies that are appropriate for their goods and services. Certain pricing methods work for introducing new products whereas other strategies are implemented for mature products that have more competitors in the market.

捆绑定价对于拥有一系列互补性产品的公司来说非常有效。例如，餐厅可以在一周的某一天上主菜时配上免费的甜点。那些即将寿终正寝的老款电子游戏通常会附带蓝光光盘销售，以使交易更有吸引力。企业需要研究和开发适合其产品和服务的定价策略。某些定价方法适用于推出新产品，而其他策略适用于市场上竞争对手较多的成熟产品。

Admittedly, there are many different and complex ways that pricing can be approached. However, the bottom-line rules of pricing are simple and straightforward. When it comes to pricing, the most important thing to remember is that prices must be set in a way that will cover costs and profits. With this in mind, pricing must be flexible, because prices should always be in line with changing costs, consumer demand, competitive pricing moves, and profit goals. When the time comes that there is a need to lower prices, the company should first find a way to lower costs, because pricing should always be done in a way that will assure sales and profit.

诚然，可以采用许多不同和复杂的方法进行定价。然而，定价的底线是简单和直接的。说到定价，需要记住的最重要的一点是，设定的价格必须能涵盖成本和利润。记住，定价必须是灵活的，因为价格应该始终与不断变化的成本、消费者需求、有竞争力的定价方案、利润目标保持一致。当需要降低价格的时候，公司应该首先找到降低成本的方法，因为定价应该始终以确保销售和利润的方式进行。

【Exercise】

1. Translate the following phrases into Chinese.

QR code_____

American Marketing Association _____

social signature_____

monthly active users(MAU)_____

search engine marketing (SEM)_____

2. Translate the following phrases into English.

企业文化_____

退货政策_____

用户黏性_____

数据分析_____

预期利润_____

3. Please explain the following words or items.

(1) marketing

(2) platform marketing

(3) SNS marketing

(4) Mobile marketing

4. Please answer the following questions.

(1) What are the tips for direct E-mail marketing?

(2) What efforts should we wake in SEO & SEM Marketing?

(3) Please write down the steps of product selecting.

(4) What are the pricing strategies?

Chapter 7　The Cross-border E-commerce Order Management
跨境电子商务订单管理

【Ability Objectives】

❑ Be able to introduce the E-commerce in English 能够用英语介绍电子商务；

❑ Be able to communicate with customers in English 能够用英语与顾客交流；

❑ Be able to read and comprehend some articles related to cross-border E-commerce 能够阅读和理解与跨境电子商务有关的文章。

【Knowledge Objectives】

❑ Master typical expressions about cross-border E-commerce 掌握跨境电子商务的经典表达；

❑ Memorize new words and phrases in the texts 能够记忆文章中的单词与短语。

【Key Words】

order processing（订单处理）；electronic order（电子订单）

Section 7.1　Order Processing 订单处理

New Words

processing	*v.*	处理；加工；〈口〉排队走；初步分类
	n.	过程；加工处理；处置；进行
collective	*adj.*	集体的；共同的；集合的；集体主义的
	n.	集团；集合体；集合名词
fulfill	*vt.*	履行；实现；满足；使结束
acceptance	*n.*	接纳；赞同；容忍
accurately	*adv.*	精确地，准确地
invest	*vt.*	投资；覆盖；耗费；授予；包围
	vi.	投资，入股；花钱买
strategy	*n.*	战略，策略
vary	*vi.*	变化；变异；违反
	vt.	改变；使多样化；变奏

complexity	n.	复杂，复杂性；复杂错综的事物
instantaneous	adj.	瞬间的；即时的；猝发的
render	v.	提供；给予；提交；翻译
physical	adj.	物理的；身体的；物质的；根据自然规律的，符合自然法则的
	n.	体格检查
submit	vt.	使服从；主张；呈递；提交
	vi.	服从，顺从
route	n.	路线；路途；固定线路；途径
	v.	按某路线发送
facilitate	vt.	促进；帮助；使容易
strategically	adv.	战略性地；战略上
inspect	vt.	检查；视察；检阅
	vi.	进行检查；进行视察
resolve	v.	决心；决定；解决（问题或困难）；（经正式投票）做出决定
	n.	决心；坚定的信念
frame	n.	帧；支架；骨架；画面
	v.	给……做框；给……镶边；作伪证陷害；制订
	adj.	[美]木造的
crucial	adj.	重要的；决定性的；定局的；决断的
chaotic	adj.	混沌的；混乱的，无秩序的
unreliable	adj.	不可靠的；靠不住的
guidelines	n.	指导方针
satisfaction	n.	满意，满足；赔偿；乐事；赎罪
representative	adj.	典型的，有代表性的；代议制的；表现的，体现的；与表象有关的
	n.	代表；典型；众议员；销售代表
vital	adj.	至关重要的；生死攸关的；有活力的
fabric	n.	织物；布；组织；构造；建筑物
accessible	adj.	易接近的；可进入的；可理解的
upfront	adj.	预付的；在前面的；正直的，坦率的
	adv.	在前面；提前支付（工资）

Phrases

to be associated with	与……有关系；与……相联系
distribution centers	配送中心
to fill out	填写；变丰满，变大

all of a sudden   突然

Sentences

1. There was total agreement to start the peace process as soon as possible.
   全体同意尽快启动和平进程。

2. We have developed rapid order processing to expedite deliveries to customers.
   我们已创造了快速处理订单的方法以便迅速将货物送达顾客。

3. It was a collective decision.
   这是集体的决定。

4. Social science is a collective name, covering a series of individual sciences.
   社会科学是一个总称，涵盖一系列独立学科。

5. These cleaners could fulfill all customers' demands.
   这些清洁剂可以满足所有顾客的需求。

6. If one believes in himself, all he needs is just a little bit of luck to fulfill all his dreams.
   一个人只要相信自己，他就只需要一点点运气，所有的梦想就都有可能实现。

7. A very determined effort by society will ensure that the disabled achieve real acceptance and integration.
   社会坚定不移的努力将确保残疾人得到真正的接纳，并使其融入社会。

8. Many people don't like to invest in stocks.
   许多人不喜欢投资股票。

9. I've just been explaining the basic principles of strategy to my generals.
   我刚才一直在向我的将军们解释战略的基本原则。

10. As they're handmade, each one varies slightly.
    由于它们是手工制作的，每一件都会略有不同。

11. I was astonished by the size and complexity of the problem.
    这个问题的复杂性和涉及面之广使我感到惊讶。

12. It's a concept that is difficult to render into English.
    这个概念难以用英语表达。

13. Trains are taking a lot of freight that used to be routed via trucks.
    火车正在运送过去由卡车运送的大批货物。

14. He traced the route on the map.
    他在地图上勾画出了路线。

15. The new airport will facilitate the development of tourism.
    新机场将促进旅游业的发展。

16. Officers making a routine inspection of the vessel found fifty kilograms of cocaine.
    对船只做例行检查的警官们发现了 50 千克可卡因。

17. Estelle kept a photograph of her mother in a silver frame on the kitchen mantelpiece.
    埃丝特尔把她母亲的一张照片放在厨房壁炉架上的银质相框里。

18. The traffic in the city is chaotic in the rush hour.

在上下班高峰时间，城市的交通混乱不堪。

19. His judgment was unreliable.

他的判断是不可靠的。

20. Both sides expressed satisfaction with the progress so far.

双方都对目前的进展表示满意。

21. The port is vital to supply relief to millions of drought victims.

这个港口至关重要，给数百万干旱灾民提供救济物资。

22. The fabric of society has been deeply damaged by the previous regime.

社会结构已被上届执政者严重地破坏了。

23. The centre is easily accessible to the general public.

该中心对于广大公众来讲很便利。

24. He's been upfront about his intentions since the beginning.

他从一开始就明白地说出了他的意图。

Conversations

1. Online Ordering

A: I'm thinking of buying some satin sheets, but I find that your price is on the high side.

B: Dear customer, I think our price is very favorable. You can hardly get such an attractive price from other shop.

A: If you can go a little lower, I'd be able to give you an order on the spot.

B: Which one are you talking about?

A: Here is the link.

B: For this one, the best I can do is to give you a 5% reduction.

A: That's great. This is my first time to purchase goods on Amazon. I'm not sure how to place an order.

B: Let me show you how to order. First, open the item's page and select the quantity number, color, size. Then click the "Buy Now" button.

A: What's the use of the "Add to Cart" button above the "Buy Now" button?

B: Click the "Add to Cart" button, you've added the item on the current page to your cart, and then you can keep browsing for other items. When you need to place an order, you can access the contents of your cart by clicking the "Cart" button.

A: Okay, I see. Thank you.

1. 在线订购

A：我在考虑订购一些丝绸床单，但是我觉得你们的价格有些偏高。

B：亲，我认为我们店的价格是很优惠的。你从其他店里很难找到如此有吸引力的价格。

A：如果你能把价格降低些我现在就订货。

B：您说的是哪款产品呢？

A：这是链接。

B：这一款我们最多只能降价 5%。

A：那太好了，对了，这是我第一次在亚马逊上购物，我不太明白怎么下订单。

B：我为您示范如何操作。首先在产品页面选择数量、颜色和尺寸，然后点击"现在购买"按钮就可以了。

A："现在购买"按钮上面的"加入购物车"按钮有什么用呢？

B：点击"加入购物车"按钮，就可以将当前页面的商品添加到您的购物车里，然后继续浏览其他商品。需要下订单时，直接点击"购物车"按钮就可以访问购物车里的商品内容。

A：好的，我知道了，谢谢！

2. Introducing the Payment Procedure

A: Hello, there?

B: Yes, what can I do for you?

A: Well, it's my first time purchasing goods on Amazon. I like a watch in your store. Can you tell me how to pay for it?

B: Of course, I'd love to. First, you should complete the order information for the item, such as quantity, style, and color. Then click the "Buy Now" button to enter the new page. Select the shipping address on the new page, and you can enter a new shipping address, or choose the default address.

A: Please wait a moment. I have entered my shipping address when registering.

B: Then you can click on the "Ship to this address" button and go to the next page to select the payment method. There are many payment options. You may choose a credit card or debit card, and then click the "Continue" button to proceed step by step.

A: Well, it doesn't sound complicated either.

B: Yes, you will be very skilled if you do it a few more times.

A: Thank you for your help.

2. 介绍付款程序

A：你好，在吗？

B：是的，请问有什么吩咐？

A：是这样的，我第一次在亚马逊上买东西，我在你们店内看好一款手表，能告诉我付款步骤是怎样的吗？

B：当然，我很乐意。首先您要选择商品的基本属性，比如数量、款式和颜色。然后单击"现在购买"按钮，进入新的页面。在新的页面选择送货地址，可以选择默认地址，也可重新添加地址。

A：请稍等，在注册时我已经输入我的收货地址了。

B：那您可以直接单击"送货到该地址"按钮，进入下一个页面选择付款方式。您可以选择信用卡或借记卡，然后单击"继续"按钮，按步骤操作。

A：听起来也不是很复杂。

B：没错，您多操作几次就会很熟练了。

A：谢谢你的帮助。

Text

7.1.1　Introduction of Order Processing 订单处理简介

Order processing is the term used to identify the collective tasks associated with fulfilling an order for goods or services placed by a customer. The processing procedure begins with the acceptance of the order from the customer, and is not finished until the customer has received the products and determined that order has been delivered accurately and completely. Companies often invest a great deal of time and effort in designing an efficient strategy for processing orders, thus establishing a long-term relationship with its customers.

订单处理是一个术语，用于标识与履行客户下的商品或服务订单相关的集体任务。处理过程从接受客户的订单开始，直到客户收到产品并确定订单已准确、完整地交付时才结束。公司经常投入大量的时间和精力来设计有效的订单处理策略，从而与客户建立长期的关系。

The actual approach to order processing will vary, depending on the complexity of the order, and the type of products ordered. In some cases, it can be almost instantaneous. For example, if a buyer places an order for a software download or an E-book, the order processing usually involves nothing more, than the buyer rendering payment for the product, the seller registering the sale and accepting the payment, and the immediate delivery of the E-book or software by means of a download.

订单处理的实际方法会有所不同，具体取决于订单的复杂性和订购的产品类型。在某些情况下，它可能几乎是瞬间发生的。例如，如果买家下了下载软件或电子书的订单，订单处理通常只涉及买家为产品付款、卖家登记销售并接受付款，以及通过下载立即交付电子书或软件。

When physical goods are involved in order processing, a more complex approach is commonly employed. Customers may place orders by submitting a written request, by phone, or by using online order forms that are routed directly to the seller. Each order is then routed to a distribution center, where the type and quantity of items requested by the customer are collected and prepared for shipping. In order to facilitate this process, larger companies often operate multiple distribution centers that are strategically located, allowing for the shipment to be delivered to the customer as soon as possible.

当订单处理涉及实物商品时，通常使用更复杂的方法。客户可以通过提交书面请求、电话或使用直接发送给卖家的在线订单来下订单。然后，每个订单都被送到配送中心，在那里收集客户请求的商品的类型和数量，并准备发货。为了促进这一过程，较大的公司通常运营多个位于战略位置的配送中心，以便将货物尽快交付客户。

When receiving the ordered items, the customer completes the order processing by inspecting the items that are delivered. If the items are in fact what the customer ordered, and are not damaged in any way, then the order processing cycle is considered complete. Should the received items be incorrect, or are damaged, in any way, then the processing is not considered complete until the issues are resolved.

当收到订购的物品时，客户通过检查交付的物品来完成订单处理。如果物品实际上是客户订购的，并且没有任何损坏，则认为订单处理周期已完成。如果收到的物品不正确或以任何方式损坏，则在问题解决之前，处理不会被视为完成。

Efficient and accurate order processing is essential to the success of any type of business. A truly efficient system will require that orders must be verified with customers to ensure that there are no questions about what the customer wants. Once the order is verified, the items needed to fill the order accurately must be collected in a timely fashion. After collecting the necessary products, they must be packaged securely and delivered to the customer within the time frame promised. Failure to manage efficiently any of these tasks increases the chances of disappointing the customer, and thus losing any possibility of repeat business.

高效、准确的订单处理对于任何类型的业务的成功都至关重要。一个真正有效的系统要求必须与客户核实订单，以确保对客户的要求没有疑问。订单一经核实，准确完成订单所需的物品一定要及时领用。收集了必要的产品后，必须安全包装，并在承诺的时间范围内交付客户。不能有效地管理这些任务中的任何一个都会增加客户失望的可能性，从而失去回头客。

In short, order processing is the process or work-flow associated with picking, packing and delivery of the packed items to a shipping carrier. Order processing is a key element of order fulfillment. Order processing operations or facilities are commonly called "distribution centers".

简而言之，订单处理是与挑选、包装和将包装好的物品交付运输承运人相关的过程或工作流程。订单处理是订单履行的关键环节。订单处理设施通常称为"配送中心"。

7.1.2　Steps of Order Processing 订单处理步骤

Developing steps for processing orders is crucial for your business. Without proper order-processing work flow, the order processing within your business will be chaotic and unreliable. Take the time to develop the proper order-processing guidelines and your business will run more smoothly and you will have higher customer satisfaction.

开发订单处理步骤对您的业务至关重要。如果没有适当的订单处理工作流程，您的企业内部的订单处理将会混乱和不可靠。花点时间制定适当的订单处理指南，您的业务就会运行得更顺畅，客户满意度也会更高。

1. Use a Standardized Form When Taking Orders 在接受订单时使用标准化的表单

Whether your company uses a customer service representative to take orders or the customer enters orders directly through your website, it is vital that you have a standardized form.

无论您的公司使用客户服务代表接受订单，还是客户直接通过您的网站输入订单，拥有标准化的表单都是至关重要的。

Each of your inventory items may have slightly different order details.

您的每个库存项目的订单详细信息可能略有不同。

It is important that incomplete order forms are not accepted. If an order form does not have the needed information, it must be returned and completed before it can be processed.

不接受不完整的订单是很重要的。如果订单没有所需的信息，则必须将其退回并填写后才能进行处理。

2. Confirm the Order 确认订单

After an order form has been submitted, it should be confirmed with the customer. This can be accomplished by sending an E-mail with the order details. It is not necessary to require that the customer verify the order. Instead, make it clear that the customer should contact your company if there are any problems with the order. Be sure to make your company's contact information easily accessible to the customer.

提交订单后，应与客户确认，可以通过发送包含订单详细信息的电子邮件实现客户确认。没有必要要求客户核实订单。相反，请明确表示，如果订单有任何问题，客户应与您的公司联系。确保客户可以轻松访问您公司的联系信息。

3. Distribute the Order Form Internally 内部订单分配

Once the order form is filled out, it should be forwarded to everyone who needs to perform an action related to fulfilling the order. This includes the warehouse, the accounts receivable department and the manufacturer, if the order is being fulfilled by a third-party. The expected fulfillment date should be clearly indicated so that everyone involved knows the timetable.

填写订单后，应将其转发给需要执行与履行订单相关的操作的每个人。如果订单由第三方履行，这包括仓库、应收账款部门和制造商。预期的完成日期应该清楚地标明，以便每个参与的人都知道时间表。

4. Communicate with the Customer 与客户沟通

It is vital to clearly communicate with the customer. Tell the customer if there is a delay in the fulfillment of the order. Being upfront and honest with the customer when there is a problem is much better than ignoring it. Also, inform the customer when the order ships. Tell him the carrier, the tracking number and the expected delivery date. Ask for feedback from the customer after he receives the order. Have a customer service representative call to make sure the customer is satisfied with the purchase or use an online survey to gain feedback. Either way, the customer feedback will give very useful insight into your order-fulfillment process.

与客户进行清晰的沟通至关重要。告诉客户订单的履行是否有延迟。当出现问题时，坦率和诚实地对待客户比忽视它要好得多。另外，在订单发货时通知客户。告诉他承运人、跟踪号和预计的交货日期。在客户收到订单后，要求他提供反馈。请客户服务代表致电以确保客户对购买感到满意，或使用在线调查获取反馈。无论哪种方式，客户反馈都将为您的订单履行过程提供非常有用的见解。

Section 7.2　Electronic Order 电子订单

New Words

receipt	*n.*	收到；收据；收入
	vt.	收到
assume	*vi.*	设想；承担；采取
	vt.	假定；僭取；篡夺；夺取；擅用；侵占
commodity	*n.*	商品，货物；日用品
validity	*n.*	【计】有效性；正确；正确性
invalid	*adj.*	无效的；有病的；残疾的
modify	*vt.*	修改，修饰；更改
	vi.	修改
inquiry	*n.*	调查；询问；追究；询盘

Phrases

electronic order	电子订单
electronic platform system	电子平台系统
system administrator	系统管理员

Sentences

1. I wrote her a receipt for the money.
   我为那笔钱给她开了张收据。

2. He was tallying the day's receipts.
   他正在结算当天的收入。

3. We are taking action, having been in receipt of a letter from him.
   收到他的信之后，我们开始采取行动。

4. Mr. Cross will assume the role of CEO with a team of four directors.
   克罗斯先生将担任由 4 位执行官组成的一个团队的首席执行官一职。

5. Prices went up on several basic commodities like bread and meat.
   面包、肉等几种基本商品的价格上涨了。

6. Crude oil is the world's most important commodity.
   原油是世界上最重要的商品。

7. Shocked by the results of the elections, they now want to challenge the validity of the vote.
   震惊于这些选举的结果，他们现在想质疑投票的可信性。

8. The period of validity of the agreement has expired.
   本协议的有效期已过。

9. The trial was stopped and the results declared invalid.

审判被终止了，其结果被宣布无效。

10. We think that those arguments are rendered invalid by the facts.
    我们认为那些论点在事实面前站不住脚。

11. The club members did agree to modify their recruitment policy.
    俱乐部成员确已同意修改他们的入会政策。

12. A judge has suspended the ban pending a full inquiry.
    一名法官已暂时取消了此项禁令，等待一次全面调查。

Conversations

1. Maintenance Service

A: Hi, are you there?

B: Hello. Welcome to my shop.

A: Well, I bought a necklace in your store three months ago, but now the clasp had broken. How could that happen? Only three months later, the quality of your goods is too poor.

B: Dear customer, I'm sorry for this, but our necklace has been tested for quality, and it won't easily break if there's nothing wrong with it.

A: I don't need this right now. Just want to know whether you can fix it or not? If not, I'd like a refund.

B: Sorry, since the goods have been sold for three months, there is no refund. However, we do offer maintenance services.

A: Well, then I don't have to pay for the freight, right?

B: I'm sorry, we can offer you repair service, but you need to pay the freight by yourself.

A: What? That doesn't make sense. Why don't I go to the jewelry store nearby?

B: Sorry, dear customer, we're doing this by our store's rules. As your request exceeds the stipulated time, there is nothing we can do. The only thing we can do is to give you a 20% discount if you visit our shop next time.

A: That sounds sincere enough, and I'll let it go at that.

1. 维修服务

A：你好，在吗？

B：您好，欢迎光临。

A：是这样的，3 个月前我在你们店里买了一款项链，不过现在钩环坏了。怎么会这样呢？才 3 个月，你们的商品质量也太差了吧。

B：亲，发生这样的事我感到很抱歉，不过我们的项链是经过质量检测的，如果不是有什么意外的情况是不会轻易坏掉的。

A：我不想听这些，我只想知道你们能修好吗？如果不能我希望能退款。

B：抱歉，由于商品已售出 3 个月了，所以不能退款。不过我们确实可以向您提供维修服务。

A：这样啊，那运费不需要我出吧。

B：不好意思，我们可以为您提供维修服务，不过运费需要您自己出。

A：什么？这也太不合理了，与其这样，我还不如去附近的珠宝店修呢？

B：不好意思，亲，我们也是按规定来的，主要是因为您用的时间超过了规定的时长。您如果下次光顾本店，我们可以为您打 8 折。

A：你们还挺有诚意的，好吧，我也不再追究了。

2. Returning Goods Unconditionally

A: Hi, what is your policy on returns?

B: Hello. If the return is caused by the product quality or the mistake from us, you will be guaranteed to get 100% refund. May I help you?

A: Yes, I would like to return this earphone.

B: Dear customer, is there anything wrong with this earphone? We do not accept merchandise for return unless items are defective, in which case they will be replaced, subject to availability, or refunded at buyers discretion.

A: There is much noise in this earphone. Can I return it?

B: Of course, you can apply for return directly, and then return the goods to the following address.

A: Do I have to pay for the freight?

B: There will be no charge at all. The balance will be refunded back to you after we receive the items.

2. 无条件退货

A：你好，你们怎么规定退货的事宜？

B：您好，若因商品质量或由于我们的失误而导致的退货，将会保证得到 100% 的退款。我能为您效劳吗？

A：对，我想退回这只耳机。

B：亲，请问这只耳机有什么问题吗？若非商品有瑕疵我们不接受退货，而瑕疵品将视情况替换或是按您的意愿退款。

A：这只耳机有杂音，我可以退货吗？

B：当然可以，您直接申请退货，然后将商品退回以下地址就可以了。

A：那我需要支付运费吗？

B：完全不用收费。我们在收到退回的货物后，会退回款项。

Text

7.2.1　Introduction of Electronic Order 电子订单简介

An electronic order is a shopping request issued by the product demand side, which can be used as payment, delivery and receipt. The electronic order of cross-border E-commerce generally includes basic information and product information of electronic order. In cross-border E-commerce, electronic orders also assume the function of electronic contracts. Therefore, when the deal reached, the buyer must send an electronic order to the supplier.

电子订单是产品需求方发出的购物请求，可以作为支付、发货和收据。跨境电商的电子订单一般包括电子订单的基本信息和产品信息。在跨境电子商务中，电子订单也承担着电子合同的功能。因此，当交易达成时，买方必须向供应商发送电子订单。

7.2.2　Steps of Electronic Order Processing 电子订单处理步骤

An electronic order is generated from the cross-border E-commerce platform, and its generation process is mainly reflected in the four steps:

电子订单是从跨境电商平台生成的，其过程主要体现在四个步骤：

1. User Issues an Order 用户发出订单

Customers are allowed to modify or cancel their orders during the period that the orders have submitted and have not confirmed.

在订单已提交且未确认期间，允许客户修改或取消订单。

2. Confirm the Order 确认订单

After the customer order is submitted to the electronic platform system, the platform system administrator confirms the order data, while the large goods will be confirmed by telephone or mail. The contents of the confirmation include whether the customer's address is true or not, and commodity distribution related information. The system administrator confirm the validity of the order, invalid orders will be canceled directly. Orders that have been confirmed will no longer be modified.

客户订单提交到电子平台系统后，平台系统管理员确认订单数据，大件商品通过电话或邮件确认。确认内容包括客户地址是否真实、商品配送相关信息。系统管理员确认订单有效，无效订单将直接取消。已确认的订单将不再修改。

3. Order Distribution 订单分配

After the order confirmation, platform administrator will distribute the order to supplier or delivery section to stock and delivers goods. Logistics of the order operates offline, and the platform administrator will modify the goods status from the system for buyer to inquiry.

订单确认后，平台管理员将订单下发给供应商或发货部门入库发货。订单物流离线操作，平台管理员将商品状态从买方系统修改为查询。

4. Order Receipt 收单

The order receipt step of cross-border E-commerce is independent of the other steps. It mainly deals with cash on delivery method. After confirming receipt of payment, combined with the feedback of the distribution staff, the financial staff modifies the order status of payment.

跨境电商的收单环节独立于其他环节，主要处理货到付款方式。财务人员确认收款后，结合配送人员的反馈，修改付款订单状态。

The electronic order in this book is the automatically generated order after the first two steps, which includes the important information such as detailed product information, customer's information, payment information, and etc. The electronic order will work as an important proof of goods shipment, delivery and money collection to guide the Step 3 and Step 4.

　　本书中的电子订单是走完前两步后自动生成的订单，包括详细的产品信息、客户信息、支付信息等重要信息，电子订单将作为货物发货、发货、收款的重要凭证，指导第三步和第四步。

【Exercise 】

　　1. Translate the following phrases into Chinese.

　　　　distribution centers_____

　　　　electronic order_____

　　2. Translate the following phrases into English.

　　　　电子平台系统_____

　　　　系统管理员_____

　　3. Please answer the following questions.

　　　　(1) What are the steps of order processing?

　　　　(2) What are the steps of electronic order processing?

Chapter 8 The Services of Cross-border E-commerce
跨境电子商务服务

【Ability Objectives】

❑ Be able to introduce the E-commerce in English 能够用英语介绍电子商务；

❑ Be able to communicate with customers in English 能够用英语与顾客交流；

❑ Be able to read and comprehend some articles related to cross-border E-commerce 能够
阅读和理解与跨境电子商务有关的文章。

【Knowledge Objectives】

❑ Master typical expressions about cross-border E-commerce 掌握跨境电子商务的经典
表达；

❑ Memorize new words and phrases in the texts 能够记忆文章中的单词与短语。

【Key Words】

product information inquiry（产品信息查询）；price negotiation（价格谈判）；payment
（支付）；product packaging（产品包装）；disputes and settlement（纠纷与解决）；comments
on products（产品评论）；customer maintenance（客户维护）

Section 8.1 Pre-sale Services 售前服务

New Words

specification	*n.*	规格；规范
reliable	*adj.*	信赖的；可依靠的
consistency	*n.*	一致性；连贯性
proficient	*adj.*	熟练的；娴熟的；精通的；训练有素的
promotional	*adj.*	广告宣传的；推销的
foundation	*n.*	基本原理；根据；基础
sustainable	*adj.*	可持续的
corresponding	*adj.*	相应的；相关的
release	*v.*	公开；公布；发布
eliminate	*v.*	排除；清除；消除

exclude	*v.*	不包括；不放在考虑之列
ignore	*v.*	忽视；对……不理会
troublesome	*adj.*	令人烦恼的；讨厌的；令人痛苦的
bargain	*v.*	（和某人就某事）讨价还价；商讨条件
initiative	*n.*	主动性；积极性；自发性
reject	*v.*	拒绝接受；不予考虑
reputation	*n.*	名誉；名声
considerable	*adj.*	相当多（或大、重要等）的
supervisor	*n.*	监督人；指导者；主管人
approval	*n.*	赞成；同意；提议
negotiate	*v.*	磋商；协商
retain	*v.*	保持；持有；保留；继续拥有
integrity	*n.*	完整；完好

Phrases

to intend to	打算（做）……；想要（做）……
to be concerned about	关心；挂念
conversion rate	转化率
core competitiveness	核心竞争力
to meet one's demand	满足某人的需求
individual needs	个人需求
domestic sales	内销
to arise from	产生于；起因于
to result from	产生于……；由……引起
to cut the price	降价
positive cycle	良性循环
bulk price	批发价
to make clear	弄清楚；解释

Sentences

1. The toy has been produced exactly to our specifications.
   这些玩具完全按我们的规格生产。

2. We are looking for salesmen who is reliable and hard-working.
   我们正在物色可靠且勤奋的推销员。

3. We can use the logo in all our promotional products.
   我们可以将这个标志用于所有的促销产品。

4. Communication and understanding provide a solid foundation for customer relationship.
   沟通和理解是客户关系的牢固基础。

5. Our focus is on sustainable development.

我们的焦点在可持续发展上。

6. Given each picture a number corresponding to its position on the page.
按所在页面位置给每一幅图片编上相对应的号码。

7. Credit cards eliminate the need to carry a lot of cash.
有了信用卡就无须携带大量现金。

8. We should not exclude the possibility of negotiation.
我们不应该排除谈判的可能性。

9. They completely ignore these facts as if they never existed.
他们完全忽略了这些事实，仿佛它们不存在似的。

10. The economy has become a troublesome issue for the conservative party.
经济已成为保守党的一大难题。

11. I intend to take full advantage of this App to buy the things we need.
我打算充分利用这个 App 购买所需的物品。

12. A high customer conversion rate depends on many factors.
高客户转化率取决于多种因素。

13. Discounts and promotional activities will draw more consumers.
折扣和促销活动将吸引更多的消费者。

14. In the market, dealers were bargaining with growers over the price of coffee.
在市场上，经销商正在与种植者就咖啡价格进行商谈。

15. She hopes to seize the initiative to deal with the problem.
她希望能够主动处理这个问题。

16. A supervisor in enterprise needs to be familiar with running method.
企业的管理者要深谙管理之道。

17. The chairman has also given his approval for an investigation into the case.
主席也已同意对此案进行调查。

18. They refused to negotiate unless three preliminary requirements were met.
如果三项先决条件得不到满足，他们就拒绝谈判。

19. The interior of the shop still retains a nineteenth-century atmosphere.
这家商店的内部装修仍然保留着 19 世纪的风格。

Conversations

1. Retail and Wholesale

A: Hello, I'm interested in your wool carpet. I wonder if you could allow me any discount for this commodity.

B: As a rule, we don't allow any discount. How much would you like?

A: I want a 6 sq.m. wool carpet to decorate the living room.

B: A higher discount will be given for a big order. Your order is too small, so it's hard for me to give you a discount.

A: What if I buy another one for my bedroom?

B: Generally speaking, we offer a discount of 8% to buyers who order over 10,000 square meters, which is our wholesale price. I am sorry I can't make an exception unless you buy in bulk. This is our lowest price. We can't give you any more discounts.

1. 零售和批发

A：你好，我对你们的羊毛毯很感兴趣。我想知道你能给我打折吗？

B：一般来说，我们没有打折。您打算买多少呢？

A：我想要一张 6 平方米的羊毛毯来装饰客厅。

B：订单量越大，折扣越高，您的订单量太少了，所以我很难给您打折。

A：那我再买一张放在卧室如何呢？

B：一般来说，我们会给订单量超过 10 000 平方米的买家 8% 的折扣，就是我们的批发价。抱歉，除非您批量购买，否则我不能破例，我们的价格已经很低了，所以不能再给您任何折扣了。

2. Choose a Suitable Necklace

A: Hi, there?

B: What can I do for you, dear customer?

A: I need a necklace to go with my dress, but I haven't decided for a long time. Any recommendations?

B: There are several necklaces in classic styles in our store. Here is the link.

A: Well, they are so extravagant that I prefer simple and elegant ones.

B: What color is your dress, please?

A: A black full-length skirt.

B: How about this one? The necklace consists of two strings of pearls. It goes well with the black skirt.

A: I don't like pearl necklaces very much. It's too oldish for me.

B: Do you like this necklace of crystal? It has high clarity and no bubbles. Here is the detail. The design of this necklace is also very simple.

A: It looks not bad.

B: This necklace and a pair of earrings are in one set. If you like, you can buy a whole set, which is more economical.

A: I do like it. I'll take it all.

B: Okay, here's the link. Just click in and pay for it.

2. 选择合适的项链

A：在吗？

B：亲，我能帮您什么吗？

A：我想选一条项链搭配裙子，不过选了很久还没有主意，你有没有可推荐的呢？

B：有几款是我们店里的经典款，这是链接。

A：嗯，这几款给人的感觉太过奢华了，我更喜欢简单大方的。

B：请问您的裙子是什么颜色的？

A：黑色拖地长裙。

B：这款双层珍珠项链怎么样？很配黑色的裙子。

A：我不太喜欢珍珠项链，有点老气，不太适合我。

B：您喜欢这款水晶项链吗？透明度很高，而且没有气泡，这是细节图。这款项链的设计也非常简单。

A：看起来不错。

B：这款项链还有一副耳环是配套的，您如果喜欢，可以一起买了，更划算。

A：我很喜欢，这一套我都要了。

B：好的，这是链接，您点进去支付就可以了。

Text

8.1.1　Product Information Inquiry 产品信息查询

On the cross-border E-commerce platform, the seller will usually introduce the products (or services) in details on the description page, including product quality, color, specifications, size, materials, modes of sale, and etc. Customers buy goods (or services) by choosing a platform, intending to buy the commodity (or service) that is cost-effective, safe, reliable, and with comprehensive information.

在跨境电商平台上，卖家通常会在描述页上详细介绍产品（或服务），包括产品质量、颜色、规格、尺寸、材料、销售方式等。客户通过选择平台购买商品（或服务），意在购买性价比高、安全可靠、信息全面的商品（或服务）。

As customers cannot see the real products (services) through online shopping, they can only judge the products through the pictures, descriptions and customer reviews on website (or App). Customers are more concerned about the consistency of the products and the advertising. In this case, customers will inquire of the customer service staff about the products through E-mail or social media. Customer service staff should be proficient in professional knowledge about all the products, have good promotional skills, respond timely and effectively, so as to put away customers' worries before buying products, promote customers to purchase and improve customer conversion rate.

由于客户无法通过网购看到真实的产品（服务），因此只能通过网站（或 App）上的图片、描述和客户评论判断产品。顾客更关心产品和广告的一致性。在这种情况下，客户会通过电子邮件或社交媒体向客服人员查询产品。客服人员要精通所有产品的专业知识，有良好的促销技巧，反应及时有效，在客户买产品前打消其后顾之忧，促进客户购买，提高客户转化率。

Product quality is the foundation and source of healthy development of E-commerce, and the core competitive of sustainable management of company. As the E-commerce platforms only provide pictures and description of products, buyers are unable to determine the quality. Before ordering the products, the buyer may inquire about the quality of them. Customer service staff should be patient and truthfully answer the corresponding questions about quality, trying to win orders.

产品质量是电子商务健康发展的基础和源泉，是企业可持续经营的核心竞争力。由于电商平台只提供产品的图片和描述，因此买家无法确定质量。在订购产品之前，买家可以询问产品的质量。客服人员要耐心地如实回答相应的质量问题，争取订单。

When sellers release a product, they should describe the product materials accurately, especially for products like bags and shoes. The price will differ a lot for different materials they use. The price of some leather products like bags and shoes are high, so the buyer will worry about the authenticity of the material. Receiving such inquiries about the material, the seller should communicate with the buyer sincerely. It is best to attach some relevant customer reviews to eliminate buyers' doubts and promote the transaction.

当卖家发布产品时，他们应该准确地描述产品材料，特别是像包和鞋子这样的产品。它们使用的材料不同，价格会有很大不同。一些像包和鞋子这样的皮制品的价格很高，所以买家会担心材料的真实性。收到此类材料询价后，卖方应与买方真诚沟通。最好附上一些相关的客户点评，消除买家疑虑，促进成交。

Besides product quality and materials, color is also an important factor to attract buyers to place an order. Some buyers may be interested in the product, but the color provided may not meet their demand. For these buyers, the seller should carefully understand the individual needs, and actively guide them to place an order.

除了产品质量和材料，颜色也是吸引买家下单的重要因素。一些买家可能对产品感兴趣，但颜色可能不符合他们的需求。对于这些买家，卖家要仔细了解其需求，积极引导他们下单。

As for product specifications and size issues, the seller will generally describe on the product details page, but it does not exclude some buyers who will ignore this information. In the event of inquiries about product specifications and size, the seller should repeat the detailed specifications and size of the product and guide the buyer to confirm the specifications and size on the product details page again. In addition, some products of cross-border E-commerce are for domestic sales, so there will be size issues, especially for products like clothing and shoes. There are many disputes arising from different size standards, so it is a troublesome problem for many sellers. How can we avoid such disputes? In addition to carefully set the size chart, the seller should respond the size questions in details and with patience, which will play a significant role in avoiding disputes and improving customer experience and satisfaction.

至于产品规格和尺寸问题，卖家一般会在产品详情页进行说明，但不排除一些买家会忽略这些信息。在询问产品规格和尺寸时，卖方应重复产品的详细规格和尺寸，并引导买家再次在产品详情页确认规格和尺寸。此外，跨境电商的一些产品是内销的，所以会有尺码问题，特别是像服装和鞋子这样的产品。由于大小标准不同而引起的纠纷很多，这对许多卖家来说是个麻烦的问题。如何避免这样的纠纷？除了仔细设置尺码图表，卖家还应详细耐心地回答尺码问题，这对避免纠纷、提高客户体验和满意度将起到显著作用。

8.1.2　Price Negotiation 价格谈判

Unlike domestic online customers, most cross-border customers do not bargain with sellers in most cases. Most of the buyers will decide whether to place the order based on the released price. Some of the unpaid orders may result from the high price of the product or shipping. The seller may communicate with the buyer timely and understand the reasons for the unpaid order. If you do not get a reply, you may take the initiative to adjust the price of the product or shipping to regain buyers' focus and improve the conversion rate.

与国内在线客户不同，大多数跨境客户在大多数情况下都不会与卖家讨价还价。大多数买家将根据发布的价格决定是否下单。一些未付订单可能是由于产品或发货价格过高造成的。卖方可以及时与买方沟通，了解订单未付的原因。如果没有得到回复，需要主动调整产品或发货价格，重新获得买家的关注，提高转化率。

But some customers will bargain with the seller for discount before placing an order. For them, the seller should analyze the purpose of bargaining, respond and deal with it specifically. For some products with limited profit margin, the seller should reject the request by emphasizing quality advantage, price advantage over similar products or good reputation, and guide buyers to increase the order number to obtain a discount. For some products with considerable profit margin, the seller should not immediately cut the price after the counter-offer from the customer, but should pretend to ask the supervisor's approval and reply later, so that buyers do not think the released price unrealistically high.

但一些客户会在下单前与卖家讨价还价以求打折。对于他们来说，卖方应该分析讨价还价的目的，并做出具体的回应和处理。对于部分利润率有限的产品，卖家应通过强调质量优势、价格优势或同类产品的好口碑来拒绝要求，并引导买家增加订单量以获得折扣。对于一些利润率较大的产品，卖家不应在客户还价后立即降价，而应假装征得主管批准后再回复，以免买家认为发布的价格不切实际地高。

In addition, there are some small wholesale customers on the cross-border E-commerce platform. Many small foreign buyers favor online orders because of the delivery speed, payment after arrival of products, low risk and relatively high security etc. For them, the seller should give special attention and actively follow up with the inquiry. They should negotiate about the wholesale price according to the quantity and try to retain these small wholesale customers, which will bring great advantages to the positive cycle of online stores. On the one hand, the seller can set the wholesale price when publish the product, so that the buyer can click on the "Bulk Price" button to see the product's default wholesaler. On the other hand, in order to attract small wholesale customers, the seller can also make clear the wholesale discount or indicate the buyer to write to negotiate about the discount on the home page or product description page. When faced with inquiry from a large wholesaler, the seller must seize the opportunity and reply in details, including the style, the amount of purchase and the corresponding offer. The offer usually includes shipping, and should have price advantage, making the buyer feel that he receives a large discount.

　　此外，跨境电商平台上还有一些小型批发客户。不少国外小买家因为发货速度快、货到付款、风险低、安全性相对较高等特点，青睐网上订单，对他们来说，卖家要特别关注，积极跟进询价。他们应该根据数量协商批发价，尽量留住这些小的批发客户，这会给网店的正向循环带来很大的好处：一方面，卖家可以在发布产品的时候设定批发价，让买家点击"批发价"按钮就可以看到产品的默认批发商；另一方面，为了吸引小额批发客户，卖家也可以在首页或产品说明页面明确批发折扣或提示买家写信洽谈折扣事宜。面对大型批发商的询价，卖方必须抓住机会，详细答复，包括款式、采购金额和相应的报价。报价通常包括运费，而且应该有价格优势，让买家觉得他得到了很大的折扣。

Section 8.2　On-sale Services 售中服务

New Words

indispensable	*adj.*	不可或缺的；必不可少的
original	*adj.*	原来的；起初的；最早的
option	*n.*	可选择的事物；选择；选择权；选择的自由
procedure	*n.*	（正常）程序；手续；步骤
accordingly	*adj.*	依据；相应地
redundant	*ad.*	多余的；不需要的
incorporate	*v.*	将……包含在内；包含；吸收；使并入
hesitate	*v.*	（对某事）犹豫；迟疑不决
available	*adj.*	可获得的；可购得的；可找到的
appropriate	*adj.*	合适的；恰当的
collision	*n.*	碰撞；相撞
recycle	*v.*	回收利用；再利用
withstand	*v.*	承受；经受住
decompose	*v.*	（使）分解
humidity	*n.*	热；高温潮湿
endurance	*n.*	忍耐力；耐久力
polystyrene	*n.*	聚苯乙烯
polyethylene	*n.*	聚乙烯
polyurethane	*n.*	聚氨酯
annoying	*adj.*	使恼怒的；使生气的；使烦恼的
punctuality	*n.*	守时；准时
intact	*ad.*	完好无损；完整
harsh	*adj.*	恶劣的；艰苦的

| waterproof | *adj.* | 不透水的；防水的；耐水的 |

Phrases

to serve as	充当；担当
in the process of	在……过程中
to engage in	经营；参加；从事；忙于
to dedicate to	献给
to involve in	参与；涉及；卷入
long-distance transportation	长途运输
to stand out	突出；出色
negative feedback	负面反馈
to get more kicks than half pence	得不偿失
to be packed with	挤满……；装满……；塞满……
to be likely to	可能

Sentences

1. An intelligent computer will be an indispensable diagnostic tool for doctors.
   智能计算机将成为医生不可或缺的诊断工具。

2. I bought the coat as it was considerably reduced from its original price.
   这件外套大减价，因此我就把它买下了。

3. Cooperation was more than just an attractive option, it was an obligation.
   合作不仅是一种有吸引力的选择，更是一种责任。

4. He minuted the procedure of the meeting.
   他对会议议程做了记录。

5. It is a difficult job and they should be paid accordingly.
   这是份棘手的工作，他们应得到相应的报酬。

6. This word is redundant, it can be left out.
   这个字是多余的，可以去掉。

7. Don't hesitate to make comments or suggestions if you have any.
   有意见尽管提出。

8. New types of multi-tasking software are now available.
   新型多任务处理软件现已上市。

9. If the answer is "yes", then we must decide on an appropriate course of action.
   如果答案是肯定的，那么我们必须商定合适的行动方案。

10. The car was completely wrecked by the force of the collision.
    这辆汽车受到很大的撞击力，完全损坏了。

11. The collision took place in the busiest shipping lanes in the world.
    撞船事故发生在全世界最繁忙的航道上。

12. A lot of the plastics that carmakers are using cannot be recycled.

汽车制造商使用的许多塑料制品是无法回收利用的。

13. They can withstand extremes of temperature and weather without fading or cracking.

它们能够经受极端的气温和天气状况而不褪色、不开裂。

14. All substances, except those which decompose when heated, may be changed from one state into another.

除加热时分解的物质外，所有物质都可以从一种状态变为另一种状态。

15. Nearly all TV is commercial and it is very annoying to be interrupted by advertisement at intervals.

几乎所有的电视节目都是商业性的，而且每隔一段时间就会被广告中断，十分烦人。

16. Punctuality is a necessary habit in all public affairs of a civilized society.

准时是文明社会各项公共事务中一个必不可少的习惯。

Conversations

1. Inventory Shortness

A: I think the price of this suspender skirt is little bit higher, can you give me a discount?

B: Sorry, dear customer, there's no discount in our store.

A: That's a pity. In that case, I can only buy it next month.

B: If you do like it, I suggest you place your order as soon as possible. This suspender skirt sells well, and only the last few pieces are left.

A: Is it?

B: This is a skirt that we mainly promote in this quarter. It will not be sold after we empty the inventory.

A: In that case, maybe I should buy one.

B: Ok, click on this link to place your order.

1. 库存短缺

A：这件吊带裙价格有一点儿高，可不可以打折呢？

B：不好意思，亲，我们店里都不打折哦。

A：那太遗憾了，这样的话，我只能下个月来买了。

B：如果您真的喜欢的话，建议您尽快下单，这款吊带裙我们买得很好，只剩最后几件了。

A：是吗？

B：这是我们这一季度主推的一款裙子，清空库存后就不再卖了。

A：如果是这样的话，我想我应该买一条。

B：好的，点进这个链接就能下单了。

2. Transfer Goods Elsewhere

A: Hello?

B: What can I do for you?

A: I want to order a large number of tennis rackets. How many tennis rackets do you have in stock?

B: In some cases, such as the basketballs, which always occupy market steadily, we keep a stock all the time. For the tennis rackets, we have produced some this year, so we should be able to fulfill your requirements. How many do you intend to order?

A: We need 5,000 tennis rackets.

B: We only have 1,000 rackets in stock at present, but it can be delivered from the warehouse in Guangzhou.

A: Is it? That would be great.

2. 到别处调货

A：在吗？

B：有什么可以帮您的吗？

A：我要订购大量的网球拍，你们店里有多少库存呢？

B：有的商品比如篮球，市场很稳定，我们一直保持库存。就网球拍来说，今年我们生产了一些，所以应该能够满足您的需求。您打算订购多少呢？

A：我们需要 5000 支网球拍。

B：我们这边暂时只有 1000 支库存，不过我们可以到广州的仓库去调货。

A：是吗？那太好了。

Text

8.2.1　Payment 支付

Order payment serves as the indispensable key part throughout cross-border E-commerce, covering both online and offline approach. Offline bank approach is essentially the same as the original payment in international trade, except that the platform of business shifts from offline exhibitions to B2B(Alibaba.com, Made in China, Global sources etc.) and B2C websites (AliExpress, eBay, Amazon etc.). Offline payment methods include cash, letter of credit(L/C), payment on delivery, Western Union Transfer and documentary collection as well documents against payment(D/P), installment, payment on credit and deferred payment, among which the first four are generally the main options.

订单支付是整个跨境电商不可或缺的关键部分，涵盖了线上和线下两种方式。线下银行方式与国际贸易原有支付方式基本相同，只是业务平台从线下展会转向 B2B（阿里巴巴、中国制造、环球资源等）和 B2C 网站（全球速卖通、eBay、亚马逊等）。线下支付方式包括现金、信用证、货到付款、西联汇款、跟单托收以及付款交单、分期、信用证付款和延期付款，其中前四种通常是主要选择。

Comparatively, online approach mainly refers to the payment model of E-account to E-account, touching upon such methods as Alipay, PayPal and MoneyBookers, and etc.

相比之下，在线方式主要是指电子账户对电子账户的支付模式，涉及支付宝、贝宝、MoneyBookers 等方式。

Some buyers that are new to online shopping may turn out to be not familiar with the payment procedures of cross-border E-commerce platforms, and thus fail to complete the order after initiating one. In this case, sellers should give in-time communication and patient explanation to related questions. Meanwhile, suppliers should contact purchasers to first of all thank them for their support, then to enquire about any possible problems occurred in the process of payment and inform them of the procedures and offer help accordingly, when some unpaid orders especially those repeated ones from one buyer are spotted.

一些刚开始网购的买家可能不熟悉跨境电商平台的支付程序，因此在发起订单后无法完成订单。在这种情况下，卖家应该及时沟通并耐心解释相关问题。同时，供应商应联系采购商，首先感谢它们的支持，当发现一些未支付的订单，特别是来自一个买家的重复订单时，还应询问付款过程中可能出现的任何问题，并告知它们程序，提供相应的帮助。

Though most of the buyers are able to see through this process, some still may have payment failure after multiple attempts. Therefore, when asked for assistance, sellers shall let buyers know potential reasons for the failure and help them through the payment to finally win the order back. Additionally, some may have no clue to use the shopping cart to combine the purchasing and payment for various types of products in one store, which leads to the inconvenience on both sides caused by redundant orders from one buyer. In this sense, sellers shall guide them to reasonably use the cart and to incorporate the order payments.

虽然大多数买家都能看透这一过程，但也有一些人在多次尝试后仍可能付款失败。因此，卖家在请求协助时，应让买家知道失败的潜在原因，并通过付款帮助买家最终赢回订单。此外，有些人可能不知道如何使用购物车将一个商店的各种产品的购买和支付结合起来，从而导致一个买家的重复订单给双方带来不便。从这个意义上说，卖家应该引导他们合理使用购物车，并将订单付款纳入其中。

Some buyers may hesitate to make orders due to the doubts over the security of cross-border online payment. For those, sellers shall dispel their concern and enhance their trust by telling them the security insurance of online payment.

由于对跨境在线支付安全性的疑虑，一些买家可能会在下单时犹豫不决。对于这些人，卖家应该通过告诉他们网上支付的安全保险来打消他们的担忧，增强他们的信任。

For example, secure payment of Alibaba.com aims to provide a safe payment service for all parties engaged in international trade. By partnering with an independent online payment platform(Alipay), secure payment provides security to online payment and to online transaction for both buyers and suppliers, and also it ensures money dispute resolution. Efficient transaction is realized here by supporting drafting freight order, online wholesaling and trading as well as online ordering of purchasers, with real-time order process available over platform of alibaba.com. Secure payment also offer diverse payment methods as credit cards, Western Union and bank transfers to guarantee the convenient payment for buyers.

例如，阿里巴巴的安全支付旨在为从事国际贸易的各方提供安全的支付服务。通过与独立的在线支付平台（支付宝）合作，安全支付为买家和供应商提供在线支付和在线交易的安全性，并确保资金纠纷的解决。通过支持货运订单的起草、在线批发和交易以及采购商的在线订购，实现了高效的交易，并通过阿里巴巴平台实现了实时订单流程。安全支付还提供信用卡、西联汇款、银行转账等多种支付方式，保证买家支付的便利性。

8.2.2　Product Packaging 产品包装

As cross-border E-commerce sellers, besides long-distance transportation, it is more important to ensure the integrity of goods when delivered to customers. Appropriate packaging can determine the integrity of goods. Good product packaging can affect the customer's review of the product, and make it stand out from other products.

作为跨境电商卖家，除了长途运输，更重要的是保证商品在交付给客户时的完整性。适当的包装可以决定商品的完整性。好的产品包装可以影响顾客对产品的评价，使其从其他产品中脱颖而出。

1. Appropriate Box Size 适当的盒子尺寸

Oversized boxes will cause higher freight and need more filler. Appropriate box size can reduce the collision between the goods and the box. Pick the appropriate box and try to pack the goods in different ways.

超大的箱子会导致更高的运费，需要更多的填充物。适当的箱体尺寸可以减少货物与箱体的碰撞。选择合适的盒子，试着用不同的方式包装货物。

2. Use Recycled Materials for Package 使用回收材料进行包装

Many sellers have the habit of using carton boxes repeatedly, but please never use cracked carton boxes. Once cracked, the weight that cartons can withstand will be reduced by 70%. Many sellers use recycled or poor quality carton boxes in order to save cost, and often receive buyer's negative feedback, or request for return or replacement, and thus get more kicks than half pence. After exposed to the air for a long time, these decomposable packaging materials will be naturally decomposed because of the temperature and humidity. The repeated use of wrapping paper and packaging foam will also reduce its endurance. Sellers must be very cautious when picking up the packaging materials.

许多卖家有重复使用纸箱的习惯，但请不要使用破裂的纸箱。一旦开裂，纸箱能承受的重量将减少 70%。许多卖家为了节约成本，使用回收的或质量低劣的纸箱，经常收到买家的负面反馈，或要求退货或更换，因此得不偿失。这些易腐烂的包装材料在与空气长时间接触后，会因为温度和湿度而自然分解。反复使用包装纸和包装泡沫也会降低其耐久性。卖家在选取包装材料时一定要非常小心。

3. Select Packaging Materials with Good Quality 选择质量好的包装材料

Polystyrene can only withstand collision for one time, while polyethylene and polyurethane materials are relatively much stronger. Because these materials are thin, strong, and can be as strong as other packaging materials with smaller size, so you can choose smaller box to pack and save some shipping fee. For products like oven or TV, sellers must use foamed plastic or polystyrene foam to prevent the collision on the corner.

聚苯乙烯只能承受一次碰撞，而聚乙烯和聚氨酯材料相对坚固得多。因为这些材料薄、结实，可以和其他尺寸较小的包装材料一样结实，所以您可以选择较小的包装盒来包装，这样可以节省一些运费。对于烤箱或电视机等产品，卖家必须使用泡沫塑料或聚苯乙烯泡沫塑料，以防止拐角处发生碰撞。

Fragile goods must be packed with polystyrene-filled particles or bubble wrap. If necessary, you can use double packaging. If the two products are wrapped in the same box, be sure to add some foamed plastic in the middle of them to avoid collision. Finally, please mark "fragile" outside the box.

易碎品必须用聚苯乙烯填充颗粒或气泡包装。如有必要，您可以使用双层包装。如果两个产品都包装在同一个箱子里，一定要在中间加一些泡沫塑料，以免发生碰撞。最后，请在包装盒外注明"易碎品"。

4. Wrap Products for Gifts and Holidays 为礼品和节日包装产品

It is very annoying for everyone to receive a damaged product because of transportation, especially for holiday or birthday present. During holidays such as birthday, anniversary or Christmas, sellers pay more attention not only to the actuality of products, but also to the intactness of them. So it is better to spend more time on the package, and make it look better.

对于每个人来说，因为运输问题而收到损坏的产品是非常恼人的，特别是作为节日或生日礼物。在生日、纪念日或圣诞节，卖家不仅注重产品的现状，而且注重产品的完整性。所以最好花更多的时间在包装上，让它看起来更好看。

5. Wrap High-priced Products 包装高价产品

Cross-border E-commerce sellers do not want to lose high-priced products during transit, so use at least size 7 cm × 4cm × 4cm box to ship expensive jewelries and other similar products. Tiny boxes are easily misplaced or forgotten during transport.

跨境电商卖家不想在运输过程中丢失高价产品，所以至少使用7厘米×4厘米×4厘米大小的盒子运送昂贵的珠宝和其他类似的产品。小箱子在运输过程中很容易放错地方或忘了。

6. Packaging Methods to Adapt Various Environmental Conditions 适应各种环境条件的包装方法

The package is likely to be thrown into the truck or container recklessly by transport personnel. So the seller must design an experiment, in any possible harsh environment like different temperature and humidity conditions, to see whether the package is in good condition after the test. No matter what kind of products, make sure to ensure that it is well packaged and waterproof.

包裹很可能会被运输人员鲁莽地扔进卡车或集装箱。所以卖家必须设计一个实验，在任何可能的恶劣环境下，比如不同的温度和湿度条件，看看测试后包装是否处于良好的状态。无论是哪种产品，都要确保包装完好、防水。

7. Reconfirm the Address 再次确认地址

Packing notes can be printed from the "Manage Your Order" page. The address label should be attached outside the carton box, and the other packing note should be placed in the box with products.

可以从"管理您的订单"页面打印装箱单。地址标签应该贴在纸箱外面，另一张装箱单应该放在装有产品的盒子里。

It is the most basic, and the most error-prone thing to confirm the correct shipping address. It is best to add a clear return address outside the box. The address should be attached to or written directly on the box. It is best to use an oily pen to write the address. If the address is wrong, it can be easier to detect and make corrections. The problem of vagueness resulting from rain or label wrinkles can also be avoided.

确认正确的发货地址是最基本的，也是最容易出错的。最好在包装盒外添加一个清晰的回邮地址。地址应贴在包装盒上或直接写在包装盒上。最好用油性笔写地址。如果地址错误，可以更容易地检测和更正。还可以避免因下雨或标签起皱而导致的模糊问题。

Section 8.3　After-sale Services 售后服务

New Words

restriction	*n.*	限制规定；限制法规
counterfeit	*adj.*	伪造的；仿造的；假冒的
prohibit	*v.*	以（法令）禁止
impact	*n.*	巨大影响；强大作用
implement	*v.*	使生效；贯彻；执行；实施
appease	*v.*	安抚；抚慰
priority	*n.*	优先事项最重要的事；首要事情
intangible	*adj.*	难以形容（或理解）的；不易度量的；[商]无形的
profitability	*n.*	获利（状况）；盈利（情况）
rectify	*v.*	矫正；纠正；改正
evaluation	*n.*	评价；评估
negative	*adj.*	消极的；负面的；缺乏热情的
revise	*v.*	修改；修订
modify	*v.*	调整；稍做修改；使更合适
reward	*n.*	奖励；回报；报酬
loyalty	*n.*	忠诚；忠实，忠心耿耿
convincing	*adj.*	令人信服的；有说服力的
preliminary	*adj.*	初步的；预备的
maintenance	*n.*	保持

preference	*n.*	偏爱；爱好；喜爱
encounter	*v.*	遭遇；遇到（尤指令人不快或困难的事）
characteristic	*n.*	特征；特点；品质
identify	*v.*	确认；认出；鉴定
uncertainty	*n.*	拿不定的事；令人无把握的局面
psychological	*adj.*	心灵的；心理的；精神上的
flaw	*n.*	裂痕；裂隙；瑕疵
impressive	*adj.*	令人赞叹的；令人敬佩的
territory	*n.*	领土；版图；领地
density	*n.*	密集；稠密；密度；浓度
horticultural	*adj.*	园艺的
approximately	*adv.*	大概；大约；约莫
remote	*adj.*	偏远的，偏僻的
passionate	*adj.*	热诚的；狂热的
valid	*adj.*	（法律上）有效的；（正式）认可的
exemption	*n.*	（指部分收入）免税
abundant	*adj.*	大量的；丰富的；充裕的
trivial	*adj.*	不重要的；微不足道的；琐碎的
compromise	*n.*	妥协；折中；互让；和解
upheaval	*n.*	巨变；激变；动乱；动荡
pragmatism	*n.*	实用主义；务实主义
aesthetic	*adj.*	审美的；有审美观点的；美学的
tentatively	*adv.*	不确定的；不肯定的；暂定的
peripheral	*adj.*	次要的；附带的
burgeoning	*adj.*	迅速成长的；迅速发展的
prevailing	*adj.*	普遍的；流行的；盛行的

Phrases

to apply for	申请
customs detention	海关扣押
to be reluctant to	不愿意；不情愿
vicious cycle	恶性循环
to be critical to	至关重要
bottom line	底线；最低条件
be affected by	受……影响
positive ratios	好评率
make up for	弥补
brand awareness	品牌意识

based on	基于
to lie in	位于；在于
an ecological circle	生态圈
return visit	回访
sales volume	销售量；销售额
stuffed toy	填充玩具；毛绒玩具
to take into consideration	考虑到；顾虑；着想
taxation rates	税率
penetration rates	渗透率
in duplicate	一式两份
to make a concession	让步
to have faith in	相信；信任
to engage in	经营；参加；从事；忙于
to carry out	执行；进行；完成

Sentences

1. There are no restrictions on the amount of money you can withdraw.
   取款没有限额。

2. Counterfeit products hurt consumers, retailers and manufacturers.
   假冒产品伤害了消费者、零售商和制造商。

3. Cross-border E-commerce platforms prohibit the sale of intangible goods.
   跨境电商平台禁止出售无形商品。

4. The report sets out strict inspection procedures to ensure that the plan is properly implemented.
   报告设置了严格的检查程序，以确保建议得到切实执行。

5. I tried to appease them by offering to replace the product with a brand-new one.
   我试图用一款全新的产品取代这个产品以安抚他们。

6. Stocks and bonds are intangible property.
   股票和证券是无形财产。

7. Changes were made in operating methods in an effort to increase profitability.
   为了提高盈利能力，经营方式发生了改变。

8. Instead of blaming ourselves, we should try to find out what we need to rectify.
   我们不应该责怪自己，而应该试着找出我们需要改变什么。

9. Three editors handled the work of revising the articles for publication.
   三位编辑负责文章的修订出版工作。

10. Neither party shall modify the contract without authorization.
    任何一方不得擅自修改合同。

11. The company is starting to reap the rewards of long-term investments.

这家公司开始收获长期投资的回报。

12. Improving customer's loyalty and satisfaction is our goal.

提升客户忠诚度和满意度是我们的目标。

13. This is the most convincing evidence that I can find to prove my point.

这是我所能找到的最令人信服的证据，以证明我的观点。

14. The maintenance of international peace matters a lot.

维护世界和平事关重大。

15. Many people expressed a strong preference for shopping online.

许多人强烈表示喜欢上网购物。

16. If you undertake the project, you are bound to encounter difficulties.

如果你承接这项工程，你肯定会遇到许多困难。

17. Our country has a large population vast territory and abundant resources.

我国人口众多，地大物博。

18. The region has very high population density.

该地区的人口密度很高。

19. During the May Day holiday, the Xi'an International Horticultural Expo Garden was packed with visitors.

五一假期期间，西安世博园挤满了游客。

20. The journey took approximately seven hours.

旅程大约花了 7 个小时。

Conversations

1. Custom Made

A: Hi, there?

B: May I help you?

A: I want a necklace for my friend as a birthday present.

B: Do you need any recommendations?

A: No, no, I'm sorry, but I don't like the style of necklace in the store at all. I want to know if you can do DIY in your store.

A: You mean custom-made, right?

A: Yes.

B: Certainly. How should we design it?

A: It's uncomplicated at all. She likes simple style, and this is the effect I want. Can you make it?

B: Oh, this style is very simple, no problem, but it will take some time. About one week.

A: I'm ok with it. By the way, could you send a birthday card on delivery?

B: Dear customer, we will try our best to meet your requirements. However, you need to make a note in the order, otherwise we may forget since there are too many orders.

A: Thank you so much!

1. 定做

A：你好，在吗？

B：有什么能帮您的吗？

A：我想买一条项链作为生日礼物送给朋友。

B：您需要我为您推荐吗？

A：不，不，很遗憾，我不太喜欢店里的产品款式。我想了解你们店里能不能 DIY 制作。

B：您的意思是特别定制，对吗？

A：是的。

B：当然可以，您想要怎么设计呢？

A：不需要很麻烦，我朋友喜欢简单的款式，这是我要的效果，你们能够制作吗？

B：哦，这个款式很简单，当然可以，不过需要一点时间，大概一周。

A：没问题，我可以接受。另外，你们能否在发货的时候赠送一张生日贺卡？

B：亲，您的要求我们会尽量满足，不过您需要在订单里备注一下，否则订单过多，我们可能会遗忘。

A：太谢谢啦！

2. Which Express Company to Choose?

A: Hi seller, can you deliver my goods via DHL?

B: Dear customer, generally speaking, we will ship your goods via UPS.

A: What's the difference between UPS and other express companies? It seems that DHL has been chosen more.

B: Indeed, but it is relatively cost effective to send goods over 20kg via UPS.

A: What is the weight of my package?

B: Wait for a moment, I have to check the weight of your parcel first.

(A few minutes later)

B: Dear customer, your parcel is about 25kg. It's more favorable to choose UPS.

A: Okay. I see.

2. 选择什么快递公司？

A：你好，卖家，可以通过 DHL 寄送我的商品吗？

B：亲，一般而言，我们会通过 UPS 寄送您的商品。

A：UPS 和其他快递公司有什么区别吗？好像 DHL 用得更多些。

B：没错，不过用 UPS 寄送重量在 20kg 以上的商品，费用相对划算些。

A：我的包裹有多重？

B：稍等，我先称一下。

A：亲，您的包裹约 25kg。选择 UPS 运送会更优惠。

B：好的。我明白了。

Text

8.3.1　Disputes and Settlement 纠纷与解决

There are two types of disputes when buyers apply for a refund in the transaction. One kind of dispute is that buyer does not receive the goods, commonly known as no goods received. The other is that buyer receives the goods, but the goods do not match the agreement, commonly known as unmatched items.

买家在交易中申请退款时有两类纠纷。一种纠纷是买方没有收到货物，俗称没有收到货物；另一种是买方收到货物，但货物与约定不符，俗称不符物品。

The disputes of no goods received from the platform are mainly as follows: No logistics information, the logistics shows goods have been delivered but the buyer complains no goods received, the customs detention, goods in transit, original goods returned, seller secretly change the logistics method, and etc.

平台无收货纠纷主要有：无物流信息、物流显示已发货但买方投诉没收到货、海关扣留、在途货物、原货退还、卖方偷换物流方式等。

No logistics information means that no tracking information could be found on the logistics site with the tracking number provided by the seller. There are two cases about the logistics shows goods have been delivered but the buyer complains no goods received. In one case, the logistics address matches the buyer's address on the order. That is, the logistics information shows that the product has been delivered, and the delivered country, province city, zip code and signature are the same as on the order. In the other case, the logistics address does not match the buyer's address on the order. That is, the logistics shows the product has been delivered, but the delivered address or signature does not match the information on the order.

没有物流信息意味着在由卖方提供跟踪号的物流站点找不到任何跟踪信息。下面有两个关于物流的案例——显示货物已经送达，但买方抱怨没有收到货物：在一种情况下，物流地址与订单上的买家地址相匹配，即物流信息显示产品已经发货，发货国家、省（市）、邮政编码和签名与订单上的一致；在另一种情况下，物流地址与订单上的买家地址不匹配，即物流显示产品已经发货，但发货地址或签名与订单上的信息不匹配。

The goods are detained at the customs means that the logistics information shows that the goods are at the customs, due to the customs requirements of the importing country. The main reasons are as follows: The importing country has restrictions on imported goods; buyers are reluctant to pay customs clearance fees; goods on the order are fake, counterfeit, or prohibited; the declared value and the actual value of the goods do not match; seller cannot present the related documents needed by the importing country; buyer cannot present the related documents needed by the importing country, etc.

货物滞留在海关是指由于进口国的海关要求，物流信息显示货物已在海关。主要原因有：进口国对进口商品有限制；买家不愿支付通关费；订单上的商品是假的、假冒的或违禁商品；申报价值与商品实际价值不符；卖方不能出示进口国需要的相关单据；买方不能出示进口国需要的相关单据；等等。

Goods in transit means that the tracking information shows the package is between "shipped" and "delivered" on the official website of the logistics company. Original goods returned means that there is tracking information and it shows the goods have been returned. Seller secretly change the logistics method means that the seller chooses a different logistics method to ship the goods without the permission of the buyer.

在途货物指的是物流公司官网上的跟踪信息显示包裹处于"已揽收"和"已发货"之间。原货退回是指有跟踪信息，说明货物已经退货。卖方偷换物流方式是指卖方在未经买方许可的情况下，选择不同的物流方式装运货物。

Unmatched items mean that the goods received by the buyer do not match the agreement, including the goods and description do not match, quality problems, fake products, wrong goods, short-shipment, damaged products, and etc. That the goods and description do not match means that the goods received by the buyer do not match the seller's description of the product on the details page of website, in terms of color, size, product packaging, brand, style, model or other aspects. Quality problems refer to the quality problem of goods received by the buyer, or problem when in use. For example, the electronic equipment does not work, or the texture of the product is poor and so on. Fake products mean that the buyer request a refund after receiving the goods because the goods are counterfeit or suspected to be counterfeit products short-shipment means that the number of goods received by the buyer is less than the agreed quantity on the order. Damaged goods mean that the goods received by the buyer have different degrees of packaging damage (except for the packaging used by the post office or seller), or the product is damaged.

不匹配项目是指买方收到的商品与协议不符，包括商品与描述不匹配、质量问题、假冒产品、错货、短装、损坏产品等。商品与描述不匹配是指买方收到的商品与卖方在网站详情页上对产品的描述不匹配，无论是颜色、尺寸、产品包装、品牌、款式、型号等方面。质量问题是指买方收到的货物存在质量问题，或者在使用过程中出现问题。例如，电子设备不能工作或者产品质地差等。假货是指买方收到货物后，因货物是假货或疑似假冒产品而要求退款。短货是指买方收到的货物数量少于订单上约定的数量。破损商品是指买方收到的商品有不同程度的包装破损（邮局或卖家使用的包装除外），或者产品损坏。

Once the dispute is filed, it will have impacts in many aspects. It will affect not only the buyer's shopping experience, but also the buyer's trust of the platform. As buyers do not have a good shopping experience, they will question the seller, and it will indirectly affect the buyer's trust of the platform. Thus they will question the platform, other suppliers on the platform and their products, and finally it will create vicious circle.

一旦提起纠纷，将会产生多方面的影响。不仅会影响买家的购物体验，也会影响买家对平台的信任。买家由于没有良好的购物体验，他们会询问卖家，这也会间接影响自己对平台的信任。因此，他们会质疑平台，质疑平台上的其他供应商及其产品，最终会造成恶性循环。

Nearly every company receives a complaint from a customer at one point or another. Handling a customer properly is critical to the success of a company. An organization that handles complaints in the right way can increase customer loyalty and improve its brand companies failing to address customer complaints in the proper manner may harm the reputation of their business, lose valuable customers and lose money. Understanding the benefits and objectives of settling customer complaints can help a company develop and implement a proper system to handle complaints.

几乎每家公司都会在某一时刻收到客户的投诉。与客户打交道得当是公司成功的关键。以正确的方式处理投诉的组织可以提高客户忠诚度和改善其品牌，如果公司没有以适当的方式处理客户投诉，那么可能会损害其业务的声誉，失去宝贵的客户，并造成损失。了解解决客户投诉的好处和目标可以帮助公司开发和实施适当的投诉处理系统。

1. Keeping the Customer 留住客户

When a company settles a customer's complaint in a positive manner, it possesses the opportunity to increase customer loyalty. A company shows that it cares about its customers by taking time to properly listen to the issue the customer is experiencing and trying to find a workable solution that appeases the customer. Keeping a loyal customer is an important objective to many companies. It is a true fact that companies spend less money retaining existing customers than implementing marketing strategies to obtain new ones.

当一家公司以积极的方式解决客户的投诉时，它就拥有了提高客户忠诚度的机会。公司通过花恰当时间倾听客户正在经历的问题，并试图找到一个可行的解决方案来安抚客户，以表明它对客户的关心。留住忠诚的客户是许多公司的重要目标。与实施营销策略以获得新客户相比，公司花在留住现有客户上的钱更少，这是一个事实。

2. Maintaining Reputation 维护声誉

Another objective to settling customer complaints is to maintain the company's good reputation. One of the most powerful forms of advertising is through word of mouth. When your company makes it a priority to handle customer complaints, positive news will spread about your company through word of mouth. The opposite is true if your fail to handle customer complaints properly. The reputation of a company is an intangible asset that can add value to the organization.

解决客户投诉的另一个目的是维护公司的良好声誉。最有力的广告形式之一是通过口碑传播。当你的公司把处理客户投诉作为优先事项时，就会通过口碑传播有关你公司的正面消息。如果你不能正确处理客户投诉，那么情况正好相反。公司的声誉是可以为组织增值的无形资产。

3. Protecting the Bottom Line 守护底线

A customer complaint that is not settled correctly can become a financial burden for a company. When a customer affects profitability, a company must choose to attempt to keep the customer or sever ties. Times exist when company must drop customer to prevent financial damage. For example, if a customer continually complains after the company makes several attempts to rectify the situation, the company should consider letting the customer go. Customers who complain without satisfaction cost the company money by taking up the time of individuals in the human resources department.

没有正确解决的客户投诉可能会成为公司的财务负担。当客户影响盈利能力时，公司必须选择是试图留住客户还是切断联系。有时公司必须放弃客户以防止财务损失。例如，如果客户在公司多次尝试纠正情况后不断抱怨，公司应该考虑让客户离开。抱怨得不到满意的客户会占用人力资源部人员的时间，从而使公司损失金钱。

4. Encouraging Improvement 鼓励改进

An objective of settling complaints is that it allows companies to see where they need improvement. If a product or service is not living up to customer expectations, you can evaluate that product or service and attempt to make improvements. If complaints are handled quickly, it may prevent the customer from revealing the problems to the public. Settling complaints also allows the company to keep its customers because the organization recognizes the problem and can make corrections before receiving any more complaints or losing customers.

解决投诉的一个目标是让公司看到其需要改进的地方。如果产品或服务没有达到客户的期望，您可以评估该产品或服务并尝试进行改进。如果投诉处理得很快，可能会阻止客户向公众披露问题。解决投诉还可以让公司留住客户，因为组织认识到了问题，可以在收到更多投诉或失去客户之前进行纠正。

8.3.2　Comments on Products 产品评论

Comments on products refer to the service evaluation from buyers to sellers about the description accuracy of products communication quality, response speed, and delivery time of products at the end of the transaction. For cross-border E-commerce sellers, comments on products are very effective sales tools. More than 90% of buyers said they would read the comments before placing the order; more than 80% of the buyers said their buying behavior was affected by positive ratio and comments on products.

产品评论是指交易结束时，买家对卖家对产品沟通质量、响应速度、交货时间等描述准确性的服务评价。对于跨境电商卖家来说，产品评论是非常有效的销售工具。超过 90% 的买家表示，其会在下单前阅读评论；超过 80% 的买家表示，其购买行为受到正面比率和对产品的评论的影响。

If the buyer has real personal feeling and is impressed by the service after he confirms receipt, the buyer will be very happy to make a satisfactory evaluation on their own shopping experience. If the seller receives positive comments, he must express thanks, such as issuing coupons, promotion code, and special discounts to help buyers to purchase again. If the seller receives negative feedback, he must let the buyer express dissatisfaction and make up for it timely. The seller can also guide the buyer to revise the negative comments. If the buyer does not leave a comment, the seller can send a message or E-mail to urge the buyer according to different situations.

如果购物者有真实的亲身感受，确认收货后对服务印象深刻，购物者会很乐意对自己的购物体验做出满意的评价。如果卖家收到正面评价，一定要表示感谢，比如发放优惠券、促销码、特别折扣等，帮助买家再次购买。如果卖家收到负面反馈，一定要让买家表达不满，并及时弥补。卖方也可以指导买方修改负面评论。如果买家没有留下评论，卖家可以根据不同的情况发信息或邮件催促买家。

1. Directly Ask the Buyer to Leave a Comment 直接请买家留言

Directly asking the buyer to comment is the easiest way for the seller to get evaluation. But before asking, the seller should contact the buyer first and ask if he is satisfied with the shopping experience. If the buyer is not satisfied, the seller must make up in time and guide the buyer to leave a positive comment. If the buyer is satisfied with the product or service, the seller can ask the buyer to write detailed positive comments.

直接向买家征求意见是卖家获得评价的最简单方式。但在询问之前，卖家应该先联系买家，询问其购物体验是否满意。如果买家不满意，卖家一定要及时弥补，引导买家留下正面评价。如果买家对产品或服务感到满意，卖家可以要求买家写下详细的正面评价。

2. Provide Rewards 提供奖励

It will be easier for buyers to leave positive comments if sellers provide some rewards. For example, if buyers leave positive comments and upload pictures, the seller can reward them 2% or 5% off for the next purchase. Even a very small reward can attract buyers to write comments, and even improve customer loyalty. Now, most of the cross-border E-commerce websites use these methods to stimulate buyers to write positive comments, and improve brand awareness.

如果卖家提供一些奖励，买家会更容易留下正面评价。例如，如果买家留下正面评论并上传图片，那么卖家可以在其下次购买时奖励 2% 或 5% 的折扣。即使是很小的奖励也能吸引买家写评论，甚至提高客户忠诚度，现在，大部分跨境电商网站都是用这些方式刺激买家写正面评论，以提高品牌知名度。

3. Show Buyer's Comments 显示买家的评论

Sellers can put buyer's positive comments and pictures on the home page. Or the seller can share the comments on social media. In order to make the comments more convincing, the seller can also allow buyers to provide short video comments, usually within 30 seconds. When collecting comments, sellers should clearly express what kind of comments they want to receive in order to avoid collecting similar non-specific comments. Comments about buyer's personal experience are more effective than the comments that express love, because the former provides detailed information and can help drive the potential customers to place orders.

卖家可以将买家的正面评论和图片放在首页。或者卖家可以在社交媒体上分享评论。为了让评论更有说服力，卖家还可以允许买家提供短视频评论，通常在 30 秒内，卖家应该明确表示希望收到什么样的评论，以免收集类似的不具体评论。关于买家个人体验的评论，比表达爱意的评论更有效，因为前者提供了详细的信息，可以帮助驱使潜在客户下单。

All in all, asking buyers to give feedback and comments is a very important part for cross-border E-commerce. If sellers want to receive positive comments they must first provide the best quality products and services, the most effective communication, and good marketing to reduce negative comments. They should also actively help buyers solve problems, and let buyers appreciate their earnest service.

总而言之，请买家反馈和点评是跨境电商非常重要的一环。如果卖家想要得到正面评价，他们必须首先提供最优质的产品和服务，最有效的沟通，以及良好的营销，以减少负面评价。要积极帮助买家解决问题，让买家领略他们的殷勤服务。

8.3.3　Customer Maintenance 客户维护

In traditional international trade, we usually meet the customers in exhibitions. The main difference between the exhibition and cross-border E-commerce platform is that almost every customer can meet with the seller in the exhibition face to face. That is, in traditional international trade, the final transaction between buyers and sellers may actually be built on preliminary contact.

在传统的国际贸易中，我们通常在展览会上会见客户。展会与跨境电商平台的主要不同之处在于，几乎每一位客户都可以在展会上与卖家面对面交流。也就是说，在传统的国际贸易中，买卖双方的最终交易实际上可能建立在初步接触的基础上。

However, as the key characteristic of Internet, buyers and sellers have never met before the transaction if they do business on the cross-border E-commerce platforms, so we are unable to determine customers' information even before we communicate with them. Of course, the cross-border E-commerce platforms provide various ways to help buyers and sellers identify each other's information, but these methods are also based on the Internet. Consequently, the nature of Internet determines that we are still unable to determine the background, real information and other factors of both sides in the transaction through the most intuitive way.

然而，作为互联网的关键特征，在跨境电商平台上进行交易，买卖双方在交易前从未见过面，因此在与客户沟通之前，我们无法确定客户的信息。当然，跨境电商平台提供了多种方式来帮助买卖双方识别对方的信息，但这些方式也是基于互联网。因此，互联网的性质决定了我们仍然无法通过最直观的方式确定交易双方的背景、真实信息等因素。

In business, a single transaction to the business is only the value for a single time. Or a single trade to buyers and sellers means only the profit for a single time. In order to allow buyers and sellers to gain profits continuously through transactions, there must be a method to help buyers and sellers to form a strong connection. This means the value for a certain period of time, and the added value of business, because this strong connection creates new values such as brand value and service value, which is unrelated to the transaction itself.

在商业中，对企业的一笔交易仅仅是一次交易的价值。或者，买卖双方的一笔交易意味着只有一次利润。要让买卖双方通过交易不断获得利润，就必须有办法帮助买卖双方形成强联系。这不仅是指一定时期内的价值，也指企业的附加值，因为这种强联系创造了品牌价值、服务价值等新价值，与交易本身无关。

The difference between the customers on the cross-border E-commerce platforms and in the traditional international trade lies in its uncertainty. It is not difficult for us to understand that the maintenance and the establishment of customer connection on cross-border E-commerce platforms is a more complicated process than in traditional international trade. However, customer maintenance is the key to cross-border E-commerce. According to the study, the cost of developing new customer is five times as that of retaining an old one. So how do we maintain customer relationships and establish a close connection with our customers on cross-border E-commerce platforms? This requires us to consider the basis of cross-border E-commerce platforms, and carry out the following activities:

跨境电商平台上的客户与传统国际贸易中的客户的不同之处在于其不确定性。我们不难理解，跨境电商平台客户的维护和建立是一个比传统国际贸易更为复杂的过程。然而，客户维护是跨境电商的关键。根据这项研究，开发新客户的成本是保留旧客户的 5 倍。那么我们如何在跨境电商平台上维护客户关系，与客户建立紧密的联系呢？这就需要我们考虑跨境电商平台的基础，开展以下活动：

1. Collect Customer Information, Build Customer Database 收集客户信息，建立客户数据库

Sellers should collect detailed information on customers' personal information, purchase history, buying preferences and concerns. These are all "clues" that can help sellers understand customers' preferences. After knowing these, sellers can provide customers with personalized service.

卖家应该收集客户的个人信息、购买历史、购买偏好和关注的详细信息。这些都是可以帮助卖家了解客户喜好的"线索"，了解了这些之后，卖家才能为客户提供个性化服务。

2. Maintain Regular Contact with Old Customers 与老客户保持定期联系

In order to retain and maintain good relationships with customer, many cross-border E-commerce sellers will send E-mails or cards to customers on holidays or customers' birthday. It can change the business relationship into friend relationship and help the sellers to follow up with the customers.

为了保持和维护与客户的良好关系，许多跨境电商卖家会在节假日或客户生日时向客户发送电子邮件或贺卡。它可以把商业关系变成朋友关系，并帮助卖家跟进客户。

3. Reply Old Customers' E-mails without Delay 立即回复老客户的电子邮件

Old customers' E-mails must be replied on the same day. If you encounter a complicated problem, and cannot reply on the same day, you must promptly inform the customer, like: "Mail received, and is being processed." Even so, you must reply that customer no more than three days later.

老客户的电子邮件必须在当天回复。如果您遇到复杂的问题，不能当天回复，必须及时通知客户，例如："邮件已收到，正在处理中。"即便如此，您必须在不超过三天的时间内回复该客户。

4. Ensure Product Quality 确保产品质量

Products must go through strict quality inspection and the quality of products must be ensured. Only the quality is ensured will the company develop better, and the customers，will repurchase these high-quality and inexpensive products. Over time, will form a positive "ecological circle".

产品必须经过严格的质量检验，必须保证产品的质量。只有保证质量，公司才能发展

得更好，客户才会重新购买这些物美价廉的产品。久而久之，将形成一个良性的"生态圈"。

5. Pay Old Customers a Return Visit Regularly 定期回访老客户

The so-called return visit is the planned tracking service to old customers. It can be an E-mail, inviting the old customers to give feedback about the recent quality and service of products and other suggestion. In short, the aim is to let buyers know that the seller is really buyer-centered, and want the buyers to have a better shopping experience in the future.

所谓回访，就是对老客户的有计划的跟踪服务。它可以是一封电子邮件，邀请老客户反馈最近产品的质量和服务以及其他建议。简而言之，目的是让买家知道卖家确实是以买家为中心的，希望买家在未来有更好的购物体验。

8.3.4　Consumer Habits and Characteristics of Major Countries 主要国家的消费习惯和特点

Consumption habit refers to psychological of stable preference for certain object formed by consumption subject in actual long-term consumption. In short, consumption habit is the preference of consumer for a certain kind of commodity, brand or consuming behavior. In nature, it is a stable individual consuming behavior, formed gradually in the long term, and in turn influences consuming behavior.

消费习惯是指消费主体在实际的长期消费中形成的对某一客体的稳定偏好心理。简而言之，消费习惯是消费者对某种商品、品牌或消费行为的偏好。从本质上讲，它是一种稳定的个体消费行为，是长期逐渐形成的，并反过来影响着消费行为。

1. the United States 美国

Rather than the price and packaging, people in the United States prefer to quality of commodity. Quality is vital for commodity to enter the US market, where the commodity with even a slight flaw will be put in the corner and sold in discount. Packaging is another important factor. Commodity should be both in good quality and in fine-decorated packaging to present impressive visual experience to customers.

与价格和包装相比，美国人更喜欢商品的质量。商品要进入美国市场，质量至关重要，哪怕有一点瑕疵都会被放在角落里打折出售。包装是另一个重要因素。商品既要质量好，又要包装精美，才能给顾客带来令人印象深刻的视觉体验。

People in the United States highly value the efficiency, thinking wasting time as wasting life. They hope to receive satisfied goods soon after placing orders. Therefore, when setting shipping templates, it is advisable to set highly efficient logistic mode such as UPS, DHL, TNT and FedEx at the same time. If not, explanations are suggested to add in the product description, giving potential buyers preparation or letting them choose other sellers. The seller can make good impression to potential buyers even the deal is not made eventually.

美国人非常重视效率，认为浪费时间就是浪费生命。他们希望在下订单后不久就能收到满意的货物。因此，在设置发货模板时，建议同时设置 UPS、DHL、TNT、FedEx 等高效物流模式。如果没有，建议在产品说明中增加说明，让潜在买家做好准备或让他们选择其他卖家。即使最终没有成交，卖家也能给潜在买家留下好印象。

Because of the United States' large territory and its four time zones, buyers from different time zones shop online at different times. To raise the attention to the launched commodities, sellers should sum up experiences, choose and launch products in a time period when online purchasing occurs in high density.

由于美国幅员辽阔，有四个时区，来自不同时区的买家在不同的时间进行网上购物。为了提高对推出商品的关注，卖家应该总结经验，在网上购物密度较高的时期选择和推出产品。

January is the high season for apparel sales, with winter clothes sold in discount in the United States. February 14th is the Valentine's Day in this country, making horticultural products, fashion accessories, jewelry, watches bags and gifts become hot sellers. Spring in America begins in March, which is the high season for horticultural products because of Easter in March. Sales volume of household and living appliances in this month sees rapid increase and sales volume of cosmetics products rebounds strongly with the coming of new arrivals in spring.

1月是服装销售旺季，美国冬季服装打折销售。2月14日是这个国家的情人节，使园艺产品、时尚配饰、珠宝、手表包和礼品成为热销产品。美国的春天从三月开始，这是园艺产品的旺季，因为三月有复活节。随着春季新来者的到来，本月家用电器和生活电器的销售量快速增长，化妆品的销售量强劲反弹。

Horticultural products enjoy good sales volume in April in the US market. Sales for women's shoes grow drastically due to the demand of wedding. In this ideal season for wedding, bridesmaids grown and wedding supplies are hot. Mother's Day is the second Sunday of May. With this day's coming, fashion accessories, jewelry, bags and greeting cards become popular items Fathers' Day is the third Sunday of June, where in June also occurs the graduation season. Therefore refrigeration appliances such as air conditioners begin becoming hot commodities in June. Mobile phones and other electronic products are also in their high season this month. Snooker and water sport equipment sell good in spring and summer.

4月份，园艺产品在美国市场的销量很好。由于婚礼的需求，女鞋的销量急剧增长。在这个理想的婚礼季节，伴娘数量增加，并且婚礼用品很火爆。母亲节是五月的第二个星期天。随着这一天的到来，时尚配饰、珠宝、手袋和贺卡成为热门项目。父亲节是6月的第三个星期日，6月也是毕业季。因此，空调等制冷电器在6月份开始成为热门商品。手机和其他电子产品本月也处于旺季。斯诺克和水上运动器材在春夏两季卖得很好。

The United States' Independence Day is on July 4th. Furniture and other household and living appliances come into high season due to the demand for wedding. August sees students back to school, making this month a high season for clothing and shoes. Autumn comes in September, and it is the best selling season for apparel. Cosmetics are also in hot sales thanks to the autumn new products' arrival.

美国独立日在7月4日。由于婚礼的需求，家具和其他家居用品进入旺季。8月份是学生返校的月份，这使得这个月成为服装和鞋子的旺季。九月是秋天，这是服装最畅销的季节。由于秋季新品的到来，化妆品也在热销。

Halloween is on October 31st. Sports equipment sell in large discount in this month, and stuffed toys also find a good sale. Thanksgiving Day is on the fourth Thursday of November. With some major festivals' arrival in winter, cosmetics, stuffed toys, and gifts come into high season for sales. December is a high season for winter apparel and shoes. Christmas Day makes horticultural products sell hot. Sales for heating equipment come to its peak. Jewelry and watches in December occupies a quarter of the whole year. In this sense, when developing marketing strategy, sellers in cross-border E-commerce platforms should take the features of the US market into consideration.

万圣节在 10 月 31 日。这个月运动器材大打折，毛绒玩具也卖得不错。感恩节在 11 月的第四个星期四。随着冬季一些主要节日的到来，化妆品、填充玩具和礼物进入销售旺季。12 月是冬装和冬鞋的旺季。圣诞节使园艺产品卖得火爆。供暖设备的销售达到了顶峰。12 月的珠宝和手表占全年的四分之一。从这个意义上说，跨境电商平台的卖家在制定营销策略时，应该考虑美国市场的特点。

2. Canada 加拿大

Approximately 37% of cross-border online buyers throughout the whole world are in Canada. Popularity of the Internet, mobile phones and bank services are high in Canada. But because of its vast territory and thin population, logistics is quite a challenge for remote areas in this country. Fortunately, 80% of Canada's populations live in the areas less than 60 miles from the US borders, namely three major cities of Canada. Canada is a major market for the US cross-border E-commerce, for its precise delivery time, and more preferable taxation rate than that in the United States.

全世界大约 37%的跨境在线买家在加拿大。在加拿大，互联网、手机和银行服务的普及程度很高。但是，由于其幅员辽阔，人口稀少，物流对这个国家的偏远地区来说是一个相当大的挑战。幸运的是，加拿大 80%的人口居住在距离美国边境不到 60 英里的地区，即加拿大的三个主要城市。加拿大是美国跨境电商的主要市场，因为它的送货时间准确，税率比美国更优惠。

60% of Canadians purchase online from America. 38% of Canada's populations live in Ontario, where the relatively low logistic fees and exchange rates fuel the Canadian's online shopping behavior. In Canada, credit cards' penetration rate is high, and 81% of online payment is made by credit cards, followed by PayPal(42%). These factors promote the cross-border finance.

60%的加拿大人从美国网购。加拿大 38%的人口生活在安大略省，那里相对较低的物流费用和汇率助长了加拿大人的网购行为。在加拿大，信用卡的渗透率很高，81%的在线支付是通过信用卡完成的，其次是贝宝（42%）。这些因素促进了跨境金融的发展。

Canadians are passionate about sports. 54% of Canada's populations regularly take part in sports activities. As result, there is large demand for sports equipment and facilities. The top five favored sports in Canada are golf, ice hockey, baseball, swimming and basketball. As a part of many Canadians' life, sports give Canada huge sports products consumption ability with large demand for sports products. The five major sports products in Canada are gym shoes, sportswear bicycles and accessories, golf equipment, and training devices. The retail volumes of these five products show an increasing trend. Among them, two traditional sports products, gym shoes and sportswear occupy half of the sports equipment market in Canada. China has strength and potential in exporting sportswear and gym shoes. Therefore, Chinese firms who wish to explore and expand overseas market are suggested to pay more attention to business opportunities in Canadian market, especially in sportswear and gym shoes market.

加拿大人热衷于体育运动。加拿大 54%的人口经常参加体育活动。因此，对体育器材和设施的需求很大。加拿大最受欢迎的五项运动是高尔夫、冰球、棒球、游泳和篮球。体育作为加拿大人生活的一部分，给了加拿大巨大的体育产品消费能力和巨大的体育产品需求。加拿大的五大运动产品分别是运动鞋、运动服装、自行车及配件、高尔夫器材和训练器材，这五种产品的零售量呈上升趋势。其中，运动鞋和运动服这两种传统运动产品占据了加拿大运动器材市场的半壁江山，中国在运动服和运动鞋出口方面有实力和潜力。因此，建议希望开拓和拓展海外市场的中国企业更多地关注加拿大市场的商机，特别是运动服装和运动鞋市场的商机。

3. Italy 意大利

In Italy, most online buyers are at the age 18 to 44,with 55.4% male, and 44.6% female. The most frequent online shopping time in a day is from 21 to 23. 47% are virtual products or services such as paid audio and video resources and tourist services, and 53% are physical commodities. E-commerce platform is the main shopping channel.

在意大利，大多数网上买家的年龄在 18 岁到 44 岁；其中 55.4%是男性，44.6%是女性。一天中最频繁的网购时间是从 21 点到 23 点。47%是付费音视频资源、旅游服务等虚拟产品或服务；53%是实物商品。电子商务平台是主要的购物渠道。

International common payment is also valid in Italy. Credit cards and PayPal are most popular. Credit cards, in particular, enjoy high popularity and usage rate, with Visa and MasterCard as the main channels. The process of customs clearance in Italy mainly focuses on customs tariff payment and special requirements for special items. For a sample with commercial value, Italy can provide it with tax exemption, on the following four conditions: (1) The sample can be only carried into Italy by the abroad company's representatives for exhibition and display, and is to be exported on time, (2) A certificate of origin signed by a recognized chamber of commerce should be submitted, (3) Proper tariff should be paid in the customs when the sample enters, and the tariff will be returned when the sample is exported, (4) A form in duplicate should be filled in, describing each sample's weight and value in detail.

国际共同支付在意大利也是有效的。信用卡和贝宝最受欢迎。尤其是信用卡，以 Visa 和万事达卡为主要渠道，普及率和使用率都很高。意大利的通关过程主要集中在海关关税缴纳和特殊物品特殊要求方面。对于具有商业价值的样品，意大利可以为其免税，条件如下：①样品只能由国外公司代表携带到意大利展出，并按时出口；②须提交由认可商会签署的产地来源证；③样品入境时应向海关缴纳适当的关税，样品出口时退还关税；④填写表格一式两份，详细说明每个样品的重量和价值。

Italians are more flexible than Germans, and more enthusiastic than the British. When negotiating contracts and making decisions, Italians are less emotional but more cautious, and are not likely to take a position in a rush. Meanwhile they value the price, refuse to make a concession in this aspect, and prefer to implement by agent.

意大利人比德国人更灵活，比英国人更热情。在进行合同谈判和做出决定时，意大利人不那么情绪化，但更谨慎，不太可能仓促采取立场。同时，他们看重价格，拒绝在这方面做出让步，更倾向于以代理商的方式实施。

Italians have faith in domestic firms, and believe that products made by firms at home are in higher quality, and that there exists commonalities between domestic firms and themselves. In this sense, doing business with Italians requires patience in order to convince them that your products are in higher quality and lower price than their domestic products.

意大利人对国内企业有信心，认为国内企业生产的产品质量更高，国内企业与自己之间存在共性。从这个意义上说，与意大利人做生意需要耐心，以便让他们相信你们的产品比他们国内的产品质量更好，价格更低。

4. The UK 英国

The UK belongs to Western Europe. Buyers in Western European countries commonly prefer quality and pragmatism, value efficiency, and pay close attention to details. They therefore raise high demand for products, and carefully examine the description of products in detail. British buyers not only raise strict request on commodity's quality, but also lay emphasis on its aesthetic feeling, and demand fine-decorated packaging. British retailers like trial orders. They like to order one or two samples tentatively before placing bulk orders. This suggests no ignoring any small retail order, for a large order might hide behind it.

英国属于西欧，西欧国家的采购商普遍质量务实、讲求效率、注重细节。因此，他们对产品提出了很高的要求，并仔细检查了产品的详细描述。英国买家不仅对商品的质量提出了严格的要求，而且注重美感，要求包装精美。英国零售商喜欢试订。他们喜欢先试探性地订购一到两个样品，再下大宗订单。这表明不要忽视任何小规模的零售订单，因为大额订单可能隐藏在背后。

Retail Times in Britain recently indicates that according to the latest published investigation carried out by Macfarlane Packaging, a major British packaging supplier, improper packaging is most unpleasant for online buyers when receiving goods during the online shopping.

英国《零售时报》日前指出，英国主要包装供应商麦克法兰包装公司最新公布的一项调查显示，网上购物者在网购过程中收到商品时，最不愉快的是包装不当。

According to the result of this investigation, 25% of the online buyers complain about the excessively big package or boxes they have received which far exceed the sizes of commodity. Due to the large package, small commodities cannot be delivered as a letter into the mailbox. Thus receivers can only choose expressage or other deliveries, or have to pick up goods in person in a certain site. In addition, 22% online buyers show their upset and disappointment when receiving broken or damaged package, for damaged package may result in spoiled commodity inside. Also, the risk of losing packages makes online buyers feel stressed. In the meantime, 19% of consumers are dissatisfied with poor protective effect of packaging.

根据这项调查的结果，25%的网购者抱怨他们收到的包裹或盒子太大，远远超过了商品的大小。由于包裹很大，小商品不能以信件的形式投递到邮箱。因此，收货人只能选择快递或其他送货方式，或者必须亲自在某个地点提货。此外，22%的网购者在收到破损或损坏的包裹时表现出沮丧和失望，因为破损的包裹可能会导致里面的商品变质。此外，丢失包裹的风险让在线买家感到压力。与此同时，19%的消费者对包装保护效果不佳表示不满。

In terms of commodities of high quality and low price made in China, the British are fond of Guangdong products, especially household and individual appliances. Household appliances and furniture are in high demand and high purchase rate, and are in highest reorder rate in exporting to Britain. Mirror, lamps and lanterns also sell in large quantity. Commodities with high value such as television and its peripheral products also witness a large market in Britain.

就中国制造的物美价廉的商品而言，英国人喜欢广东的产品，特别是家用电器和个人家电。家用电器和家具需求量大，采购率高，在对英出口中再订购率最高。镜子、灯具也大量销售。电视及其周边产品等高附加值商品在英国也有很大的市场。

5. Russia 俄罗斯

As an emerging cross-border E-commerce market, Russian cross-border E-commerce market is burgeoning. The statistics indicate that the online sales volume of foreign commodities in Russia reached to 4.3 billion US dollars in 2016, compared with 3.4 billion US dollars in 2015. 90% of these online trade orders in Russia were for Chinese commodities according to the statistics issued by AKIT in 2017. Chinese commodities are attracting a large amount of Russian online shoppers with high quality, low price and varied categories.

作为新兴的跨境电商市场，俄罗斯跨境电商市场方兴未艾。统计数据显示，2016年俄罗斯外国商品网上销售额达到43亿美元，而2015年为34亿美元，根据AKIT 2017年发布的统计数据，这些俄罗斯的网上贸易订单中有90%是针对中国商品的。中国商品以其高质量、低价格和多样化的品类吸引了大量的俄罗斯网购者。

Russia has a cold climate. In this sense, considering the large temperature differences in different seasons in Russia, sellers can highlight the keyword "Best Seller of the Season" in the title when publicizing the commodities' information online.

俄罗斯气候寒冷。从这个意义上说，考虑到俄罗斯不同季节的温差很大，卖家在网上宣传商品信息时，可以突出标题中的关键字"当季畅销品"。

In addition, due to the cold winter in Russia, keeping warm outdoors is very important for Russians. In winter, hats scarves and gloves are necessities there, and Russian women are also fond of fur coats.

此外，由于俄罗斯冬季寒冷，户外保暖对俄罗斯人来说非常重要。冬天，帽子、围巾和手套是那里的必需品，俄罗斯妇女也喜欢毛皮大衣。

Same as North China, there are central heating installations indoors in Russia. So in winter, the temperature difference is quite huge between outdoor and indoor. Thus Russians' indoor clothing is another extreme compared with outdoor clothing. Leisure wears are hot sellers in winter, and robes after bath and light pajamas in bedtime are also popular Russian home dress in winter.

和中国北方一样，俄罗斯的室内也有集中供暖装置。所以在冬天，室内外的温差是相当大的。因此，与户外服装相比，俄罗斯人的室内服装是另一个极端。休闲装在冬天很畅销；沐浴后的长袍和睡前的轻薄睡衣也是冬天流行的俄罗斯家装。

Sport is an important part in Russians' life. Russians often purchase specialized sport clothes, gym shoes and accessories. Russians are good at gymnastics and ice sports. In addition, Russians also love prevailing sports like running, balls and fitness training as other countries people do. Therefore, climbing wears, sneakers, swimming wears, and skiing wears are popular commodities attracting Russian sports fans. Besides sports, Russians are also quite good at enjoying their lives. The young generations have formed the habit of vacation, and often they choose to go to beach. For the demand of vacation therefore, swimming wears, beach shoes and sun bonnets are best sellers loved by many Russians.

体育运动是俄罗斯人生活中的重要组成部分。俄罗斯人经常购买专门的运动服、运动鞋和配件。俄罗斯人擅长体操和冰上运动。此外，像其他国家的人一样，俄罗斯人也喜欢像跑步、踢球和健身训练这样的流行运动。因此，登山服、运动鞋、游泳服和滑雪服是吸引俄罗斯体育迷的热门商品。除了体育，俄罗斯人也很会享受生活。年轻一代养成了度假的习惯，他们经常选择去海滩。因此，对于度假的需求，泳装、沙滩鞋和太阳帽是许多俄罗斯人喜爱的畅销品。

【 Exercise 】

1. Translate the following phrases into Chinese.

    conversion rate＿＿＿＿＿＿＿＿＿＿＿＿＿＿＿＿＿＿＿＿

    core competitiveness＿＿＿＿＿＿＿＿＿＿＿＿＿＿＿＿＿

    positive cycle＿＿＿＿＿＿＿＿＿＿＿＿＿＿＿＿＿＿＿＿＿

    customs detention＿＿＿＿＿＿＿＿＿＿＿＿＿＿＿＿＿＿＿

    negative feedback ＿＿＿＿＿＿＿＿＿＿＿＿＿＿＿＿＿＿

2. Translate the following phrases into English.

    底线；最低条件＿＿＿＿＿＿＿＿＿＿＿＿＿＿＿＿＿＿＿

    好评率＿＿＿＿＿＿＿＿＿＿＿＿＿＿＿＿＿＿＿＿＿＿＿＿

    品牌意识＿＿＿＿＿＿＿＿＿＿＿＿＿＿＿＿＿＿＿＿＿＿＿

    销售量；销售额＿＿＿＿＿＿＿＿＿＿＿＿＿＿＿＿＿＿＿

    税率＿＿＿＿＿＿＿＿＿＿＿＿＿＿＿＿＿＿＿＿＿＿＿＿＿

3. Please explain the following words or items.

(1) comments on products

(2) consumption habit

4. Please answer the following questions.

(1) What should we notice during the product packaging?

(2) How can we maintain customers?

References
参考文献

[1] HANG Y. Analysis on the Electronic Commerce Talent Training Mode for Application Oriented University under the Environment of Masses Entrepreneurship and Innovation[J]. DEStech Transactions on social science, education and human science, 2016.

[2] HUANG W, ZHOU S. Electronic Commerce Innovation and Development Strategy of Travel Agency Under Low-Carbon Economy[M]//Proceedings of the International Conference on Information Engineering and Applications(IEA)2012. Springer London, 2013.

[3] 王群，卢传胜，沙鹏飞.跨境电商专业英语[M].上海：立信会计出版社，2016.

[4] 张式锋，孙圣涵.跨境电子商务专业英语[M].上海：立信会计出版社，2018.

[5] 王乃彦.对外经贸英语函电[M].6版.北京：对外经济贸易大学出版社，2017.

[6] 王维平，蒋轶阳.跨境电商英语[M].北京：中国商务出版社，2017.

[7] 盛湘君.跨境电商交际英语[M].北京：外语教学与研究出版社，2016.

[8] 冯媛媛.跨境电子商务英语[M].北京：人民邮电出版社，2018.

[9] 李莹莹，杨雯娟.电子商务英语教程[M].北京：中国轻工业出版社，2016.

[10] 苏凤杰.跨境电子商务英语人才的培养[M].北京：中国建材工业出版社，2017.

[11] 王琼.跨境电商实用英语[M].北京：中国人民大学出版社，2018.

[12] 李卫，李韦婷，赵秀丽.外贸英语函电[M].北京：中国财富出版社，2018.

[13] 徐凡.跨境电子商务基础与实务中国财富出版社[M].北京：中国铁道出版社，2019.

[14] 罗芳.跨境电商英语口语实例大全[M].北京：中国铁道出版社，2019.

[15] 陈英.电子商务英语[M].哈尔滨：哈尔滨工业大学出版社，2009.

[16] 刘玉霞，岳丹.电子商务英语[M].北京：清华大学出版社，2013.

[17] 陈艳.国际物流（双语）[M].北京：化学工业出版社，2016.

[18] 创想外语研发团队.跨境电商英语必会口语表达[M].北京：中国水利水电出版社，2018.

[19] 中国国际贸易学会商务专业培训考试办公室.跨境电商英语教程[M].北京：中国商务出版社，2016.